d

Robert Wilson, the leading American avant-garde theatre director, revolutionized the stage by making visual communication more important than words. His productions cut across the boundaries that traditionally have defined theatre, dance, opera, and the visual arts to create a total work of art. Wilson forces the spectator to question what theatre is and how it communicates.

This book, the first comprehensive study of Wilson, traces the evolution of the director's astonishing career as well as his complex relationship to language and his visual rhetoric. It explains how he renovated the stage and describes in detail major productions such as: *Deafman Glance, Einstein on the Beach,* and *the CIVILwarS.* Also, the psychological significance of Wilson's work, largely ignored until now, is considered along with his artistic goals, and a detailed analysis of the major themes and images that recur in his works.

The author, Arthur Holmberg, worked personally with Wilson and as a result of numerous interviews and first-hand observations of his creative process, has written an intimate, behind-the-scenes view of one of our greatest and most original directors.

Photographs and sketches from Wilson's private collection are included, along with a chronology of his work.

DIRECTORS IN PERSPECTIVE

General Editor: Christopher Innes

The theatre of Robert Wilson

What characterizes modern theatre above all is continual stylistic innovation, in which theory and presentation have combined to create a wealth of new forms – naturalism, expressionism, epic theatre and so forth – in a way that has made directors the leading figures rather than dramatists. To a greater extent than is perhaps generally realized, it has been directors who have provided dramatic models for playwrights, though of course there are many different variations in this relationship. In some cases a dramatist's themes challenge a director to create new performance conditions (Stanislavski and Chekhov), or a dramatist turns director to formulate an appropriate style for his work (Brecht); alternatively a director writes plays to correspond with his theory (Artaud), or creates communal scripts out of exploratory work with actors (Chaikin, Grotowski). Some directors are identified with a single theory (Craig), others gave definitive shape to a range of styles (Reinhardt); the work of some has an ideological basis (Stein), while others work more pragmatically (Bergman).

Generally speaking, those directors who have contributed to what is distinctly "modern" in today's theatre stand in much the same relationship to the dramatic texts they work with as composers do to librettists in opera. However, since theatrical performance is the most ephemeral of the arts and the only easily reproducible element is the text, critical attention has tended to focus on the playwright. This series is designed to redress the balance by providing an overview of selected directors' stage work: those who helped to formulate modern theories of drama. Their key productions have been reconstructed from promptbooks, revues, scene-designs, photographs, diaries, correspondence and – where these productions are contemporary – documented by first-hand description, interviews with the director and so forth. Apart from its intrinsic interest, this record allows a critical perspective, testing ideas against practical problems and achievements. In each case, too, the director's work is set in context by indicating the source of his ideas and their influence, the organization of his acting company and his relationship to the theatrical or political establishment, so as to bring out wider issues: the way theatre both reflects and influences assumptions about the nature of man and his social role.

Christopher Innes

Seated on his *Parzival Sofa*, Robert Wilson compleat man of the theatre: director, dancer, playwright, performer, painter, sculptor, video artist, sound artist, set designer, lighting designer, choreographer.

The theatre of
Robert Wilson

ARTHUR HOLMBERG
Assistant Professor, Department of Theater Arts
Brandeis University, Massachusetts

CAMBRIDGE
UNIVERSITY PRESS

PUBLISHED BY THE PRESS SYNDICATE OF THE UNIVERSITY OF CAMBRIDGE
The Pitt Building, Trumpington Street, Cambridge, United Kingdom

CAMBRIDGE UNIVERSITY PRESS
The Edinburgh Building, Cambridge CB2 2RU, UK
40 West 20th Street, New York, NY 10011–4211, USA
477 Williamstown Road, Port Melbourne, VIC 3207, Australia
Ruiz de Alarcón 13, 28014 Madrid, Spain
Dock House, The Waterfront, Cape Town 8001, South Africa

http://www.cambridge.org

First published 1996
Reprinted 2000, 2002

Printed in the United Kingdom at the University Press, Cambridge

A catalogue record for this book is available from the British Library

Library of Congress Cataloguing in Publication data
Holmberg, Arthur.
The theatre of Robert Wilson / Arthur Holmberg.
p. cm. – (Directors in perspective)
Includes bibliographical references and index.
ISBN 0 521 36492 2 (hardback)
1. Wilson, Robert, 1941– – Criticism and interpretation.
I. Series.
PN2287.W494H65 1997
792′ .0233′092–dc20 95–51227 CIP

ISBN 0 521 36492 2 hardback

SE

Dedicated to Robert Wilson

il miglior fabbro

A theatre which subordinates the *mise-en-scène* and production, i.e., everything in itself that is specifically theatrical, to the text, is a theatre of idiots, madmen, grammarians, grocers, antipoets and positivists . . . There can be no complete theatre . . . which does not add to our fully known feelings the expression of states of mind belonging to the half-conscious realm, which the suggestions of gestures will always express more adequately than the precise localized meanings of words.

Antonin Artaud, *The Theatre and Its Double*

Contents

Illustrations

All pictures supplied by the Byrd Hoffmann Foundation unless otherwise indicated

Acknowledgments

Deep is my gratitude to the following people without whose kind assistance the battle to write this book would certainly have been lost: Christopher Innes, Victoria Cooper, Sarah Stanton, and Alison Gilderdale of Cambridge University Press; Ronald Vance, Seth Goldstein, Barry Langford, and Geoffrey Wexler of the Byrd Hoffman Foundation; Dennis Redmond, Guillermo Alonso, and Kimberley Vernados of RW Work; Lucinda Childs, Honni Coles, Philip Glass, Suzushi Hanayagi, Hans-Peter Kuhn, Ann-Cristin Rommen, Sheryl Sutton, and Tom Waits – Wilson collaborators; Robert Brustein, Rob Orchard, Jan Geidt, Jeremy Geidt, Remo Airaldi, Maribeth Back, Frank Butler, Tom Cole, Thomas Derrah, Lynn Jeffery, Christine Joly de Lotbinière, Abby Katz, Henry Lussier, Charles Marz, Kati Mitchell, Joan Moynagh, Bonnie Raphael, Liz Rosier, Jessica Sayre, and Ruth Sternberg of the American Repertory Theatre; Richard Feldman, American Repertory Theatre company photographer; Greg Boyd, Mike Wilson, and Nina Chwast of the Alley Theatre; Chris Baker of the Shakespeare Theatre at the Folger; Ann Owens of Houston Grand Opera; President Jehuda Reinharz, Provost Irving Epstein, Dean Robin Feuer Miller, Associate Dean Elaine Wong, Barbara Cassidy, Mary Broderick, Anne Livermore, Professors Michael Murray, Karl Eigsti, John Bush Jones, and Steven Dowden of Brandeis University; Professors William Alfred, Donald Fanger, Alice Jardine, Judith Ryan, Susan Suleiman, and Dean Michael Shinagel of Harvard; Myra Mayman and Susan Zielinski of the Harvard Office of the Arts; Vlada Petric of the Harvard Film Archive; Jeanne Newlin and Catherine Johnson of the Harvard Theatre Collection; Constance Christo and Margaret Keyes of the Harvard Modern Language Center; Rudolph Ellenbogen of Columbia University's Rare Book and Manuscript Library; Joanna Britto and Ann Shumard of the Smithsonian Institution's National Portrait Gallery; Sylvie Drake, Donna Frazier, Bret Israel, Richard Rouilard, and Lisa Thackaberry of *The Los Angeles Times*; Eva Hoffman, Constance Rosenblum, and Andrea Stevens of *The New York Times*; Peter Zeisler and Jim O'Quinn of *American Theatre*; Martha Coigney of the International Theatre Institute; Jeff Muskovin and Max Leventhal; Jeffrey D. Upah; Howell Binkley, Steven Strawbridge, and Jennifer Tipton, lighting designers; John Conklin, Fred Kolo, and Yoshio Yabara, set and costume designers; Letizia Brod; Professor Antonio Cao of Hofstra University; Philippe Chemin; Peter Engelhorn; Nicholas Stuyvesant Fish and Patricia Schechter Fish; Meryl Langbort; Stephan Meier; Dorothy Monet; Professor Manfredi Piccolomini of Lehman College, CUNY; Gail M. Price; Alexandra Serban and Professor Andrei Serban of Columbia's School of the Arts; Graciela and Stanley Samuels; Charles and Dagmar Thompson; F. von Broembsen; Dee Worman and Karl Reynolds; and Cristina and Lucinda Zilkha.

Robert Wilson's magnanimity, benevolence, and generosity of spirit are beyond gratitude and beyond praise. Eternally I am indebted for the many hours and many days I have shared with him during which he patiently guided me through the maze of Wilsonland.

Chronology

The following chronology lists only premieres, not revivals. It includes only theatre. Wilson often uses unconventional spelling, punctuation, and capitalization in his titles. Furthermore, on different occasions he writes the same title in different ways. These variations often arise from a concern with visual design and graphic layout. In this work, Wilson's most frequent configuration is used.

1965   *Dance Event*, New York World's Fair, NYC.

1966   *Solo Performance*, Byrd Hoffman Studio, NYC.

1967   *Theater Activity*, Bleecker Street Cinema, NYC; American Theater Laboratory, NYC.

1968   *BYRDwoMAN*, Byrd Hoffman Studio, NYC.

1969   *The King of Spain*, Anderson Theater, NYC. *The Life and Times of Sigmund Freud*, Brooklyn Academy of Music, NYC.

1970   *Deafman Glance*, University of Iowa, Iowa City.

1971   *Program Prologue Now, Overture for a Deafman*, Espace Pierre Cardin, Paris.

1972   *Overture*, Byrd Hoffman Studio, NYC. *KA MOUNTAIN AND GUARDenia TERRACE*, Haft Tan Mountain, Shiraz, Iran.

1973   *King Lyre and Lady in the Wasteland*, Byrd Hoffman Studio, NYC. *The Life and Times of Joseph Stalin*, Det Ny Theater, Copenhagen, Denmark.

1974   *DIA LOG/A MAD MAN A MAD GIANT A MAD DOG A MAD URGE A MAD FACE*, Teatro di Roma, Rome. *A Letter for Queen Victoria*, Teatro Caio Melisso, Spoleto, Italy.

1975   *DIA LOG*, II, Public Theater, NYC. *The $ Value of Man*, The Brooklyn Academy of Music, NYC. *To Street* (solo), Kultur Forum, Bonn, Germany.

1976   *DIA LOG*, III, Whitney Museum, NYC. *Einstein on the Beach*, Festival d'Avignon, France.

1977   *I was sitting on my patio this guy appeared I thought I was hallucinating*, Quirk Auditorium, Eastern Michigan University, Ypsilanti, Mich. *DIA LOG/Network*, Spazio Teatro Sperimentale, Florence, Italy.

1979   *Death Destruction & Detroit*, Schaubühne, Berlin, Germany. *DIA*

1991 *When We Dead Awaken (WWDA)* by Henrik Ibsen. American
      Repertory Theatre, Cambridge MA. *Parzival*, opera by Richard
      Wagner. Staatsopera, Hamburg. *The Magic Flute*, opera by
      Wolfgang Mozart, Opéra Bastille, Paris. *Lohengrin*, opera by
      Wagner. Zurich Opera. *Grace for Grace* by Robert Wilson.
      Cathedral of Saint John the Divine, NYC. *Malady of Death*, after
      the novel by Marguerite Duras. Schaubühne, Berlin.

1992 *Doctor Faustus Lights the Lights* by Gertrude Stein, Hebbel
      Theater, Berlin. *Danton's Death* by Georg Büchner. Alley Theater,
      Houston, TX. *Don Juan último* by Vicente Molina Foix. Teatro
      María Guerrero (Centro Dramático Nacional), Madrid. *Alice*,
      after the novel by Lewis Carroll. Music and lyrics by Tom Waits;
      text by Paul Schmidt. Thalia Theater, Hamburg.

1993 *Alice in Bed* by Susan Sontag. Schaubühne, Berlin. *Madama
      Butterfly*, opera by Puccini. Opéra Bastille, Paris.

1994 *Der Mond im Gras: einmal keinmal immer* by Robert Wilson, after
      fairy tales by the Brothers Grimm and the grandmother's tale
      from   Büchner's   *Woyzeck*;   Kammerspiele,   Munich.
      Hanjo/Hagoromo. Music and libretto for *Hanjo* by Marcello Panni;
      libretto after Yukio Mishima's *Five Modern No Plays*. Music and
      libretto for *Hagoromo* by Jo Kondo, after a text by Zeami. Teatro
      della Pergola (Maggio Musicale, Florence). *T. S. E.* by Robert
      Wilson, music by Philip Glass, text by Maita de Niscemi and
      Brad Gooch. Case di Stefano, Gibellina, Sicily (Orestiadi di
      Gibellina). *The Meek Girl* by Robert Wilson and Wolfgang Wiems
      after Fyodor Dostoyevsky. Théâtre MC 93 Bobigny (Festival
      d'Automne de Paris). *Skin, Meat, Bone: The Wesleyan Project* by
      Robert Wilson and Alvin Lucier. Theater Center for the Arts,
      Wesleyan University, Middletown.

Unpublished quotations from Robert Wilson come from two sources:
taped interviews listed in the endnotes or from the notebooks I kept
during rehearsals. Since it is important to date each Wilson quotation in
terms of the development of his career and techniques (assertions from
one period may contradict those made later), the title of the production
he was working on when he made the statement appears after the quotation. The title has been abbreviated for ease of reference as shown in the
chronology above. The statement may have been made to a group of
actors, a single actor, or to me in private conversation.

1 Contextualizing Wilson: from semiotics to semantics

> The essence of great art is its infinite power of suggestion.
> Baudelaire, "Wagner et Tannhäuser à Paris"

The Merlin of the avant-garde, Wilson's career astonishes. First, the sheer size of his œuvre; he now has over one hundred productions behind him. The fecundity of his imagination and the range of his work have no parallel in contemporary theatre. Second, the multifaceted nature of his talent: director, dancer, playwright, performer, painter, sculptor, video artist, sound designer, set designer, lighting designer, choreographer, pedagogue, therapist, entrepreneur. Since he is the compleat *homme de théâtre*, his work cuts across traditional genres: drama, dance, opera, visual art, performance art, video, film, music, vaudeville. According to Jean-Marie Blanchard, former General Administrator of the Opéra Bastille in Paris, Wilson "opened a breach in the schizoid classifications of opera–theatre–dance–plastic arts to blaze a trail through a new space of representation."[1] Inevitably, the word *Gesamtkunstwerk* arises when discussing Wilson's multichannel theatre. Third, the enormous influence he has wielded, especially on the Continent, where he is regarded as America's greatest director, and where he has been one of the strongest – if not the strongest – influence on theatre for the past fifteen years. Fourth, his perseverance in pursuing – against reason, against hope – the visionary gleam. It takes more than genius to have a career like Wilson's. "The most important lesson I learned from Wilson," owns Julie Archer, who collaborated on the lights for the the *CIVILwarS Knee Plays*, "was how to fight to insure quality."[2] Fifth, the multicultural nature of his work with influences from America, Asia, and Europe – a paradigm of the global village. Sixth, his constant growth as an artist.Continually challenging himself, just as he challenges others, the development of Wilson's career is paradoxical: always the same, always different. Wilson changed the way theatre looks and talks. Unmistakable, all his productions have a unique signature. But each production is also different, and his career has evolved in unexpected and exciting ways. Talking about a living artist like Wilson – still growing, still searching – is as easy as trying to catch

Halley's Comet with a butterfly net as it streaks across the sky. He will continue to experiment, continue to astound. To appreciate the arc of Wilson's career, it makes sense to divide his development into four major periods: (1) silent operas; (2) deconstructing language; (3) from semiotics to semantics; (4) "how to do things with words": confronting the classics.

SILENT OPERAS

The first period – silent operas – culminates in 1973 with *The Life and Times of Joseph Stalin*, a twelve-hour epic with 150 performers that incorporated material from *The King of Spain*, *The Life and Times of Sigmund Freud*, and *Deafman Glance*.[3] Like all the early work, *The Life and Times of Joseph Stalin* was non-linear; the director conceived it as pictures structured architecturally. Consisting of seven acts, visual parallels linked acts I and VII, II and VI, III and V. Using a classical structure, IV was the turning point. At this time, a Wilson script consisted of stage directions.[4] Wilson thinks big. Although he has also done small chamber pieces, his mythopoetic vision inclines to epic: *KA MOUNTAIN AND GUARDENIA TERRACE* lasted seven days.

Wilson began his professional career in New York in the 60s, a bubbling cauldron of artistic experiments that changed the face of theatre.[5] Happenings, postmodern dance, performance art, Warhol's movies – trailblazers explored the borders of art, questioned genres, pushed against limits. Collective scripting, communal living, erasing the barrier between life and art, exploring the word as sound, replacing character with everyday people performing everyday activities, rejecting the literary in favor of other theatrical codes, non-linearity, a return to ritual – these war cries of the avant-garde sum up the climate in which Wilson forged his first works.[6] "There was an energy in New York then," Wilson reminisces, "certain things going on that everyone fed off – painters, poets, writers, dancers, composers, directors. Cage liberated all of us" (*Lear*).[7]

But Wilson quickly points out how different his theatre was from the usual downtown fare. Once I suggested that his theatre came from the sixties. He replied:

No I came out of it. I hated the theatre in the 60s. I was never part of that movement. What I was doing did not resemble the Living Theatre, The Open Theatre, or the Performance Group. I went against everything they were doing. I loathed the way their theatre looked. I had more in common with nineteenth-century theatre and vaudeville than with those groups. I was formalistic. I used the proscenium arch. My theatre was interior, and I treated the audience with courtesy. When New York was going for minimalism in a big way, I was doing rich, baroque pieces like *Stalin* and *Deafman Glance*. (*Faustus*)

After graduating from the Pratt Institute of Art in 1965, Wilson worked with people suffering from a wide range of physical and mental handicaps.

I worked with hyperactive and brain-damaged children. Then I started working with people in iron lungs, many of whom were catatonic. I was hired to get the patients to talk. The director of the hospital thought it was important for the patients to communicate with each other and the staff. I worked there for two years, and at the end of that time I came to the conclusion that it wasn't necessary to try to encourage those people to speak. I worked with pre-school children in Harlem, with aged people in New Jersey, and with patients in mental institutions. In all these classes I wasn't there to teach anything, but to listen to find out what they were interested in and help them do whatever they wanted to do.[8]

The important point is that Wilson did not impose society's standards of normality on the people he worked with. Rather, by listening and looking attentively, by trying to understand them, he met them on their terms, not his, not society's. "I believe in autistic behavior," he declared.[9] Wilson recognized and respected differences, and this sensitivity to difference would later enable him to restructure theatre according to alternate modes of perception and communication.

Meeting one handicapped youth – Raymond Andrews, a deaf-mute, African American teenager – was the critical turning point in Wilson's career. Walking down a street in Summit, New Jersey, in 1968, Wilson saw a policeman beating a twelve-year-old boy over the head with a club. The boy was making strange, inarticulate sounds. Wilson intervened and accompanied the officer and boy to the police station. Later, he found out that the boy lived in two rooms with twelve other family members and had been declared uneducable. Wilson adopted the child to try to educate him. As it turns out, the child also educated Wilson. "He began to make drawings to point out various things to me that I wouldn't notice and that he would be more sensitive to because of his being deaf. Then I realized that he thought, not in words, but in visual signs" (*Quartet*). Wilson explored Raymond's body language in workshops; deaf-mutes rely heavily on movement to communicate. From Raymond, Wilson learned how subtle and sophisticated body language can be. These explorations were to culminate in *Deafman Glance* – a play without words based on the drawings Raymond made to communicate with Wilson.

Using non-professionals and gathering round a group of disciples called the Byrds, Wilson created his early pieces through workshops that centered on movement and body awareness. "We felt we were working as much on the self as on the work," Sheryl Sutton recalls. "It was a process of personal growth. We started with movement to learn to listen with the body. It was like a laboratory. We were doing research on perception and communication. And each of us had a forte, something we did especially well, and he would incorporate it into the play. My shtick was floating."[10] By floating Sutton means a virtually seamless, invisible movement, movement so slow, so smooth, so controlled that the spectator is not aware that the person has been moving until, with a jolt, he realizes that the performer is on the other side of the stage.

"Directing," Wilson says, "is like bringing together in a kitchen different kinds of people who ordinarily wouldn't meet – different ages, talents, physical types, backgrounds. To make dinner you find out who can make chicken soup. Who can make spaghetti? Salad? Apple pie? Put it all together, and you have a good meal. Making theatre is an exchange. You learn from each other" (*Quartet*). Wilson keeps growing as an artist because he keeps learning from the people he works with. Wilson creates his pieces through a workshop process, generating the material by working closely with collaborators. "I don't think in the abstract," he says. "I have to see it in the concrete to respond. I create best in a rehearsal room filled with people, not alone in my loft" (*WWDA*).

Deafman Glance – the signature piece of this first period – begins with a silent prolog: on a white platform, her back to the audience, a mother (Sutton dressed in a black Victorian gown) stands next to a bottle of milk on a high, white table (see figure 1). Reading a comic book, a little boy sits on a low stool. On the floor, a little girl sleeps, covered by a white sheet. The mother, wearing red gloves, puts black gloves over them. In extreme slow motion (the prolog takes forty-five minutes), she pours milk, gives it to boy, returns to table, picks up knife, gently stabs boy, wipes knife clean. Stage left, an older brother (Raymond Andrews) witnesses the event. He screams. The ritual – first milk, symbol of life, then murder – is repeated on little girl. Older brother screams again. The mother puts her hand over his mouth. Traumatized by witnessing the murders, he loses the gift of speech. Gray drop, showing a cracked wall, goes up, revealing a magic forest with a pink angel walking backwards. Nine ladies, elegantly clad in white Victorian gowns with white birds on their fingers, listen to "The Moonlight Sonata." The boy enters this dreamworld. Wonders ensue: A giant frog – dapper in velvet smoking jacket and cravat – lounges at a banquet table, sipping martinis nonchalantly. Men with yellow fish on their backs float across a red river. A magic bench flies the boy through the air (see figure 2). A giant bee and giant bunny wiggle and bump to the

1 The slaughter of the innocents: Sutton performing the ritual murder in the prolog to *Deafman Glance*.

pop tune "Mutual Admiration Society." An ox swallows the sun, his stomach glows, his head falls off. Nine apes crawl up from the ground. As Fauré's *Requiem* sounds, apes pick up red apples. George Washington and Marie Antoinette stroll in. The queen's parasol bursts into flames. Apples float into space. Stars fall from the heavens. Drop comes down as a banjo strums "When You Are in Love, It's the Loveliest Night of the Year."

Designed by Fred Kolo, one of Wilson's principal collaborators in the early days, the set drew on nineteenth-century stage craft: scenery painted on flat canvases using classic perspective. Kolo also cites the painting techniques of René Magritte and Edward Hopper as influences. Both painters represented objects with a simplified realism based on form, color, and light. "By being grounded in *trompe-l'œil* painting, the set created a place you had never been before but where all these strange events seemed plausible," Kolo says.[11]

Launching Wilson's international career, the work stormed America and Europe. European critics showered kudos on it. Louis Aragon lauded

2 *Deafman Glance*. Raymond Andrews sailing through the air in Wilson's magic forest. By comparing the trees in this scene with those in *The Forest* (figure 37), one can gauge how the geometric aesthetic came to dominate. In later productions, tall abstract verticals signify trees. For the sake of contrast, in his highly abstract *King Lear*, Wilson used a real tree for Gloucester's death scene. The old man walked into the tree and merged with nature, joyfully seeking the release of death. Wilson loves trees and pores over books with photographs of trees from all over the world.

it as a "miracle," a work to "heal congealed art": "The spectacle has recourse to new methods of light and shadow, to machines reinvented from before the Jansenism of the eyes . . . It criticizes everything we have become accustomed to. *Deafman Glance* is an extraordinary mechanism of liberation, liberation of the soul, liberation of the body."[12] In discussing *Deafman Glance* Susan Sontag recalled:

My first encounter with Bob's work was *Deafman Glance* in Paris in 1971. I went to the opening and went back every night. I was enraptured. I saw it with a shock of recognition. I had never seen anything like it before, but it was what I had always longed to see without knowing it. I needed to experience theatre with that rhythm, that intensity, that beauty. Why is Wilson's work important? It's profound and profoundly visionary. It has the signature of a major artistic creation. I can't think of any body of work as large or as influential. To be so prolific, to have such a large palette, to do so many different things is part of his genius. His is the great theatre career of our time.[13]

After the success of *Deafman Glance* Wilson, who had considered himself a painter, contemplated a career in theatre.

Underneath the surrealistic fairy tale, the images bodied forth an archetypal pattern of death and rebirth. Inspired by Raymond's drawings, *Deafman Glance* dramatizes a child's attempt to grapple with the mysteries of life ending and life beginning. Before their murder, Bird Woman, albeit detached, shows concern for her children's physical well-being: she feeds them. Who is this Bird Woman, she who gives life and death? "I don't know," Wilson demurs. "By turns I see her as a mother, a priest, an angel of death. Maybe she's Medea. It's not a violent murder. It's tender. She's a mystery. I try to open up, not narrow down meanings. There are many interpretations" (*Quartet*). "I never thought of it as evil," Sutton notes. "No emotion was implied. No anguish. No suffering. It was more subliminal. I thought of it as a ritual, like a mass. Raising and lowering the knife was like raising and lowering a chalice." Sutton's allusion to the chalice used in the mass cuts to the heart of *Deafman Glance*. The mass – Fauré's *Requiem* is the musical climax of the piece – centers on the violent murder of a Passover lamb: Christ. His blood, symbolized by the wine in the chalice, purifies, cleanses, renews. This symbology knits up together in a *complexus oppositorum* images of destruction and creation, death and rebirth. Through death, life lives. Through violence, violence is transcended. Images of violence and ritual sacrifice thread through the work: the hut burns and collapses into the earth, the innocent ox, like a scapegoat, is offered up. The sacrificial victims are both human and animal. As a symbolic act, sacrifice exhibits contradictory aspects: it is both a sacred duty and a criminal act. "Violence and the sacred," René Girard argues, "are inseparable."[14] From the outset, Wilson's imagination has been epic, poetic, mythic, and deeply spiritual.

Part of the appeal of the early work was its naivete, a naivete that, while never totally lost, ebbed as formality and refinement increased. Technically, *Deafman Glance* shows characteristic Wilson touches. A stage divided into horizontal zones parallel to the proscenium (see figure 3). Processional movement in straight lines across these zones, creating layers of activity. The additive process, which gradually fills a space with energy and people, then gradually empties it out. Formal design replaces a chronological story line. A kaleidoscope of images explodes on stage.

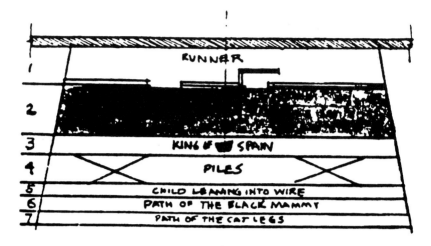

FLOOR PLAN (7 LAYERS OF ZONED ACTIVITY)

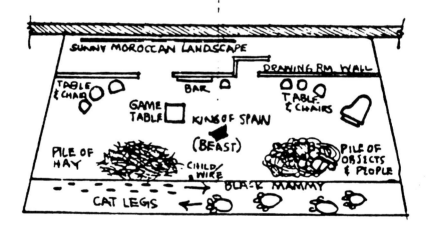

FLOOR PLAN

3 The floor plan for *The King of Spain,* showing the stage divided into zones of layered activity parallel to the picture plane.

Instead of a traditional narration, these images explore a sensibility: they express the inner life. Wilson moves the theatre away from drama towards lyric poetry.[15] The play took place in what Wilson calls "the time of the mind"; the slow movement installed a trance-like state. And from this stage, language was banished. Silence reigned. In the program Wilson quoted Ezra Pound: "And the fourth, the dimension of stillness and the power over wild beast . . ."

DECONSTRUCTING LANGUAGE

If in the first period Wilson ignored language, in the second he deconstructed it, toying with its foibles. If in the first period Raymond, a deaf-mute, was his muse, in the second Chris Knowles inspired him, an autistic child who plays with language like a jigsaw puzzle, arranging and rearranging the pieces into unexpected patters and patterns according to sounds, visual architecture, and mathematical formulas. The second period begins with *A Letter for Queen Victoria*, although Wilson's interest in the theatrical use of language had begun somewhat earlier, in, for example, the dinosaur chant for *KA MOUNTAIN AND GUARDenia TERRACE*.[16] Some of Raymond's unconventional writings had piqued Wilson's curiosity about breaking linguistic codes and creating new ones. At this time, Wilson disbanded the Byrd Hoffman School of Byrds and began working more with professionals. He also assumed the role of playwright, generating scripts with Chris, including the DIA LOGS (see figure 4), and writing plays of his own like *I was sitting on my patio this guy appeared I thought I was hallucinating*, which incorporated rags and tatters of found language. Visually, his style evolves as well. In the first period, the stage pictures referred playfully to nineteenth-century illusionistic theatre (*The King of Spain*); to Edward Hicks and America folk painting (*Life and Times of Sigmund Freud*); and to childhood fantasy – children's drawings and storybooks. In the second period, Wilson's geometric aesthetic – minimalist in sympathy – sharpens. The range of color narrows: black and white and gray prevail. By restricting color, Wilson privileges architecture, line, design. The use of sidelight increases, etching the body in space. Visually the work becomes less "naive," more sophisticated and formal, more abstract and elegant. In *I was sitting on my patio* all these elements are magnificently on display.

Einstein on the Beach (1976), the most celebrated work from this period, marks a date in cultural history. A mystical farce, *Einstein on the Beach* rampages through the absurdity of the human condition with unflagging brio and comic élan. It brings together music, dance, drama, and visual

4 Wilson, a tall Texan in a tall cowboy hat, and Christ Knowles, autistic savant, perform *DIA LOG / Curious George*. Note the concrete poetry scribbled on the walls like childish graffiti. *Curious George* was inspired by a child's book about an impertinent monkey that Chris loved.

art in one big bang – the nuclear fission of theatre. The neutrons and protons of drama are still flying through outer space. Writing in *The New York Times*, Robert Brustein observed, "With this work, [Wilson] is launching the theatre into the unknown and the unknowable, in a way that makes our contemporary domestic plays look like ancient artifacts of a forgotten age . . . Like Molière's Monsieur Jourdain, we are beginning to discover that we have been speaking prose all our lives – and we have been listening to too much prose as well. But the nonlinear theatre fulfills some of the conditions of poetry by introducing us to the unexpected, and bringing us beyond the prosaic formulas of our social–psychological universe."[17]

Einstein's theory has given the twentieth century its name – the Age of Relativity, summing up our myths and shibboleths.[18] Relativity has so permeated the way we view the world that it is the one dogma we believe absolutely. Relativity of perception, of language, of meaning – no wonder Wilson would be drawn to the man who best symbolizes our confused, distracted century, adrift in an absurd, unstable universe. Wilson turns Einstein into a latter-day Doctor Faustus, whose will to know leads him and the rest of us to the abyss. *Einstein on the Beach* ends, not with a whimper, but with a big nuclear bang.

Pitting the dreamer in Einstein against the scientist, Wilson investigates two diametrically opposed ways of knowing the world: art and science. Using reason, the man of science uncovers the laws that govern the universe. With his triumphs he leads us to the brink of annihilation. "If I were a young man again beginning my career," Einstein confessed in a pang of guilt shortly before he died, "I wouldn't be a scientist but a plumber or a peddlar." (Alluding to this remark, the furniture was fashioned from plumbing pipes.) In contrast to the scientist, the artist uses the imagination to explore the mysteries of existence through poetry and myth. Time becomes a metaphor for this dichotomy. On the one hand, mechanical clock time: in *Einstein on the Beach* people are obsessed, comically, by their wristwatches. On the other hand, interior time, time as consciousness – Bergson called it duration[19] – cannot be measured by clocks and calendars. Wilson's slow motion dramatizes time, not as a discrete unit ticked off by a chronometer, but as a flowing succession of states, melting invisibly, indivisibly into each other – time as consciousness. Since consciousness fuses past, present, and future, this is also the cyclical time of myth and ritual, of eternal return. Of the past found again, of Proust's privileged moment: a moment inside and outside time.

Erroneously, many critics consider Wilson's works non-narrative. They are non-linear but not non-narrative. In fact, one characteristic of a Wilson production like *Einstein on the Beach* is the profusion of narrative fragments that cross, crash, and collide on stage. These narrative fragments, however, may be difficult to recognize. The gaps between the fragments are larger than the fragments, giving the spectator who wants a story acres of empty space in which to construct one. Moving theatre away from narrative toward lyric poetry, Wilson privileges formal patterns; he foregrounds spatial and temporal, not narrative, structure. By emphasizing artistic devices rather than story line, he veils narrative. In Wilson, the aesthetic organization interrogates and celebrates itself. For all that, ghosts of stories haunt Wilson's works. But ghosts – elusive and ethereal – are not always easy to spot. The stories in Wilson may not have beginnings or ends, but the seeds of numerous narrations are there.

Analyzing narration, the Russian Formalist critics made a useful distinction between *fabula* (story) and *syuzhet* (plot). The *syuzhet* is a specific discourse that realizes an abstract story in a concrete, sequenced form. The *fabula* is the myth, which can manifest itself in many different works of art, with varying omissions, additions, sequences, emphases. Thus the *fabula* of the tragedy of tragedies – *Œdipus Tyrannos* – existed long before Sophocles, and long after. Artist after artist has retold the same myth, recasting it in a new *syuzhet*. In our century, Freud (one of the greatest novelists), Cocteau, Gide, D. H. Lawrence, Stravinsky, and Martha Graham all took a stab at it, each creating a work of art that, on the surface, may or may not bear much resemblance to the others but which, underneath the superstructure, relives the same story. The abstract *fabula* – a story the reader creates in his mind by putting the narrated events into a logical order – must be extrapolated from the concrete *syuzhet*, which can reorder time sequences or make deletions.[20] The *syuzhet*, which foregrounds artistic devices, can scramble the *fabula* to such a degree that the latter becomes difficult to unravel. The *fabula* is a mental construct built from clues embedded in the artistic organization of the *syuzhet*. It is a story we create through assumptions and inferences. We abstract the *fabula* as we progress through the work of art and retroactively. Hindsight helps immeasurably in concocting the *fabula*. The *syuzhet* (plot) parcels out information about the *fabula*; the spectator organizes these clues into the *fabula* or story.[21] In Wilson the *syuzhet* draws attention to itself, obscuring the *fabula*.

Einstein on the Beach was constructed around three visual motifs: the train, the trial, the spaceship. Each occurs thrice. With music by minimalist composer Philip Glass, most critics classify this work as opera. The work, however, transgresses the boundaries of traditional dramatic genres: theatre, ballet, opera, pantomime, performance art, ritual. Some of the questions *Einstein on the Beach* raises are central concerns of theatre semiotics. What can a stage do? How many different sign systems can it deploy? How does it generate and communicate meaning? Wilson organized the work in spatial terms borrowed from the traditions of painting and cinema. The perception of depth changes from close-up portrait (the intimate knee plays, Wilson's word for preludes and interludes) to mid-shot still life (train, building, courtroom, prison) to the spaceship scenes viewed as long-shot landscapes. In the following discussion of *Einstein on the Beach*, the letter "A" refers to the train motif; the letter "B" to the trial; the letter "C" to the spaceship, which is always accompanied by a dance.

Knee play 1: Stage right, two women (Lucinda Childs and Sheryl Sutton) count out loud. Sitting at tables, their fingers wander over an invisible keyboard. The chorus enters the orchestra pit and counts. Everyone is dressed the same: baggy pants, shirts, suspenders, sneakers – the Einstein uniform. The opening is slow, quiet, meditative. We seem to have stumbled into the Eleusinian mysteries transplanted to a spaceship.

Act I, scene 1A (train 1). This scene – Wilson at his most exhilarating – dramatizes the director's love affair with long lines – verticals, horizontals, diagonals. A tall abstract crane – it might be a fragment of a bridge or a launching pad – towers over the stage, looking like a Minimalist sculpture in the industrial vein. Einstein as a little boy stands atop, launching paper planes. Dressed in the Einstein uniform of baggy gray pants, white shirt, suspenders, and sneakers (*Einstein on the Beach* is an opera in black sneakers), Lucinda Childs, stage left, walks monomaniacally back and forth on a diagonal. She clutches a pipe. Her hyperkinetic arm movements do not illustrate the throbbing, hypnotic pulse of Glass's pounding music, but she is equally compelling, equally intense. Her leg work is an object lesson in controlled rhythm. A large, flat cutout of a nineteenth-century locomotive – painted naively – inches in. Its horizontal line emphasizes the vertical crane. A vertical line of light appears at the top of the backdrop. Descending to the floor, it splits the stage in two. Blackout.

In the second section, Childs's diagonal has moved more stage center. A second girl enters and crosses the stage, banging away on an invisible typewriter with spastic glee. From time to time she vaults into the air like a jack rabbit that has seen a rattlesnake. Again, the horizontal train (during each blackout the train recedes into the wings) creeps towards center. A scrim drops with a painting in the Currier and Ives tradition, depicting a train cutting a winter landscape in two on a strong diagonal. This diagonal moves in the opposite direction of Childs's. Childs's arms become more frenetic, tilting against invisible windmills. Over the instruments, one hears voices, indistinctly. Someone sings the vowel "o." Someone repeats 1966. Someone asks "What is it?" The vertical light streaks down the backdrop again. Blackout.

In the third section, Childs's diagonal has moved slightly right of stage center. Stage left a man writes furiously in the air on an invisible blackboard, probably scientific formulas like $E=mc^2$. Sutton – dressed identically to Childs – crosses the stage, head stuck inside a newspaper. Someone listens to a sea shell. Three performers form a triangle with strings. The horizontal train snails its way across the stage. Following Childs, it moves further right. It is difficult to make out the words, but they sound like scraps of radio ads. "Crazy Eddy" and "self-service" stand out clearly, but the language hems and haws, refusing to make much sense. Boxing an invisible enemy, Childs's arm movements have transmogrified into a postmodern tarantella. Singers intone numbers that correspond to the rhythmic structure of the music. The vertical light slices the backdrop in half. The crane tips forward. The boy Einstein – dressed in a sailor suit – sails through the air. Blackout.

This scene – intense, pulsating, rousing – elucidates Wilson's techniques. First, he organizes space in terms of the shifting dynamics of horizontal, vertical, diagonal. Second, he achieves unity through repetition, variation, and reversal. Third, people do not relate to each other. Loneliness settles over the stage like a pall. Fourth, the people are not characters, but performers engaged in physical activities. "Lucinda and I were dressed alike, and we were both called Einstein," Sutton recollects, "but we didn't think of it as a character. We had a series of actions to perform – mechanical gestures pilots or computer engineers would use." Fifth, language starts and stops. Sometimes it communicates, sometimes it sneezes. Its reliability is questioned at the same time its materiality as sound is heightened. By juxtaposing different means of representing a train – the cutout, the painting, the propelling music, language – Wilson interrogates all systems of representation, indicating their relativity. If our systems of representation are unreliable, so too is every stab at communication. *Einstein on the Beach* dramatizes the glory and lunacy of trying to talk to each other.

Act I, scene 2B (trial 1). A large white bed, forming a long horizontal line on the floor, lies in the middle of the courtroom. A beam of light on high repeats the horizontal. Two white globes – lamps on the judges' bench – contrast with the horizontals. Stage right, the jury box and stenographer desks. What looks like the dial of an enormous clock hangs over the judges' bench. It has no numbers, and the design derives from a Persian bowl. The chorus takes its place in the jury box. The stenographers file their fingernails. Halfway between the orchestra pit and the performers on stage Einstein fiddles on the violin, imperturbable. The judges – an elderly black man and a young white child – enter with slow and stately gait. Black robes and white wigs – symbols of the august dignity of the law – adorn them. They take their places on the bench. Another Einstein (Childs) takes her place as witness on the high *Einstein Chair*. Made of plumbing tubes, it is one of Wilson's most celebrated pieces of sculpture/furniture. Calling the court to order with their gavels, the judges solemnly repeat six times: "This court of common pleas is now in session." As the scene winds up, one hears simultaneously the chorus singing numbers and the lawyer (Sutton) reciting the "Mr. Bojangles" monolog, a text by the autistic poet Chris Knowles. From time to time a voice pierces this dense acoustical environment by screaming, "No!" A lawyer with an illuminated briefcase enters and balances himself on one leg. A giant test tube descends. A black disc covers the white face of the clock, a reference to the eclipse that corroborated Einstein's theory of relativity. Coming forward to the edge of the stage with brown bags, the performers eat lunch and drink coffee from plastic cups. One girl reads a book, nervously jerking her head to and fro. The hypnotic rhythms of the music stop suddenly. Everyone raises his wristwatch close to his face and stares at it. Freeze frame as performers, turned to stone, continue to stare at watches. Then they rub their foreheads, as if troubled by a dark, secret thought. They return to the jury box. The elderly judge (Samuel Johnson wrote the speech as well as read it) recites a monolog about romance in Paris.[22] A drop of a nude woman descends. Blackout. For the 1984 revival, Johnson wrote an alternate speech about women's liberation. In the 1992 revival, the 1976 speech was used in Paris; the 1984 speech, everywhere else.

Knee play 2: Childs and Sutton sit on angular, minimal chairs stage left and place their hands rigidly on their knees like polite little girls in a convent. Out of sync with each other, they recite the "Wind for the Sailboat" monolog, an autistic text Knowles quilted together from found language fragments. The two women bend forward slowly, crouch on the floor, then resume their positions on the chairs. They proceed to count, chanting different numbers at different rhythms. Childs slaps her thigh sharply with manic, self-destructive energy. Sutton's fingers dance over an invisible keyboard. In one of the most famous visual images from the play, the two lean on a steep diagonal over the chairs, defying gravity, hands hovering in the air. Someone shouts 1905. Blackout (see figure 5).

Act II scene 1C (spaceship/ballet 1). On an empty stage, representing an open field, the performers go through simple, postmodern choreography, running, jogging, leaping, spinning. The spinning leaves the dominant impression: a mystical trance. In the background a spaceship. Andy de Groat choreographed the original production; Lucinda Childs, the revivals. Childs's choreography is more precise and emotionally cool. His choreography resembled natural movement; hers displays virtuosity. She emphasizes strong, clean lines and is mathematical rather than mystical.

Act II, scene 2A (train 2). In act I scene 1A, we saw a locomotive from the side. In this scene we see an antique caboose from behind. Dealing with relativity, the opera shows the same object from different angles. A dark blue night has set in. During the scene the quarter moon waxes to full before an eclipse snuffs it out. An elegant couple, accoutered in turn-of-the-century evening clothes – appears to sing a love duet. Actually they are lip syncing. The real singers are in the pit; therefore, there is a

5 Sutton and Childs in a knee play from *Einstein on the Beach*.
Photograph: Copyright © 1976, 1995, Babette Mangolte, all rights of
reproduction reserved.

strange dislocation of sound. Smiling, the lady pulls a gun on her
companion. Blackout. The train reappears but it has moved far off into
the night.

Knee play 3. The two women, backs to the audience, stand at a control
board where lights flash geometric patterns. The chorus brushes their
teeth and sticks out their tongues.

Act III, scene 1B (bed/trial 2). The set looks like trial 1. The defendant
(Childs) now confusingly wears a dress, not Einstein's baggy pants. She
walks over to the bed and lies on it. She gets up, changes into a Patty
Hearst guerilla outfit, and points a machine gun at the audience. A prison
cell, occupied by a male and a female jailbird, slides in and occupies half
the stage. The defendant (Childs) resumes her position on the witness
chair and recites Knowles's monolog "I Feel the Earth Move."

Act III, scene 2C (spaceship/ballet 2). We return to the open field, but the spaceship has moved closer. While it is crossing the stage, the dance, similar to dance 1, unfolds.

Knee play 4. Lying on two glass tables, the two women, lit from below and above, swivel and pivot and gyrate. They seem to be swimming through ether.

Act IV, scene 1A (building/train 3). The shape of the building – which Wilson could see from the window of his loft – recapitulates the shape of the night train, calling into question our perception of object constancy. In an upper window a man – is he Einstein? – scribbles calculations in the air, demonically. Writing on the wind is a recurrent Wilson image. One by one, the other performers come in, form an anonymous crowd, and stare at the scribbler – the mad genius separated from the common herd. One girl lost in the lonely crowd reads a book. The mob ambles off.

Act IV, scene 2B (bed/trial 3). An organ cadenza opens the scene. The bed that dominated the courtroom has been reduced to a glowing beam of horizontal light on the floor. Slowly it levitates into a horizontal and, accompanied by soprano solo, it wafts into the heights in mystical longing.

Act IV, scene 3C (spaceship/ballet 3). The spaceship has moved closer with each succeeding ballet. Now we are inside, facing a giant control board divided into cubicles for the astronauts. Banks of lights flash geometric figures (see figure 6); two glass coffins move back and forth on horizontal and vertical lines; a small boy sits impassively in the vertical box. Wilson turns himself into a human semaphore, dancing with the fury of hell. Someone flies through the air. The flashing lights go berserk in a burst of atomic energy (see figure 7). The beat, beat, beat of the frenzied music puts one into a trance. Two plastic bubbles on the floor belch forth smoke. The two women (Childs and Sutton) crawl out. They keel over. The spaceship has sailed into the void. A drop, representing an atomic explosion, falls, terminating the scene. Einstein's formula – the icon of our age – is emblazoned on the drop: $E=mc^2$.

Knee play 5. A quiet scene after the big explosion. (Wilson prefers to let the tension out of the space slowly.) The end of the play recapitulates the beginning: the director likes circular dramatic structure. The two women, now presented as lovers, sit peacefully on a park bench, stage right. Their fingers move in a digital ballet that recalls knee play 1. A bus, similar to the train of act I, scene 1A, enters stage left and moves towards them. The last words we hear – the bus driver has a narrative monolog – are "'Kiss me, John,' she implored. And leaning over, he pressed his lips warmly to hers in fervent osculation . . ." The story, couched in a level of diction too elevated for its banality ("fervent osculation"), brings *Einstein on the Beach*

6 The interior of the spaceship in *Einstein on the Beach*. The allure of
Armageddon. The whirligigs of self-destruction hypnotize, seducing
us into their madness. Photograph: Copyright © 1976, 1995, Babette
Mangolte, all rights of reproduction reserved.

to a close, not with a whimper, not with a bang, but with a joke on language and its relationship to reality.

In this work – Wilson calls it a poetic meditation on Einstein – the director's mythic view of history encompasses the evolution of the species by
juxtaposing various means of transportation: walking, sailboats, trains,
buses, planes, spaceships. Just as the nineteenth-century locomotive –
belching smoke – symbolizes the Industrial Revolution, so too does the
spaceship represent the Age of Relativity. Man's quest to conquer the universe appears as heroic and quixotic, bold and dangerous. Each step
forward takes us one step nearer extinction. "Walking back and forth on
the diagonal," recalls Childs, "always meant for me the need to start over
again and again, the need to strive, endlessly, and perhaps not get anywhere."[23] "We thought of the play as a journey," says Sutton. And the
journey leads to the nuclear holocaust.

Einstein on the Beach shows Wilson's concern not only for trespassing

7 Wilson, dancing with the fury of bedlam and Beelzebub as the
spaceship hurtles out of control in *Einstein on the Beach*. Photograph:
Copyright © Lynn Kohlman.

the boundaries that define artistic genres but also for erasing the distinction between high art and popular culture, forcing the audience to examine the assumptions behind these categories. One of the most salient aspects of Wilson's work is the broad and disparate range of material – visual and verbal – he weaves together. He scavenges from innumerable centers of culture: canonical literary texts; newspapers; opera; pop songs; advertisements; stock market reports; cinema; dance; historical documents; autistic poetry; paintings by old masters and new; architecture; industrial design; the drawings and body language of a deaf-mute boy; the choreography of tap-dance legend Honni Coles; sculpture; postcards; and the banal conversations he overhears on the street. Leafing through one of the black notebooks in which Wilson sticks anything that tickles his fancy is to confront a higgledy-piggledy mass of incongruous images. Much of the language and many of the images in *Einstein on the Beach* are pillaged from the debris of mass culture. All of these heterogeneous materials create a centrifugal energy, but Wilson controls them through his monumental architectural sense of visual structure.

Referring to *Einstein on the Beach*, Philip Glass noted,

Artists today see their work as firmly rooted in the culture of our time. This started with Andy Warhol. Pop art taught us to take a very American vocabulary and turn it into an idiom of the fine arts. In the early sixties, the idea that the vernacular of popular culture could become the language of high art was unimaginable. The aesthetics of pop art affected people like Wilson and myself. We were all beneficiaries of that.[24]

In 1992 a third revival of Wilson's production of *Einstein on the Beach* toured America, Germany, Australia, Spain, Japan, and France. 60,000 spectators cheered the work that Alan Kriegsman of *The Washington Post* hailed as "one of the *Zeitgeist*-defining artistic creations" of the twentieth century.[25] In *Newsweek* Alan Rich saluted the second revival in 1984 as "one of the truly pivotal artworks of our time,"[26] and John Rockwell in *The New York Times* asserted "*Einstein on the Beach* remains a masterpiece; it has, thus far, triumphantly withstood the test of time. I find it constantly involving and almost religiously moving."[27]

In addition to significant textual and choreographic changes, *Einstein on the Beach* looked and felt differently in each successive revival. Some of the costumes, for instance, had changed. The corps de ballet in 1992 danced like professionally trained ballet dancers (in 1976 the dancers were largely non-professionals), and the clothes they wore, while still casual, had become more upscale. The original production – twenty years ago – felt like a seventies, avant-garde production. In the seventies, vanguard companies wanted to erase the distinction between art and life. Consequently, they stressed ordinary people in ordinary clothes performing ordinary tasks. That look now seems dated, and in revival, *Einstein on the Beach* has become measurably more elegant, refined, and professional. These changes raise the issue of the identity of a theatrical work of art. Even with the same major collaborators, this identity is neither as simple nor as stable as one would believe. Each revival of the same production and each performance of that revival is a set of contingencies.

Glass reflected on the occasion of the third revival:

Einstein on the Beach strikes me as more radical in 1993 than it did in 1976 because theatre has become much more conventional. In the seventies, a lot of experimentation was going on, but, owing to the influence of TV drama, theatre in America has degenerated. And now everyone keeps one eye on the box office. *Einstein on the Beach* was written with idealism. Our intentions were absolutely pure. We weren't thinking about money. We were thinking about aesthetics, not success. We had no idea where the piece would go after we finished it. All our decisions were made for aesthetic reasons. *Einstein on the Beach* has a tremendous impact on young audiences today. They have no idea you could get away with making theatre in such a non-traditional way.

I like working with Bob. We have similar backgrounds, coming out of the New York art world at the time we did. We were born from the same creative womb – Cunningham, Cage, Jasper Johns, Warhol. And we both have an accurate sense of time. When Bob and I talk about a work, what we talk about is time – how long a piece will last. In theatre the dramatic structure and the time structure are never separate. *Einstein on the Beach* was important in my development because I had to learn how to write music that had a dramatic structure that could extend and build over time. Time is the common medium between music and theatre. The most important lesson I learned from Bob was to let things take the time they take, that it's okay to write a scene in which nothing happens except a sense of being, not a sense of dramatic movement. Bob has the strongest signature you'll find on the stage today. He has changed forever the way people think about theatre.[28]

Although *Einstein on the Beach* was created around Wilson's designs, three times the Library of Congress refused to copyright the visual portion of the work, saying that *Einstein on the Beach* was a suite of drawings, not theatre. International critics rank the work as one of America's most important and innovative operas. Ironically, it saw the light of day thanks to a grant from the French government, and it premiered at the theatre festival in Avignon. Wilson wanted *Einstein on the Beach* to be seen in the States, but to bring it to New York's Metropolitan Opera House, which he rented in 1976 for two nights, the director ended up with a personal debt of $140,000 – despite sold-out performances. When Wilson's father heard of the loss, he said, "Son, I'm impressed. I didn't know you were smart enough to lose so much money."[29]

FROM SEMIOTICS TO SEMANTICS

The muse of the third period – Heiner Müller – changed Wilson's relationship to language. Müller, regarded by many as one of the greatest living playwrights,[30] collaborated with Wilson on the Cologne Section of *the CIVILwarS* (1984), which incorporated parts of Müller's play *GUNDLING'S LIFE FREDERICK OF PRUSSIA LESSING'S SLEEP DREAM SCREAM*.[31] Dense, elliptic, and abrasively lyrical – Müller's script uses language in a literary way. A text of Müller's lends itself to exegesis. Words have meanings. Where they are put on a page and who says them has something to do with semantics. Something we recognize as character exists, and something we recognize as a tale is told. Characters engage each other in something we recognize as dialog. Hardly conventional, Müller does not take the tools of the dramatist's trade at face value, but in his theatre plot, character, and dialog live and breathe in postmodern paradox: elusive and fragmentary, colored by parody and pastiche. Fast and furious come the allusions in Müller's texts. To fight your way through his labyrinth of words requires erudition and imagination. The script of *the CIVILwarS* differs significantly from Müller's original play, which appears only in fragments and as part of Wilson's larger mosaic. Wilson himself contributed texts to the Cologne Section, as did thirteen other authors. But it is clear that the metaphors, suggestiveness, and ripe ambiguity of Müller's work elbowed Wilson into the world of semantics.

During this period Wilson directed two other major plays by Müller, *Hamletmachine* and *Quartet*. In addition, he used Müller's "Description of a Painting" as prolog and intertext for *Alcestis*. Müller was supposed to write a text for *Death Destruction & Detroit II*, but (typically) did not. Instead, he sent Bob a letter, which was read as a prolog. Wilson also incorporated a text by Müller into *The Forest*.

In the seventies Wilson wanted to create "new works for our time . . . I was asked to direct plays and operas, but I still didn't like theatre and wasn't interested in pursuing that field as a career. I refused to direct other people's plays. I thought it was more important to create new work." One of the major concerns behind *Einstein on the Beach* was "how do we create major new works of our time?"[32] In contrast, *the CIVILwarS* contained snippets from Shakespeare and Racine. Wilson's desire to start exploring classic texts offers additional evidence of his evolution. In 1984 he directed Charpentier's baroque opera *Médée*. Not accidentally, it deals with infanticide; child abuse haunts Wilson's psyche and his work. In 1985 Wilson – he has long expressed his admiration for Shakespeare[33] – did a workshop production of *King Lear*. Previously Wilson had claimed that plots "hamper my imagination" (*Quartet*). When I reminded him of this statement later, he replied, "It's always good to contradict yourself" (*Lear*).

After *the CIVILwarS* Wilson worked most frequently in Germany, a country that takes the arts seriously. Germany – its state-subsidized theatres are the envy of the world – nurtured Wilson's genius. Having at his disposal the financial and artistic resources of Germany's major theatres, Wilson continued to grow. Other gifted American directors of his avant-garde generation withered on the vine: talent must be cultivated. The notion of untutored genius springing full-grown with armor from the forehead of Father Zeus is a Romantic myth. To unfold, talent needs support, encouragement, and time. We need to stress more "the *institutional*, or public, rather than the *individual*, or private, preconditions for achievement in the arts . . ."[34] The director-function, like the author-function "is not formed spontaneously through the simple attribution of a discourse to an individual."[35] An art of collaboration and by the nature of its mode of production deeply implicated in the society that creates it, theatre is yoked to the "values, institutions, and practices elsewhere in the culture."[36] Ruthlessly dominated by commercial pressures and the profit motive, American theatre could not support an art as complex, refined, and innovative as Wilson's. Wilson flourished because Wilson fled America.

After the cancellation of *the CIVILwarS* at the Los Angeles Olympics Arts Festival in 1984, Wilson went into artistic exile. The twelve-hour, Texas-sized epic was the director's most ambitious work, ranging through history to plumb the origins of violence. But some of the Babbitts who control the purse strings of arts funding in America pronounced it unworthy. The French, Dutch, Germans, Italians, and Japanese had all produced segments, but Wilson could not raise the money in America to bring the work together in Los Angeles. David Bowie as Abraham Lincoln reciting the Gettysburg Address in Japanese sent American corporate donors into paroxysms of anger. A honcho at Warner Communications retorted, "If Europeans think this is so great, let them pay for it."[37]

It was a crushing defeat for the indomitable Texan. At the time, Wilson, who rarely shows emotion in public, had to fight back tears during a BBC interview. "Can you imagine all this for something that didn't happen?"

he sniffled, gesturing to hundreds of set designs scattered around the room. "I'm sad," he has lamented. "It's hard for an American to get his work done in America. Diana Vreeland says some years you're in, some years you're out."[38]

"That was the last time I tried to produce my own work," the director recalled recently. His voice meters out cadences with Prussian militarism. Everything Wilson does – on stage and off – is meticulously controlled. He folds his hands like a well-brought-up little boy in a roomful of adults. Formal, polite, distant, Wilson is a perplexing mix of diffidence and hauteur. "I was left with a tremendous debt. Work in America was scarce, and the fees are not so high. To survive artistically and to pay off my debt, I had to work in Europe. There I worked with many different companies and artists. Theatre in Europe is more sophisticated than in America. Doing so many and so many different kinds of productions extended my range. So the L.A. cancellation had positive effects, too."[39]

Working with some of Europe's most distinguished artists, Wilson, who learns through osmosis, constantly stretched himself. After directing many of Germany's greatest actors – Marianne Hoppe, Maria Nicklisch, Jutta Lampa, Otto Sander, Jutta Hoffmann – the way he works with actors and how he uses them began to evolve. Wilson's encounter with Heiner Müller was a critical turning point in his relationship to language. His collaboration with Hans-Peter Kuhn, the leading sound artist in Europe, further demonstrates how Wilson prospered in Germany. After working with Kuhn on *Death Destruction & Detroit*, Wilson's sound environments – a crucial element in his productions – became increasingly sophisticated. The technology and technicians on hand in German theatres enabled him to do more not only with sound but also with light. The large palette of colors he used in productions like *Quartet* or *Cosmopolitan Greetings* was unexpected. Increasing sophistication can be seen in all aspects of his work during this period, including costumes and the use of stage makeup – what Germans call *die Maske*.

One moral emerges loud and clear from the saga of Robert Wilson: America does not support its vanguard artists. "I'm American," Wilson sighs. "I don't want to spend the rest of my life as an expatriate, but it's hard to do innovative work at home. Creativity is being repressed in America."[40]

The philistinism of America has long driven its artists into exile: From Henry James to Hemingway, from T. S. Eliot to F. Scott Fitzgerald, from Gertrude Stein to Ezra Pound, from Orson Welles to Robert Wilson.

One of the crowning glories of his career, the Cologne Section of *the CIVILwarS* (1984) exemplifies Wilson's work in this period. In 1985 the

American Repertory Theatre (ART) remounted a version of the Cologne Section. The multimedia extravaganza mesmerized critics and audiences. It even converted Dan Sullivan, the theatre critic of *The Los Angeles Times*, whose earlier skepticism had contributed to the Olympics debacle. Reviewing the Cambridge production, Sullivan wrote, "Clearly, this is a major work by a master theatre maker . . . Wilson really does offer a new way to look at theatre . . . a theatre where suspense to see the next thing that will happen is replaced by pleasure in this thing, for as long as it takes to happen."[41]

The following description refers to the American Repertory Theatre's production of the German section of Wilson's mammoth epic. The acts refer to their position in the overall work.

Act III, Scene E

The break of day, a group of army tents huddled near a battlefield. Confederate soldiers wake up and prepare for battle. A vaudeville comic dances across the stage. An antique car, bearing a load of antique bourgeois, crosses the stage. Frederick the Great stands up in back seat of car. Soldiers march off to battle. At various times one hears discontinuous dialog.

Act IV, Scene A

Section 1: Members of a prototypical American family come in and sit around a table. Behind a screen Frederick the Great watches. The American father reads a stern letter of reprimand Frederick's father sent his son. The family leaves the table. Section 2: "Machinery." A film of a giant turtle swimming underwater is projected on the screen, which fills the proscenium arch. The White Scribe, walking up and down the *hanamichi*, recites over and over a text by Heiner Müller. Music by Hans-Peter Kuhn. Section 3: "Two Tables with Spaceship." A film of an Arctic landscape. Girl sits at table, assiduously applying fingernail polish. Young man enters, spouting numbers about ball bearing production. He switches abruptly to Hamlet's ardent declaration of love to Ophelia. A spaceship lands. Section 4: "Beardance." The film changes to volcanoes erupting. Two bears enter. Submariners appear through traps in the floor and repeat commodities future prices. Frederick enters and, playing his flute concerto, dances with bears. Section 5: "Frederick the Great." A throne is placed over Frederick, who crawls with it on his back. Franz Kafka's letter to his father, explaining the psychological damage the patriarch had inflicted, is read. Section 6:

"Film Montage." Section 7: "Drugstore." Downstage a drugstore counter. High above an old man recites Timon of Athens's misanthropic diatribe against humanity. A woman smokes a cigar. A man with an idiotic smile walks up and down the *hanamichi* carrying a law-and-order sign. In the drugstore a fight ensues over whether or not the radio should blare music. Old man (Timon) tears pages out of a book and hurls them down at the squabblers. Music by David Byrne. Section 8: "Death Scene." Frederick the Great dies, surrounded by courtiers. Black Scribes, representing history, write in invisible books and whisper the names of famous battles. Music by Hans-Peter Kuhn. Section 9: "Frederick and Katte." Frederick and his homosexual lover act out a fragment of Racine's *Phaedra*. A film of polar bears. Section 10: "Dog's Death." Frederick shoots his dog. Submariners intone commodities future prices. Traditional, fifth-century Japanese flute music.

Section 11: "Erlkönig" (see figure 8) (music by Schubert, lyrics by Goethe.) A giant eagle flies across the screen. Frederick the Great rises up from a trap in the floor on a white stallion. Dressed in full red, white, and blue military regalia, medals shining like gold florins, he covers his face with a mask – a scowling devil. High upstage behind the screen, a young girl dangles, a rope around her neck. Across the screen a film is projected of a giant eagle gliding through space. Sophie Dorothea, Frederick's mother, is carried in on a Louis-Quinze chaise. Dressed in a white satin gown trimmed with ermine, hair stuffed into a *dormeuse* bonnet, she looks like a rococo teddy bear. In her lap she coddles a Pekinese. In her mouth she pops bonbons. Schubert's lied "Erlkönig" sounds. First, the hanging girl recites Goethe's lyrics in English. Then, as a deep baritone sings the German, Sophie Dorothea lipsyncs, gesticulating wildly, like Sarah Bernhardt in *Elizabeth the Queen*. While his mother sings with male voice, Frederick bends backwards on his horse, turning the mask upside down and clutching his fists with psychotic intensity. At the end of the song, Sophie tries to rise, but, given her corpulence, cannot. Furniture movers cart her off.

Goethe's ballad tells a tale about a father who, failing to understand his child's needs and fears, lets him die. In the context of *the CIVILwarS*, this scene dramatizes one of Wilson's abiding concerns: the emotional abuse of children by parents who, lacking sensitivity, crush the child's imagination and personality. One can kill the soul as easily as the body. Frederick's mother is self-contained and distant. Upstage a murdered child hangs. Downstage Frederick covers his real face with the mask of a devil. By juxtaposing these visual, verbal, and musical images, Wilson suggests that by crushing Frederick's spirit, by assassinating his true self,

8 "Erlkönig" from *the CIVILwarS*, a multi-media farandole, staggering in its brilliance and depth. By bombarding the senses, Wilson vouchsafes the spectator a glimpse of the sublime, an emotion the modern world has repressed. From left to right: Sophie Dorothea (Frances Shrand); Young Woman, hanging (Diane D'Aquila); Frederick the Great (Priscilla Smith). American Repertory Theatre.

his parents turned him into a monster. Although the theme is anything but lighthearted, the impact of the scene was not lugubrious. To the contrary, the mother made one laugh with her vaudeville turn. All of Frederick's movements were beautiful to watch, and the devil face – inspired by an Etruscan mask Wilson had seen in the Cologne museum – had its own grotesque allure. The combination of Schubert's music, Goethe's lyrics, and the image of that soaring eagle bombarded the senses with joy. Perhaps the child with the rope around her neck has not been crushed after all. Perhaps her spirit is winging away from the parents who try to stifle it. Wilson elicits complex and contradictory emotions always. And always, as in this *scène à faire*, the dense sensory input overwhelms. Too much is going on to begin to describe. Wilson, after all, is one of the world's great showmen. He has many stops, and he knows how and when to pull them all out.

Section 12: "Smilers." Film shows one building after another tumbling into dust. Philip Glass's music accompanies the cast as they enter, smile, and exit.

Act IV, Epilogue. Abraham Lincoln, King Lear, Earth Mother, and a Snow Owl all coincide on the same deserted battlefield.

the CIVILwarS marked Wilson's first collaboration with Suzushi Hanayagi, a Japanese choreographer trained in Kabuki and Noh as well as in postmodern American dance. If in his early works Wilson presented ordinary people engaged in ordinary physical tasks, his movements were now becoming more formal, more stylized. His collaboration with Hanayagi encouraged this trend.

Precisely because of this growing concern with formal matters, some critics attacked Wilson's work as apyschological. Despite the fact that Wilson foregrounds formal strategies, his theatre resonates with psychological significance. Wilson translates the drama of the soul into visual metaphors; spatial relationships and movements in Wilson reveal psychological secrets. Although most of Wilson's directions are technical, starting in the third period of his career and depending on the play and the actors, Wilson does on occasion discuss plays in explicitly psychological terms. I first noticed this change at the *Quartet* rehearsals, during which Wilson elaborated on the blitzkrieg that explodes when people fall out of love. "Has Bob been reading Stanislavski?" puzzled Jenny Rohn, the actress who played the young girl and had worked with Wilson in *Hamletmachine* and *Salome*.

During the *When We Dead Awaken* rehearsals, Wilson again expatiated on the dynamics of breaking up with Stephanie Roth (Maya) and Alvin Epstein (Rubek). But these psychological analyses always come long after the visual book is well advanced. Wilson is also willing now to let actors – rarely and only in special moments – express emotion directly. "I was stunned," notes Thomas Derrah, who had worked with Wilson in *the CIVILwarS* and *Alcestis* and, after a hiatus of five years, in *Danton's Death*. "In the past he just talked about choreography, the angle of your fingers, and how much space to leave between your arms and the body. Now he's more interested in exploring what an actor has in his tool chest, and, especially in note sessions, he now investigates subtexts and emotions." Clearly, Wilson's relationship to actors, as well as his relationship to texts, has evolved and continues to evolve.

HOW TO DO THINGS WITH WORDS

In Wilson's fourth period – how to do things with words – he confronts the classics. Opera and musicals loom large in his schedule. Since Wilson has always been interested in language as sound, opera helped him to make the transition to the classics. Opera uses language as sound as well as sense, and since it is a highly stylized genre, it suits Wilson's formal aesthetic. But most operas also have linear plots, characters, and dialog, as well as lyrical arias that, through music, express interior states better than language. As in each period, the seeds for subsequent development were sown in the previous period. Wilson's collaboration with Müller, as well as his staging of operas and ballets with stories that bow to the Aristotelian model of beginning, middle, and end – *Alceste, Salome, Le Martyre de Saint Sébastien* – prepared the ground for his current work on the classics. This period starts with *Orlando* and includes *King Lear, Swan Song, When We Dead Awaken, Parzifal, Lohengrin, The Magic Flute, Danton's Death,* and *Madama Butterfly*. Wilson continues to direct new works inspired by old myths: *The Black Rider* (based on the German folktale used in Weber's opera *Der Freischütz*), *Alice in Wonderland, Don Juan*. He has cast his eye on *Paradise Lost*, a project he is percolating with literary icon William Burroughs. He and Glass are planning an opera based on *The Arabian Nights,* and the two have virtually completed *The White Raven*, an opera about the heroic age of exploration, when Spain and Portugal pushed against the limits of the known world. Wilson has long admired Gertrude Stein. Since her stance toward language parallels his, he feels drawn to this muse of Modernism. In the wake of the extraordinary international success of *Doktor Faustus Lights the Lights,* he is preparing productions of *Four Saints in Three Acts* and *Saints and Singing*.

When Wilson approaches contemporary authors like Stein, Heiner Müller, or Susan Sontag, the performance script is virtually as printed. When fashioning a performance script from a novel, Wilson takes an active and crucial role from the outset in determining what stays in and what goes out. A real collaborator, he works closely with dramaturgs, playwrights, and actors, but he is the one who controls the script: it reflects his vision.

When Wilson directs classic plays by Shakespeare, Büchner, or Ibsen, he may move a scene to or fro, reassign a speech, repeat words, or intercalate another text. He may add an interlude between acts – Wilson calls them knee plays, and they provide an anti-structure to question the main text – but he tinkers around with the text relatively less than other avant-garde directors. Some of these texts rankle a contemporary audience's ear with classical rhetoric. Because film and television have conditioned the way we process information, we take in theatrical signs differently from either Shakespeare's audience or Ibsen's. For this reason and given his own artistic bent, Wilson prunes words with Draconian severity.

Reflecting on his collaboration with Wilson to prepare the performance script of *When We Dead Awaken*, Robert Brustein writes, "The text was radically cut . . . The major task was to pare away everything extraneous, repetitive, or explanatory – everything, that is, that could not be rendered through the symbology of the stage . . . We ended with a text about half the length of the original, without, I believe excising anything vital to the action, the characters, or the theme."[42]

Wilson does not do a play he does not like by a dramatist he does not respect, the word the director always uses when referring to Shakespeare. "I don't have to make theatre with *Lear*," Wilson said during rehearsals. "Shakespeare already made the theatre. What I have to find is a way to put his theatre on a stage with enough room around those words so that people can hear them and think about them. I don't believe in talking back to a masterpiece. I let it talk to me."

What a masterpiece says when it talks, however, depends on who is listening. Different ears hear different things. Consequently, the relationship between any text to a concrete realization of it in performance is never simple. Performance is mediation. It always interprets. It translates language into many different codes and many different sensory modalities.

Saussure's distinction between language and speech helps to clarify the relationship between text and performance. Saussure makes a fundamental distinction between language (*langue*) and speech (*parole*). For Saussure, language is an abstract language-system common to a community of speakers. It manifests itself in speech – individual utterances in actual situations. Language makes speech possible, speech gives language concrete life. To use Saussure's vocabulary, then, any text is an example of language; any production, an example of speech. To use Victor Shklovsky's vocabulary, the text is the *fabula*; the production, the *syuzhet*. Confusion ensues when critics collapse these two distinct categories into a simplistic Platonic ideal of the extratemporal meaning of a text, shining forth to the pure in heart with celestial radiance from words on a page. Like language, which can generate an infinite number of individual speech utterances and idiolects, a text can generate an infinite number of concrete performances, none of which can be definitive. Like speech, performance is contingent.

Bearing in mind Saussure's distinction between speech and language, a scene from Wilson's production of *King Lear* at the Frankfurt Schauspielhaus will demonstrate how the director approaches a classic text. Originally Heiner Müller had agreed to do a new translation into German – one of the main reasons Wilson wanted to do the production.

But Müller had become embroiled in directing *Hamlet* intercalated with his own *Hamletmachine* at the Deutsches Theater, Berlin; consequently, he never got around to it. Wilson, therefore, turned to a standard German translation by Wolf Graf Baudissin. The director divided the play into a prolog (a poem by William Carlos Williams about the death of his grandmother) followed by the division of the kingdom (act I, scene i) and fifteen scenes, with an intermission after scene six (act III, scene vi).

Near the end of the play Wilson, who at times intercuts scenes to create simultaneity, conflates act IV, scene ii, lines 84–86 and act V, scene i, lines 18–20 "But [my sister's] being widow, and my Gloucester with her, / May all the building in my fancy pluck / Upon my hateful life . . . / I had rather lose the battle than that that sister / Should loosen him and me," (Goneril, stage right) with act IV, scene iv, lines 23–29: "O dear father, / It is thy business that I go about; / . . . No blown ambition doth our arms incite, / But love, dear love, and our ag'd father's right. / Soon may I hear and see him!" (Cordelia, center) and act V, scene i, lines 7–16 R: "Now, sweet lord, / You know the goodness I intend upon you: / Tell me but truly, but then speak the truth, / Do you not love my sister?" E: "In honor'd love." R: "But you have never found my brother's way / To the forfended place?" E: "That thought abuses you." R: "I am doubtful that you have been conjunct / and bosom'd with her – as far as we call hers." E: "No, by mine honor, madam." R: "I never shall endure her. Dear my lord, Be not familiar with her." E: "Fear me not." (Regan with Edmund, stage left). By bringing the three sisters together, he emphasizes the clash of their conflicting desires: Cordelia thinks of her father; the other two, of how they can get Edmund into bed.

Here Wilson does not overlap the speeches – a technique he sometimes uses. But by making big cuts and by staging the three scenes as one, he creates an hallucinatory, frenetic pace that pushes the play towards its climax. The sisters stand in three separate zones of light. Each zone represents a different space. Although the sisters are on stage at the same time, each inhabits a different world. Seeing the three together but at such cross-purposes creates a strange atmosphere of dissonant realities.

Until now, Goneril has been a political steam engine, unflinching in her pursuit of political power. Wilson directed Jutta Lampa to show, for the first time, a crack in Goneril's adamantine purpose. Her lust for Edmund is seducing her into committing political *faux pas*. Encased in armor, she looks like a Samurai ready to lead her calvary into the fray. The director asked the actress to express psychic tension with her body by making a violent, war-like gesture with one hand while simultaneously caressing the white handkerchief she associates with Edmund tenderly. "This scene must be a surprise," the director said. "Up to here we have seen you only as a strong woman. Now you must begin to break." At the end of her scene, Wilson instructed her to cover her face with the handkerchief. From this point on the actress starts to look somewhat crazed, with bizarre physical tics.

Cordelia, turned three-quarters away, looks at the audience over her shoulder. While verbalizing her hope of rescuing Lear, she peels a large onion. The first day he rehearsed the scene the director said, "It's nice to hear the sound of the peeling onion, but it's the wrong kind of onion. The audience must be able to see the layers. The action of the onion is totally different from what's going on in your mind. In your mind you picture Goneril and Regan, and you're saying 'Fuck you' to them over and over. Don't look at the onion. Look over your shoulder as if you're staring into the eye of time. When you finally look down at the onion, nothing is there." Cordelia's thoughts, words, and gestures follow three separate paths. Whereas Wilson wanted Goneril's weakness to show in this scene, he wanted Cordelia's strength to come to the fore. While Regan showers sexual blandishments on Edmund, he caresses a rich jewel Goneril has given him. "Think to yourself," Wilson said, "I don't love either one, and smile seductively." To Regan he said, "Hold your finger straight up close to his back, but don't touch him. It creates more tension."

Difficult to stage, the blinding of Gloucester (act III, scene vii) gauges any director's imagination. Wilson placed the scene after the break, opening part two. Blackout. A vertical shaft of white light, ceiling to floor, crosses stage left to stage right (moving in the opposite direction, the same shaft of light had opened the play). When it reaches stage centre, from the darkness upstage, Regan's voice rings out, first laughing psychotically, then modulating into a cry of pain, then into a shriek of sexual pleasure. In the middle of the black stage a square of scalding white light – like a minimalist boxing ring – appears. Black velvet covers the wall in back. Dim lights go up so that we barely detect the outline of Regan, standing by the bottom corner of the square, stage left, and Cornwall by the upper corner, stage right. The square seems so hot they are afraid to touch it. In one hand he holds vertically a shining steel stick about ten feet high. In the other, a square of white paper that repeats the white square on the floor, the only two objects brightly lit. Without looking at it – a letter to Albany – he reads. Regan takes the letter. Purring with feline desire, she gives it to Edmund. The catcalls animalize her and express what cannot be verbalized: her adulterous lust. Cornwall wears a black, double vested suit (no shirt); Regan, a red suit with a sheath to her ankles. Two servants bring in Gloucester, wearing a long black robe. They place him in the hot white square and disrobe him to the waist. A ring of steel falls round him, then rises as a spiral cage, gleaming cruelly in the bright light. Gently and seductively, Regan approaches Gloucester. With an abstract, formal gesture, she plucks a hair from his face without touching him. When Gloucester says "Because I would not see thy cruel nails pluck out his poor old eyes," he pauses for a long time after "not." His mouth falls open. In that moment, he foresees his end, the end of the play, the end of the world. Slowly, he turns around in his wire cage like a trapped fox. Cornwall inches the long steel stick towards Gloucester's eye. Gloucester bends forward to meet it. No contact is made, but light – blood red – floods the white square. Gloucester quivers, as if the steel cage is sending bolts of electricity through his body. The servant who intervenes walks slowly on a diagonal to Cornwall to stab him. As he starts to move, so too does Regan, tracing a circle around the other side of the square, meeting the servant as he returns to his starting point. Stabbing him with an elegant swing of the arm, she cries out "A peasant stand up thus?" (See figure 9.) When Cornwall tells Regan how sorely he is wounded, she holds out her hand to support him. Just before touching, she withdraws it abruptly and laughs. The two exit. The spiral cage drops to the floor. On a straight vertical (Wilson calls it the strongest line), Gloucester – alone on stage – walks slowly toward the audience. The stage has darkened completely except for a tight spot on his face and bare torso. Thrust into darkness, Gloucester becomes a boulder of stoicism. Suddenly, the black velvet cloth hanging in the back drops, revealing a wall of translucent white, and dazzling white light bathes the stage. Blind, Gloucester sees. During rehearsals, Wilson told Gloucester, "Now you see because you see with your hands. The body sees, the body hears." Continuing on the vertical to the audience, Gloucester feels an invisible object in his hand. First warm and golden, the light cools to a freezing Arctic blue. Inscribed on Gloucester's bare torso is the tragedy of the flesh: the body of an old man, wrinkled, worn, worn out. After reaching the edge of the stage, he retraces the same vertical line, walking backwards. Looking like a penitent in his black robe, his hands come together in a gesture of unconscious prayer.

"A realistic approach always diminishes Shakespeare," Wilson says (*Lear*), and this scene shows the director at his best: visually stunning, deeply moving, deeply meaningful. Abstract and formal, its cold beauty terrified. Mixing elegance and sadomasochism – the steel cage, the steel spear, Gloucester's leaning forward to receive the steel point – Wilson unsettles. The instruments of torture were *objets d'art*. We do not normally perceive violence as beautiful, but here beauty enhanced the brutality

9 The blinding of Gloucester. Regan stabs the peasant who protests the monarchs' cruelty. From left to right: Regan (Astrid Gorvin); servant (Mario Melzer); Gloucester (Jürgen Holtz); Cornwall (Hans-Jörg Assmann). Photograph Frankfurt Schauspiel, photographer: Abisag Tüllman.

and suggested its irresistible appeal. With bold stroke, Wilson intensified the horror of this, the most horrible scene ever written.

In the summer of 1993 Wilson workshopped *Hamlet*, in which he acts and directs. Wilson turns Shakespeare's play into a sixty-minute mono-drama; it is a memory played over and over in someone's mind. Hamlet's? Horatio's? Shakespeare's? Or our collective unconscious? It seems to be an exorcism and an act of penance. The set is a pile of rocks that shift in size and shape during the performance. A black curtain moves from time to time, redefining the playing space. The production is scheduled to open at the Alley Theatre in Houston in 1995, and changes will inevitably occur as Wilson workshops the piece further. Establishing a reliable text for *Hamlet* presents grave problems: the first quarto, second quarto, and first folio present, in essence, three wildly different versions. There is no definitive edition. Most standard editions – usually a confla-tion of the second quarto and first folio – run to slightly over 3,900 lines. Wilson has shaved the text down to approximately 1,500 lines (the first quarto is much shorter than the second quarto or the first folio). All the words in Wilson's *Hamlet* will be Shakespeare's – no interpolated texts. But lines are transposed. Wilson favors circular ends. Therefore, the play opens with Shakespeare's conclusion. From the beginning we know the end, and the entire play becomes an elegiac meditation on Hamlet's death: "Had I but time . . . / O, I could tell you – but let it be. / Wretched queen, adieu. / I follow thee" (act V, scene ii, lines 332ff). Wilson will not play different roles, but he will assume different voices and different speaking positions.

If the relationship of a play to any performance of it is complex, bringing a novel to the stage presents a new set of problems. Migrating from one medium to another, even the language must change. One cannot carve off slices of dialog from a novel and shove them into actors' mouths. The rhythm of prose fiction is antithetical to the stage. Dialog that sparkles in a book – Jane Austen's, for example – does not breathe on a stage. Stage language – Verdi called it *la parola scenica* – must precipitate a theatrical event. Unlike novelistic dialog, it is not an end in itself; it seeks completion on a stage. Furthermore, on stage it exists in a complex relationship to other theatrical codes that change its contours and colors.

Similar problems arise when a novel becomes a film. David Mamet – playwright, director, poet, and novelist – has adapted several novels for the screen. "The process of adaptation is hard," he says. "Each medium has its own rules. The rhythm of a line of prose on a page is not the rhythm of a line of dialog on a stage. When you put it on a stage, you realize that you have broken the rhythm, and if you break the rhythm, you break the meaning. The meaning of dialog is always conveyed by its rhythm. I can't explain it, but my ear hears it."[43]

Reflecting on his adaptation of *Swann in Love* for the screen, the director Volker Schlöndorff said: "I lost my inhibitions about filming literature long ago. The only way to be faithful is to be unfaithful. If I make a movie which Proustians celebrate for its fidelity, I will have failed as a director. One must create a new work of art that stands on its own as a movie, otherwise all one has done is string together a series of dead photographs that illustrate a text like nineteenth-century engravings. Fidelity to Proust is not an aesthetic criterion to judge film with."[44]

Nevertheless, some critics still contend that any attempt to translate a novel to another medium is a perverse enterprise, doomed to miscarry. In *Subsequent Performances*, Jonathan Miller, usually the epitome of critical acumen, insists with more wit than insight that since description (prose fiction) and depiction (film and theatre) are different, the latter can never faithfully capture the former. Pictures, he argues, work differently from language – *une vérité de la palisse* no one would argue with. After many ingenious lucubrations in which he excoriates filmed novels, Miller, despite himself, stumbles across the truth. Speaking about his own film version of *Alice in Wonderland*, he writes: ". . . when the first show print came back from the labs I realized that if the film succeeded at all it was by avoiding direct adaptation. Like Robert Lowell's translations, it was an ironic *imitation* of *Alice in Wonderland*, and it is only as travesty that it has a relationship with the original novel."[45] Only after one has given up the phantom of fidelity, can one begin to discuss intelligently films or plays inspired by novels. Although Luis Buñuel's *Cumbres Borrascosas* does not "faithfully" reproduce Emily Brontë's *Wuthering Heights*, it does convey on a deep emotional level the novel's diabolism, and no one would stigmatize it as a failed film. The final sequence – a grotesque parody of *Romeo and Juliet* – has on the face of it nothing to do with Brontë's novel. Yet in its own right it is a work of genius, as brilliant and unnerving as anything the Yorkshire spinster penned. The operative word is in its own right.

Wilson has directed many productions inspired by well-known narratives. The stories that seize his imagination yield clues about that imagination. *Alice in Wonderland, The Black Rider,* and *Tales from the Brothers Grimm* all fall under the rubric of fantasy literature, works that transgress the principles of literary realism. Further, they all portray the grotesque absurdity of life. *The Forest*, based on the *Gilgamesh Epic*, depicts the tension between civilization and nature, the id and the super-ego. In addition, it explores male bonding and the existential consequences of the discovery of death. Thomas Mann's *Doktor Faustus* chronicles the descent into madness of Adrian Leverkühn, a musician who peddles his soul to the devil to create a new musical idiom. Through Leverkühn, Mann explores the blood ties between genius and insanity and the social responsibilities of art. Some critics read the novel as an allegory of the evil that took possession of Germany and led to Hitler. In the end Leverkühn retreats into a kaleidoscope of private hallucinations that cuts him off from everything except the monsters of his febrile brain. Wilson has frequently meditated on art and the artist: explicitly in *Alice, The Death of Molière, When We Dead Awaken,* and *Swan Song*; implicitly in *Doktor Faustus Lights the Lights, Deafman Glance,* and *The Life and Times of Joseph Stalin* with the lonely figure of the poet Osip Mandelshtam.

Since *Orlando* offers a particularly interesting example of Wilson's dramatization of a major novel, a closer look at his adaptation is warranted. I compare play script with novel – not in pursuit of the sylph of fidelity – but as another window on Wilson's creative process, asking not only what kinds of novels spark his imagination but within those novels what scenes.

Just as there are two sexes to Orlando, there are two sides to his–her

story: the existential and the social. Wilson, given his artistic temperament, favors the existential aspects of Woolf's novel. Woolf balances
Orlando's introspection by inserting her into the whirl of social life. Thus,
in chapter 4, Orlando (our hero–heroine spends the first half of her life as
a man; the second half, as a woman) muses playfully about gender, the
vagaries of sex, and the social, intellectual, and legal consequences of
being a woman:

When I was a young man, I insisted that women be obedient, chaste, scented, and
exquisitely apparelled. Now I shall have to pay in my own person for those
desires. There's the hairdressing. That alone will take an hour of my morning.
There's looking in the looking-glass. Another hour. There's getting into under-
clothes and lacing up, there's washing and powdering, there's changing from silk
to lace and from lace to paduasoy. And there's being chaste year in year out.[46]

In Woolf these internal meditations are set off by a life immersed in
society. Orlando is not always alone. She enjoys serving Pope and Swift
tea and gossip.

Turning 329 pages of Woolf into a two-hour monodrama requires deletions. What Wilson puts on stage and what remains in the novel,
however, is not accidental. Wilson dramatizes Woolf's elegiac vision; her
sense of passing time; her exploration of androgyny; her attack on
Victorian propriety; the rich tapestry of history; the Romantic evocation
of nature; the existential glimpse into the abyss; the sense of the multiplicity of self. He dramatizes these concerns of Woolf's because he shares
them. What does he leave out? In addition to Orlando's social life, Wilson
also deletes Woolf's sense of the continuity of English literature and her
celebration of its glory.

The novel is a valentine sent to the English language, and this feeling
for language Wilson retains. Comparing the passage from the play
quoted above with the same passage in the novel,[47] one is surprised by
how little the language has changed. The third-person narration, of
course, changes to first-person. Apart from cutting and making necessary
transitions, Woolf's unmistakable prose – complicated syntax, opulent
vocabulary, shimmering images – has found its way to the stage. Other
directors would have shortened the sentences, edited out the soaring
images, and found substitutes for the polysyllables. Many actors would
grumble that Wilson's adaptation is too "faithful, too literary." It goes
against the grain of dialog written for the theatre today. An actor needs
impeccable diction, an enormous vocal range, and the lungs of a
Wagnerian soprano to fight her way through these monumental
labyrinths. But in the right context, Wilson has a penchant for long

sentences, long tirades, and opalescent words. What he resists is realistic dialog.

The fallacy that Wilson hates language dogs him like the ghost of Banquo. Rumors circulate that Wilson had a stammer, which supposedly estranged him from language. Suzanne Lambert, Wilson's younger sister, disagrees. "In junior high and high school, you could take electives. Bob always signed up for speech classes in which students practice extemporaneous speaking, public speaking, and debates. At school his success in the speech contests made me realize how intelligent he was. He had a reputation as an orator. I don't remember any speech defect. At home he talked an awful lot."[48]

Wilson's retention of Woolf's verbal grandeur led to his minimal set. Wilson explained:

The text of *Orlando* is a novel, not a play. We had to invent a theatrical action for this text, a text replete with rich images. At first I thought I should design a set with rich images too. Then I realized that was impossible. I couldn't compete with the richness of the words. Woolf's language is music. So I made the decor minimal, like a blank canvas for the text so one could see the pictures of the text.

Although the set was abstract, Orlando's costumes were in period. "If I ever do this script again," the director claims, "I'd do it as a demented bag lady in New York, speaking all this crazy text on the streets of Manhattan. To her this weird story is real. A madness is operating all the time in Woolf's text" (*Lear*).

Woolf's novel ends with a *deus ex machina*: Orlando's husband drops from the sky to rejoin her on the last page (after having disappeared immediately after their wedding). His return lulls Orlando's dark musings. In many ways this sentimental conclusion, coming after so many meditations *de profundis*, strikes a false note. Wilson deleted it, ending his theatrical event the way it began, with Orlando's oft repeated phrase, "I am alone" (see figure 10). By bringing the play full circle and by restating the existential cry of solitude, Wilson gave his production a solemn, ambiguous end that refuses to resolve the dilemmas it propounds. Woolf's emotional gush pretends to resolve these dilemmas, but, of course, it does not:

And as Shelmerdine [Orlando's husband], now grown a fine sea captain, hale, fresh-coloured, and alert, leapt to the ground, there sprang up over his head a single wild bird.

"It is the goose!" Orlando cried. "The wild goose . . ."

And the twelfth stroke of midnight sounded; the twelfth stroke of midnight, Thursday, the eleventh of October, Nineteen Hundred and Twenty-eight.

10 Orlando (Jutta Lampe), coiling herself into an elegant twenties ballgown like a winding sheet. Wilson's production ended as it began, with a pang of solitude.

Since the last paragraph and indeed the entire last section of Woolf's novel stress the modernity of the twentieth century, contrasting it with the dank Victorian parlor (one of Wilson's recurrent themes), one gasps at her description of Shelmerdine as "a fine sea captain, hale, fresh-coloured . . ." The passage might have been lifted from a boys' weekly.[49] We must take it as parody, Woolf's mocking her own sentimental conclusion. Like Dickens's second ending to *Great Expectations*, Woolf's end does not satisfy, and she is perspicacious enough to know this; hence, the sarcasm.

With Wilson, the text to analyze is the performance; written text is only a small part of this larger text. This rattles grammarians, who fret about "fidelity to the text." By fidelity they mean a performance that reaffirms archaic interpretations of a written text. Wilson's productions connect with the words, not on a surface, but on a deep level. Since Wilson understood that Woolf's novel is not really about conjugal bliss, he changed the end. A Wilson production challenges, questions, provokes. Opening up the text, it forces the spectator to think, and rethink, the material. Wilson does not illustrate texts, he illuminates them.

Orlando represents a major turning point in Wilson's career. German critics hailed it as the director's first essay in *Sprachtheater*. But Wilson, as will be seen in chapter 2, has always been deeply engaged with language.

Nevertheless, *Orlando*, the most linear and literary work he had yet attempted, ushered in a new phase of his career during which he would train his astute eye on some of the greatest texts in the canon, enriching them, enriching us.

2   The cracked kettle

A l'extrême de toute pensée est un soupir.
Paul Valéry, Autograph Note Signed in the Author's Collection

THE LANGUAGE PROBLEM

Impatience with language rages through twentieth-century literature. From Virginia Woolf to Franz Kafka, from T. S. Eliot to Rilke, great wordsmiths have harbored suspicions about the grains of sand they use to build their castles. This mistrust of language – Flaubert's cracked kettle[1] – has, ironically, generated volumes of eloquent language, especially in novels, where narrator after narrator breaks the story to lament the impossibility of capturing life in words. Humbert-Humbert frequently interrupts his seduction of Lolita to rant against his medium of expression – language: "Oh, my Lolita, I have only words to play with! . . . I have to put the impact of an instantaneous vision into a sequence of words; their physical accumulation in the page impairs the actual flash, the sharp unity of impression . . ."[2] The linearity of language – its inability to convey the simultaneity of the whirlwind of thoughts, emotions, and sensations that bombard consciousness – exasperated Nabokov as it did Woolf.[3]

Just as modern literature – and literary theory – fret over the foibles of language, so too does philosophy. "All philosophy," sighed Wittgenstein, "is a critique of language."[4] Turning their backs on metaphysical speculation, twentieth-century philosophers organized the apocalypse of language and, consequently, of knowledge and meaning. Like literature, philosophy cast a skeptical eye on its own means of communication.

In theatre, no one has dramatized this crisis of language with as much ferocious genius as Robert Wilson. Like Wittgenstein's philosophy, all Wilson's theatre is a critique of language. But literature and philosophy are limited to the code they wish to critique; the only weapon they possess to fight language is language. Reduced to questioning words with more words, they are glued, like flies to fly paper, to the fallacies and absurdities of the system they struggle, in vain, to transcend. But since theatre has more channels of communication in its arsenal – visual and aural codes cheek by jowl with the verbal – it can elaborate a more

41

complex and sophisticated inquisition of the thousand natural shocks that language is heir to. No one has used visual signs to question words with such adamantine severity as Wilson, and no where does one experience the nervous breakdown of language as in Wilson's theatre.

The highest praise Wilson can bestow on another mortal is: "He doesn't talk." Going over a list of applicants for an assistant on *When We Dead Awaken,* Wilson selected a young man who was "Smart, fast, polite, and doesn't talk." During the workshop for *Danton's Death* the director grumbled, "Danton doesn't do anything except talk."[5] When Wilson observed that an actress in *the CIVILwarS* "never stops talking," I knew she had been banished to the lowest circle of the inferno.

In Milan during the workshop for *Doktor Faustus* at La Scala, Wilson and I dropped into the patio of Bragutta's restaurant for dinner. The hour was late, the sky clear, the breeze sensuous. Having finished their five-course meals, the elegant Milanese lingered over coffee and cognac, glowing with good food, good wine, and charm. The restaurant hummed with loud, happy voices. Wilson sat down, looked round, and grumbled, "Why do people talk so much? The human race is drowning in words. They should shut up and drink." At this point the waiter set down on the table a dish with several thin, round slices of lemon. Wilson stared in silence for ten minutes, then exclaimed, "How beautiful these lemons are!" "The color, Bob?" I asked. "No," he replied, "the structure, the pattern of the seeds."[6]

Wilson's malaise with language – his theatrical version of our *mal du siècle* – questions more radically than any other playwright or director the authority of the text and the primacy of language. Frequently, this questioning has been interpreted – erroneously – as aversion to language. Nothing could be wider of the mark. Just as all Wilson's theatre is metatheatre – asking what and how theatre communicates – so too is all his theatre metalanguage – obsessively involved with the pathology of words. Even in an early play like *Deafman Glance,* which deals with the loss of speech through trauma, language makes its presence felt by absence.

"I love Shakespeare because of his language," Wilson confesses. "I like to read Shakespeare and listen to the rhythm. Shakespeare's words are indestructible, solid as a rock. You can put them anywhere – sink them to the bottom of the ocean, fly them to Jupiter, or drop them into Vesuvius. Nothing destroys them."[7] Rarely does Wilson talk about authors, but writers who crop up in his conversation – Gertrude Stein, Samuel Beckett, Heiner Müller, William Faulkner – he claims to like for the same reason: "I love their language." A man of riddles and enigmas, Wilson's relationship to language is paradoxical. Similar to most love in the twentieth century, it is complex and tormented, like the love a man feels for a faithless mistress. Sensitive to its beauty but suspecting its virtue, Wilson simultaneosly caresses and torments language. Looking at the overall evolution of Wilson's career, one sees that he pulled language apart only to put it back together again – an attempt to "give a purer sense to the words of the tribe."[8] Unlike Humpty Dumpty, language survives many falls, and in the process of assaulting the linguistic codes he questions, Wilson reveals the full range of their possibilities. Wilson's theatre forces the audience into a different relationship with language and consequently with the systems of meanings coordinated by it.

"Words for Bob," says Tom Waits, who wrote the songs for *The Black Rider* and *Alice*, "are like tacks on the kitchen floor in the dark of night and you're barefoot. So Bob clears a path he can walk through words without getting hurt. Bob changes the values and shapes of words. In some sense they take on more meaning; in some cases, less."[9] (See figure 11.)

INTERROGATING LANGUAGE

In *A Letter for Queen Victoria*, the main character is language. This play summons language to the witness stand to investigate its malice and lies. What is language, Wilson's play asks. What is it made of? Why do we need it? How do we use it? How does it work? How does it generate meaning? To what extent is this meaning an illusion? What can it communicate? What can't it communicate? When and why does it break down? What rules govern its use? What happens when we ignore these rules? How do rules change over time? What is the relation between language and paralinguistic systems like facial expressions and body language? What is the relation between language and thought, language and consciousness, language and identity? What is the relation between speech and writing, between the physicality of language – sounds and visual signs – and mental concepts, between words and the objects they refer to? How does language represent the world? How does it misrepresent it? How can language, a social convention, communicate a private, idiosyncratic truth? Does it seduce us into believing that we can make sense of experience? Is language a crutch our intellect needs to pretend we understand the rush of the senses, the chaos of the world? Is language the original sin? Would we be better off in a pre-linguistic Eden, before the fall into language? Complex, difficult, and critical are the questions Wilson poses.

The play begins with a letter to Queen Victoria redolent of Latinate

11 Playing word games with Alice (Annette Paulmann), Charles
Dodgson (Stefan Kurt) explores the shifting boundary between sense
and nonsense in the Wilson–Waits musical *Alice*.

grandeur and Victorian rosewater: "DEAR MADAME, MOST GRACIOUS OF
LADIES, AUGUST IMPERATRICE: ALBEIT IN NO WAY POSSESSED OF THE HONOR OF
AN INTRODUCTION, AND INDEED INFINITELY REMOVED FROM THE DESERVING OF
IT, YEA, SINGULARLY UNFIT FOR EXPOSURE TO THE BRILLIANCE OF YOUR SUN,
BEING IN VERITY OF A CONDITION SO ABJECT IN ITS DESTITUTION OF GRACE . . ."
Wilson forged the remaining text from autistic arabesques and new
words that have entered English since 1947. By juxtaposing clashing
levels of diction – Miltonic opulence and contemporary lingo, crib
poetry[10] and pre-verbal screams – Wilson dramatizes a diachronic view
of language in the individual and in society. Language is not a stable
system. A social artifact, language evolves as society evolves. The
Victorian letter, bowing and scraping in linguistic self-abasement,
strikes a modern ear as jabberwocky. The Queen may have taken the
absurdly pompous diction as natural; we cannot. Given the arbitrary
nature of the linguistic sign, language never stands still. Over time it
changes and changes us.

12 Wilson, performing in *A Letter for Queen Victoria*. The drop, organizing language by visual and sound patterns, functioned as concrete poetry.

Dramatizing the language problem, the first entr'acte of *A Letter for Queen Victoria* pushes language to its limits, where it collapses into a phonetic trash can. Scripted and performed with Christopher Knowles, an autistic poet, the two do their verbal turns before a show curtain painted with a series of words they shouted HAP HATH HAT HAP – words arranged not in terms of semantics or syntax but in autistic patterns that heightened their materiality – how they sound, how they look (see figure 12). Words are not just information; they are also physical signs. Wilson refreshes our awareness of words as music and painting. The text of *A Letter for Queen Victoria* is written in capitals, aesthetically more pleasing than small letters. Capitals, the kind of lettering draftsman and architects use, figure prominently in Wilson's aesthetic. The director often uses them on drops, program covers, and posters. By molding language into a pictorial composition, Wilson emphasizes the visual beauty of written script and fuses word into image. Wilson is observing language itself, not the objects and meanings it refers to. The director focuses on language in its brute physicality.

Turned into abstract shapes, language became visual design on the curtain and pure rhythm in speech. By privileging the signifier over the signified, words ceased functioning as symbols and became objects – the referent evaporated into physical sound. As concrete as poetry gets.[11] Like concrete poetry, *A Letter for Queen Victoria* confronts printed language with pictorial language. Like concrete poetry, "it injects visual patterns with the thought element of meaningful words."[12] And like concrete poetry, it blocks the linear progression of language, stressing the multiplicity and simultaneity of possible relationships. By brushing aside discursive reasoning, the work stresses the inability of language to capture the complexity of consciousness.

Although the verbalizations at the beginning sounded like gibberish to the audience, Wilson and Chris seemed to be communicating with each other – a speech community of two.[13] Language is a social construction. It exists long before and long after the person through whom it speaks. Language is one of society's most potent weapons to control its members; its rules are mightier than any individual. But since linguistic codes are arbitrary and conventional, one can shatter and rebuild them at liberty and to infinity. What happens when one radically violates the rules that govern communication? One withdraws from society into autistic isolation. Language binds us to a community. By turning one's back on speech conventions, one turns one's back on society.

In this entr'acte language dissolves into sonic debris. Language, too, is subject to the second law of thermodynamics: "MNHJUYGTHRD VBNH V B BBNHJ BGV PJER GLOS O CHOCOLATE." The entr'acte had started with a preverbal, primal shriek, and we are still freezing in a linguistic ice age, but amid this phonetic chaos (the string of consonants is virtually impossible to pronounce), semantic light slowly begins to move over the face of the deep; the ear picks up a word – "chocolate" – clear, recognizable, lovely in the sweet simplicity of its reference. When spoken, "GLOS O CHOCOLATE" sounds like an American tourist trying to say *glâce au chocolat*, French for chocolate ice cream. The use of a foreign word – *glâce* for ice cream – again emphasizes the arbitrary nature of the linguistic sign.

After collapsing back into phonetic chaos (CVBGFHYUJKI), we hear something that sounds like a sentence, "There are these electro whe whe whe whe whe whe whe wheels." But now, although English syntax has been observed, albeit stutteringly, we are confused. The reference is muddy. What is an electro wheel? We have just been told it exists, but does it? Is it a real object or a signifier in search of a signified?

Halfway through the entr'acte, the question everyone in the audience
has been asking explodes: "WHAT ARE WE DOING?" Comes the candid
answer: "WE'RE DOING A LETTER FOR QUEEN VICTORIA . . . WE'RE DOING THE
PLAY . . . WE JUST DID ACT ONE AND WE'RE GOING TO BE DOING ACT TWO ACT
THREE AND ACT FOUR . . . AND YOU SIT ON THE BENCH AND WAIT FOR ME . . . OK."
Lights out. Curtain up. Act II. Language behaving itself – asserting, communicating – bright as the noon-day sun in its deadpan literalness.

What has Wilson wrought? Exactly what he was supposed to in an
interlude: comment humorously on the serious themes of the play to
keep the audience in their seats – entertained and braced for the next act.
Speech is the best vaudeville man puts on. Wilson has been playing
games with language, like a kid with a new bag of marbles, but, as
Wittgenstein assures us, meaning is use and the games we play with language and language plays with us are infinite.[14] In approximately five
minutes Wilson has sketched the origins and evolution of language from
jungle grunts to infant babbling, from Urlanguage to articulate art, suggesting that speech is a species-specific trait, an essential part of our
humanity.[15]

Reference – fragile, elusive – fades in and out, but language, even on
holiday, has done something. Language, in fact, has performed all the
speech acts J. L. Austin proclaimed: locutionary, illocutionary, perlocu-
tionary.[16] The language of the entr'acte has stated something ("We're performing the play *A Letter for Queen Victoria*"). It has done something
(performed the entr'acte). And it has achieved something through language: it has entertained the audience and persuaded them to prick up
their ears and listen to act II.

But Wilson has done more than is dreamed of in Austin's philosophy.
He has established a sophisticated dialog between sense and nonsense
that goes to the heart of the language question. Is language a mirage,
shining seductively in the shifting sands of the desert of meaning?
"Philosophy," Wittgenstein said, "is a battle against the bewitchment of
our intelligence by means of language."[17] *A Letter for Queen Victoria*, then,
is eminently philosophical. The specter of nonsense haunts Wilson's
works and sets up a dialectic with language that leaves one stranded in a
slough of undecidability. We are lost in a no man's land between the
nirvana of silence and the beatitude of Asphasia. Language, friend or foe?
Wilson's theatre stares the audience down, smiling like a Sphinx.

Not only does *A Letter for Queen Victoria* problematize language, it also
problematizes theatre, affronting our expectations and deferring
meaning in a carnival of contradictions.[18] "The carnival spirit," writes
Bakhtin, "destroys all pretense of an extratemporal meaning and

unconditional value of necessity. It frees human consciousness, thought, and imagination for new potentialities."[19]

In act IV, unexpectedly, a mysterious Chinese man appears as raisonneur, promulgating Wilson's artistic credo: "STILL, WHEN ONE HAS SPENT SUCH TIME AND DEALT WITH THESE . . . YES, I SUPPOSE YOU MAY CALL THEM INSCRUTABLE SUBTLETIES – ONE CAN BEGIN TO RECOGNIZE THE CONSISTENCIES, THE PATTERNS, OR AS YOU CALL IT, THE MODUS OPERANDI." This section of the play parodies *To Have and Have Not*, the *film noir* scripted by Faulkner after the Hemingway novel. Wilson had seen the movie during rehearsals.[20] That Wilson puts his credo in the mouth of a villain casts an ambiguous, humorous light over the utterance. Likewise, the pompous level of diction moves this artistic apologia towards parody. While making a serious statement, it pokes fun at itself. Like all Wilson's work, it refuses to be pinned down to a simple, single meaning.

Wilson, as the Chinese raisonneur suggests, is a man of patterns, visual and verbal, but his patterns fly in the face of Aristotelian drama. Since the Greeks, Western theatre has relied on language to transmit meaning; Wilson's theatre runs interference with language. "If I wanted to send the audience a message," shrugs Wilson, "I'd use a fax" (*Lear*). Rather than looking for simple, univocal messages, the traveller in Wilson's wonderland had better be armed with a sense of humor and start looking for patterns in the carpet. To diagnose the pathology of language, Wilson slices it up and puts it under a microscope. The director uses ten strategies to interrogate language: discarding it; disjunction; discontinuity; the play of meaning; the collapse of dialog; decontextualization; *reductio ad absurdum*; jamming; dissolving it into sound; ritualization.

THE LANGUAGE OF SILENCE

Wilson's first strategy to interrogate language is to discard it. His early works – he called them structured silence – tossed language overboard. "Language," Susan Sontag writes, "is the most impure, the most contaminated, the most exhausted of all the materials out of which art is made . . . Silence is a metaphor for a cleansed . . . vision . . . which must appear from the perspective of traditional thinking and the familiar uses of the mind as no thought at all – though it may rather be the emblem of new, 'difficult' thinking." Sontag calls the silence of art "perceptual therapy."[21]

Wilson's revolt against the tyranny of the word turns our theatrical tradition on its head. For the past two thousand years Western theatre has never cut its umbilical cord to the word. In the *Poetics* Aristotle discusses drama like a philosopher without eyes, and theatre is usually taught as a literary genre. Not surprising in a logocentric culture that privileges the verbal over the visual, associating language with reason and gendering it male, and associating the visual with the irrational and gendering it female.[22] Emancipating the stage from the dead letter, *Deafman Glance* – a play without words – brought about a Copernican revolution: language is no longer the center of the theatrical universe.

"The way actors are trained here is wrong," complains Wilson. "All they think about is interpreting a text. They worry about how to speak words and know nothing about their bodies. You see that by the way they walk. They don't understand the weight of a gesture in space. A good actor can command an audience by moving one finger" (*Lear*).

The fifteen-minute, wordless prolog Wilson added to Müller's *Quartet* demonstrates how he uses silence to question language. Wilson called the prolog "the parade before the circus. You introduce the menagerie to the audience" (*Quartet*). As the public entered the auditorium, a rococo concerto tinkled merrily away. A drop, depicting Albani's Baroque painting of *Diana and Acteon*, covered the stage curtain – an elegant rendering of this myth of sexual violation. Stage right a stark contemporary table and five chairs. The play, based on Laclos's *Les Liaisons dangereuses* takes place simultaneously in a salon before the French Revolution and in an air raid shelter after World War III.[23] Blackout. Lights up. We see a middle-aged woman in profile, holding her palm before her face as if in mourning for her life. Slowly she turns to the audience, a statue carved in ice. A silk bodice – violet – tight as a corset over a floor-length black skirt. One violet glove slinks up her right arm to her shoulder. Her face, a cloud of white powder; her eyes, slashes of black paint. A chic ghost, elegantly cruel.

In toddles an old man in formal black suit, white shirt, white face. Oblivious to the other specter, he sits down and starts reading an invisible book. An intellectual ghost. Next, in black spike heels and a green slip that reveals too much of her exuberant, eager flesh, a sexy girl wiggles in backwards – naive and sophisticated, innocent and debauched, uneasy in and uncertain of her sexuality. Then, a cocksure boy in white Versace suit struts over to the table, glaring at the old man. He wears no shirt. His body is his fortune, and he misses no opportunity to flaunt it. Last, a middle-aged man, an aging roué with outstretched arm, enters. He seems to be pulled across the stage, against his will, by an invisible bloodhound. The ghost of potency. When he sits down, several stories – flirtation, sexual role playing, lust at cross purposes, rivalry, jealousy, anger at the loss of youth and sexual desirability – start spinning so rapidly it is hard to keep track of who is seducing whom. All this through gestures and lights that constantly form, dissolve, and reform links between the players in this erotic endgame. At one point the stage goes dark and the woman and girl are linked with two spots on their faces. We see nothing else. Slowly, both perform the identical gesture. At first the girl, flirting with the man, seemed like the woman's rival. Now we wonder if she is the woman's lover or the memory of a younger self. If the audience knows Müller's script, they might think she is the niece. She shows a sexual interest in everyone at table. The slow, stylized movements dematerialize the scene. Is this a dream? It seems to be taking place before our eyes, but not here, not now – a ghost sonata of sexual frustration.

As the prolog builds to its climax, the old man pops out an invisible gun and shoots the young stud. The contrast between refined demeanor and sadistic violence unsettles. The weird, otherworldly tones of Mozart's concerto for glass harmonica waft through the theatre. The boy crawls off stage on all fours (see figure 13). The woman mounts him side-saddle, as if he were a beautiful black panther, dangerously exciting. The girl breaks into hysterial giggles. In Wilson, violence works as a potent aphrodisiac. One by one the glasses of the harmonica shatter until the music screeches to a halt in an apocalypse of broken glass. House dark. Underneath the minuet, the rumble of the guillotine.

Language does many things and does them well. But we tend to shut our eyes to what language does not do well. Despite the arrogance of words – they rule traditional theatre with an iron fist – not all experience can be translated into a linguistic code. Language can describe neither the complex movement patterns nor the simultaneous sexual antagonisms flickering around this table.

Language does not define the limits of what we think, know, and feel. Wilson's images take us to the borderland between conscious and unconscious, to a realm of feeling just below the surface of the skin. Concerning this zone of the inarticulate, T. S. Eliot wrote:

It seems to me that beyond the nameable, classifiable emotions and motives of our concious life when directed towards action . . . there is a fringe of indefinite extent, of feeling which we can only detect, so to speak, out of the corner of the eye and can never completely focus; of feeling of which we are only aware in a kind of temporary detachment from action . . . At such moments, we touch the border of those feelings which only music can express.[24]

Wilson tells a story about a French critic who, after the premiere of *Great Day in the Morning* – a dramatization of Negro spirituals – hounded the director about the final image: Jessye Norman, the soprano, walks to a table that holds an empty glass and a pitcher of water. She takes the pitcher and pours it into the glass. The glass fills up and overflows. She

13 The prolog in Wilson's production of *Quartet*. The elderly
gentleman, far left, engraving his "secret thoughts on an invisible coin
in the air" (Wilson's instructions to the actor, Jeremy Geidt), represents
the author. He only will escape alone the apocalypse of sex to tell us.
From left to right: Old Man (Jeremy Geidt), Marquise de Merteuil
(Lucinda Childs), Valmont (Bill Moor), Young Man (Scott Rabinowitz),
and Young Woman (Jennifer Rohn). American Repertory Theatre.

continues pouring and hums "Amazing Grace." The water spills off the
table and streams over the floor. Curtain. "The glass is full," the perplexed journalist shrugged. "Why does she keep pouring? Why does
water run all over the floor?" Chris Knowles, sitting next to Wilson, piped
up, "There is no reason."

There may be no reason, yet there is a meaning. Any attempt to
reduce to words the feelings this overwhelming moment of theatrical
poetry evoked falls short. The power of the spirit that sustained African
Americans in their struggle to survive. The grace of God flowing
through a dark and wayward world. No one can conjure up in words
the emotional force of that picture. "All mysticism," writes Cassirer, "is

directed toward a world beyond language, a world of silence."[25] Wilson's early works established him as a prophet of silence. Nowhere else as in Wilson does silence instill itself with such majesty. "Beckett succeeded in creating a few minutes of silence on stage," Ionesco observed after seeing *Deafman Glance*, "while Robert Wilson was able to bring about a silence that lasted for four hours. He surpassed Beckett in this: Wilson being richer and more complex with his silence. His silence is a silence that speaks."[26]

Wilson's images speak when language fails, and they take us where words cannot go. The value of a film like *Last Year at Marienbad*, Sontag points out in "Against Interpretation," lies not in meanings, but in the untranslatable, sensuous immediacy of its images and in its solutions to problems of form. "What is important now is to recover our senses. We must learn to *see* more, to *hear* more, to *feel* more . . . In place of a hermeneutics we need an erotics of art."[27]

Wilson's images – autonomous and evocative, beautiful and disturbing – dramatize how much, how quickly, and how vividly the eye understands. But this suspension of language terrorizes people who rely on words to interpret the world. Images do not make propositions; they generate, simultaneously, manifold meanings – "a plenitude of virtualities."[28] "What does it mean?" usually means, "How do I translate this play into words?" Wilson's theatre frustrates this automatic reflex; his theatre resists exchange based on a verbal gold standard. Wilson's silent images speak, but not everyone listens. In Wilson one must listen with the eyes. "Why is it no one looks?" Wilson muses. "Why is it no one knows how to look? Why does no one see anything on a stage? If you put in a program there will be five hundred red elephants in this performance, all the critics will write about five hundred red elephants, even if the elephants were white" (*Quartet*). We desperately try to reduce life to words. We spend most of our time substituting language for experience. Wilson does not create theatre for people who, in the words of Ezekiel, have eyes to see, and see not (Ezekiel 12:2).

DISJUNCTION

Disjunction is Wilson's second strategy for interrogating language. According to Heiner Müller, disjunction – or the disassociation of theatrical codes – is Wilson's most important contribution to drama. "Bob achieved what Brecht only dreamed of doing: the parting of the elements. Bob's theatre offers a more complicated pleasure than normal theatre. When you're young, you're just fucking. You don't even see the body of

the woman. But when you get old, you need more and more complica-
tions to have pleasure."[29] In Wilson the theatrical codes – lights, costumes, make-up, movement, proxemics, set, sound, language, props – all
speak different languages. Each tells a different tale.[30]

Wilson refers to disjunction as his "why-paint-a-white-horse-white
theory." The director works by layering theatrical codes against each
other.

If you place a baroque candelabra on a baroque table, both get lost. You can't see
either. If you place the candelabra on a rock in the ocean, you begin to see what it
is. Usually in theatre the visual repeats the verbal. The visual takes second place to
language. I don't think that way. For me the visual is not an afterthought, not an
illustration of the text. It has equal importance. If it tells the same story as the
words, why look? The visual must be so compelling that a deaf man would sit
through the performance fascinated. Once in a while I let the visual align with the
verbal, but usually not. Most directors begin by analyzing a text, and the visual
follows from that interpretation. This naive use of the visual code bores me. I
always start with a visual form. In most theatre the eye is irrelevant. Not in mine. I
think with my eyes. (*Quartet*)

Major consequences follow from Wilson's running the visual and
verbal on separate tracks. The first is to draw attention to the codes themselves. In contrast to slice-of-life realism, which pretends to be a transparent mirror held up to nature, Wilson's theatre never denies it is theatre. It
draws attention to its status as an art object. It celebrates its nature as
cunning artifact. Furthermore, it reflects on its own means of representation and signification. By asking how do we see and how do we hear, it
explores perception. And by confronting the audience simultaneously
with multiple realities, it dramatizes how we impose a mental construct
we call reality on the multifarious and dissonant stimuli bombarding our
mind from without. We automatically accept this mental construct,
closely linked to language, with the natural order of things.

Disjunction enables Wilson to question this natural order, which
reposes on the relationship between language and reality. A scene from
Einstein on the Beach – an opera for an atomic age – illustrates how Wilson
dramatizes the this-is-not-a-pipe conundrum.[31] Magritte made several
paintings of pipes to visualize the arbitrary nature of visual and verbal
representations. Underneath the deadpan portrait of a pipe, the artist
would write, "This is not a pipe." Neither the picture nor the word is the
thing itself.

The second trial scene of *Einstein on the Beach* (act II, scene 1B) opens
with the two judges – an elderly black man and a young white boy –
safely ensconced in their position of authority on the beach. Bewigged

and berobed, starched and stiffened, they are solemn guardians of the law. After being sworn in, Lucinda Childs takes her place atop an elongated witness chair fashioned from plumbing tubes. The lawyer (Sutton) enters and slowly approaches the witness. After stepping down and staring at the lawyer, the witness walks to a huge white bed incongruously nestled in the middle of the courtroom. In act I, Childs – dressed in Einstein's baggy-pants – represented the Jeremiah of relativity. Now she wears a simple wraparound dress, and the audience is clueless about who she might be. The judges begin to doodle in their law books. The court stenographer files her fingernails. Einstein plays a violin. Childs crawls across the bed on all fours. Then, lying down, in a voice emptied of emotion, she delivers her testimony: "I was in this prematurely air-conditioned supermarket and there were all these aisles and there were all these bathing caps that you could buy which had these kind of fourth of July plumes on them they were red and yellow and blue I wasn't tempted to buy one but I was reminded of the fact that I had been avoiding the beach."[32]

As she starts her monolog (repeated hypnotically thirty-five times),[33] the jury sings a chorus of numbers over Philip Glass's obsessively repeated rhythms. Childs's text plays against both coming before or after the beginnings or ends of musical phrases. A prison cell glides in with two jailbirds – one male, one female – and fills the right half of the stage. In the cell, the jailbirds perform a slow, angular movement sequence not related to the music (see figure 14). Childs raises herself from the bed, walks towards the cell, and executes a series of fast movements like an hysterical cheerleader. Donning a Patty Hearst guerilla outfit, she aims a machine gun at the audience. Upstage the lawyer repeats, "Hey Mr Bojangles." Childs reappears on the witness stand and launches her (or is it Einstein's?) defense: one of Knowles's autistic soliloquies:

I feel the earth move . . . I feel the tumbling down tumbling down . . . There was a judge who like puts in a court. And the judge have like in what able jail what it could be a spanking. Or a whack. Or a smack. Or a swat. Or a hit . . . So if you know that fafffffff facts . . . This would be some all of my friends. Cindy Jay Steve Julia Robyn Rick Kit and Liz . . . I FEEL THE EARTH MOVE CAROLE KING. So that was one song this what it could in the Einstein On The Beach with a trial to jail. But a court were it could happen. So when David Casidy tells you all of you to go on get going get going. So this one in like on WABC New York . . . JAY REYNOLDS from midnight to 6 AM HARRY HARRISON from 6 AM to L. I feel the earth move from WABC . . . JOHNNY DONOVAN from 6PM to 10 PM. CHUCK-LEONARD from 3 AM to 5 AM. JOHNNY DONOVAN from 6 PM to 10 PM. STEVE-O-BRION from 4 30 AM to 6 AM. STEVE-O-BRION from 4 30 AM to 6 AM. JOHNNY DONOVAN from 4 30 AM to 6 AM.

14 Childs, launching her famed beach monolog in which language
refuses to make much sense. *Einstein on the Beach* dramatizes the
splendor and misery of talk. Photograph: Copyright © 1976, 1995,
Babette Mangolte, all rights of reproduction reserved.

This soliloquy is repeated three times. Like a mantra, it puts the spectator
into a trance. A blackout cuts Childs off. When the lights came up on a
bare stage, a postmodern ballet structured around hypnotic spinning
catches us unawares. An abrupt contrast, it seems to have nothing to do
with what preceded.

   In this scene, Wilson presents two views of language: sometimes it
works, sometimes it does not. The numbers the chorus sings represent
reality in a clear, unambiguous way. They refer to the rhythmic structure of
the music. During the ballet that follows, the chorus sings solfège, referring to the notes they are singing. In this context, each syllable (do, re, mi,
fa, so la, ti do) names a discrete, determinate entity – a specific sound. But
what we have is one artificial, arbitrary system referring to another artificial, arbitrary system. Only people familiar with the tradition of western
music would recognize either the signifier or the signified. Our musical
notes are not cross-cultural. Although other cultures slice up the sound
spectrum differently, we accept our arbitrary system as natural.

Although Knowles's "I Feel the Earth Move" soliloquy violates syntax, semantics, and pragmatics, it still communicates some important information. It tells us what the performance we are experiencing is all about: "So that was one song this what it could in the Einstein On The Beach with a trial to jail." What we are witnessing is an opera (song) entitled *Einstein on the Beach*, which puts the mop-haired physicist of doom on trial to determine if he should be sent to prison for having made possible the toys we have stockpiled to blow ourselves to kingdom come.

But the rest of the text confounds this instrumentalist view of language. Other words we hear do not communicate in a clear, unambiguous way. What we hear and what we see have nothing to do with each other. In the first trial scene, the judges had ceremoniously proclaimed, "This court of common pleas is now in session." Language told us we would witness a serious trial. But language lied. What we experience in both trial scenes is a comic vaudeville.[34] And where better to relish the ambiguity of language than in a courtroom? Since our legal system is tied to rational argumentation, its efficacy depends on language. If language turns out to be ambiguous, slippery, and unreliable, then the law itself begins to crumble, based not on fact but on words.

The words speak about supermarkets and bathing caps and beaches. What we see is a woman lying down on a bed. And what is a bed doing in the middle of a courtroom? And what does Patty Hearst have to do with Einstein, who fiddles away with demonic glee during these shenanigans? We want language in the form of rational discourse to come to our aid and explain these visual puzzles.

Instead, Sutton repeats narcoleptically, "Hey Mr Bojangles." When no tap dancer or any one else appears, reference gets muddier. Wilson's problematization of the relation between name and referent refutes the classical description theory of Bertrand Russell as well as the modern description theory of John Searle.[35] In this scene word and meaning – signifier, signified, and referent – drift apart in the great semantic divide. By ripping asunder word from world, Wilson dramatizes that language is not a transparent window on reality. In fact, as Lacan theorized it may be a wall separating us from reality, what Heidegger called a "closing-off."[36]

Language – always a fiction – changes whatever experience it recounts. Our basic assumption about language is that it is meaningful and that it tells the truth. We look to language to interpret the world, but in Childs's bathing cap tirade, language runs amok, an artificial construct creating its own reality while pretending to represent the world. Wilson mocks our naive belief in language. The end of the "I Feel the Earth Move" soliloquy, for example, seems on the face of it a straightforward transmission of information: a radio timetable. A slice of banal reality. But examined closely, the schedule once again calls into question language's reliability. We are told that Donovan is on from 6 to 10 and that O-Brion is on from 4.30 to 6. But language then proceeds to contradict itself. It makes two mutually exclusive propositions. We are also told that Donovan is on from 4.30 to 6. If we listen in at 4.30, whose smiling voice will greet us, Donovan's or O-Brion's? We cannot rely on language to inform us. Language can say whatever it pleases: reality does not keep it on a leash. Language always retains the ability to lie. We have to turn the radio on to be sure.

Humans use language, Whorf asserts, "to weave the web of Maya or illusion, to make a provisionable analysis of reality and then regard it as final."[37] Is all language, then, merely a figure of speech? "The 'literal' meaning of writing," Derrida claims, "is metaphoricity itself."[38] In this scene language does not reflect or explain what we see and experience, nor does it convey reliable information. Wilson has dramatized how we use language as a narcotic to dull the senses and lull the mind into denying that it cannot domesticate the riddle or penetrate the mystery. Perhaps the beauty of language, muses Wilson's theatre, is its opacity, not its transparency.

Wilson complicates the dilemma by dramatizing the gaps between two incommensurate systems of representation: language and pictures. "Writing and pictures do not call on the same type of consciousness."[39] "Neither can be reduced to the other's terms: it is in vain that we say what we see; what we see never resides in what we say."[40] The visual story board for *Einstein on the Beach* was written long before the text – the reverse of traditional theatre, which begins with an author's text that dictates all other aspects of production. But Wilson, through disjunction, demonstrates how both word and image create the worlds we think they reflect. By confronting two modes of representation – visual and verbal – that compete and conflict, that challenge and contradict each other, Wilson highlights the arbitrary and inadequate nature of all systems of representation. In *Einstein on the Beach* representation represents itself as an existential circus. Wilson's theatre, however, never denies the referential possibilities of language. By creating a "valid order accommodating contradictions of a complex reality," Wilson's theatre dramatizes the "simultaneous perception of multiplicity"[41] – language as both sense and nonsense.

Although the visual and verbal may contradict in Wilson's works (sometimes they bisect, but usually they run on separate rails), there is nothing arbitrary about the way he puts them together. A new aesthetic order arises. In this new order word and image strangely interpenetrate, informing each other. At the heart of Wilson's vision, paradox grins.

The third strategy Wilson uses is discontinuity. On the level of words, sentences, and narrative, Wilson fragments language. A snippet from *the CIVILwarS* illustrates this pulverization (the numbers refer to the actors who spoke the phrases; E is a recorded voice over: "5E: don't be nervous I'm just scared to death one two three four five six seven eight a thousand dollars / 21: mama / 20: he looks pale / 19: yeah / 18: sister / 17: pages sewn in signature / 19: signatures / 17: daddy / 19: a spot in known / 18: boys / 17: a stopping place / E: (*sound of coyote in distance*) / 16: nearest place / 17: please / 18: family makes two no / 19: many others / 10: still pictures are forever records results of family incredible ears in a field of many shows signatures made others still"[42]

Instead of continuous dialog, tatters of sentences. They tumble forth in a verbal collage of *non sequiturs*. Words about to coalesce into a complete sentence collapse into silence. Several stories are hinted at, but they stop almost before starting. Signs refusing to signify; words refusing to relate to other words; language refusing to make sense; stories refusing to tell themselves. Meaning – erratic, obtuse – playing itself out. Obscure? Incomprehensible? Much of life is. The nature of language is ambiguity, and ambiguity is the language of our experience. Augustan prose cannot capture the sense of estrangement contemporary man feels in the world described by Camus, from which meaning, unity, and clarity have evaporated.[43] "Why should the stories we tell on stage be clearer than the stories we live?" the director asks (*Quartet*).

As in this passage, Wilson eliminates the function words that make logical connections and subordinations – the words that organize language into meaningful statements. Doing so, he emphasizes the sensory aspect of language and moves from metonymy to metaphor.[44] Wilson's haunting adaptation of Euripides' *Alcestis* illuminates how he elbows literature from the syntagmatic to the paradigmatic axis. Cutting the narrative to the bone, he stressed the metaphoric structure. Reiterated verbal motifs, not cause and effect, ordered the performance text.

Wilson violates grammar, semantics, syntax, pragmatics, and the rules of rhetoric that enable a coherent argument to unfold. "When I write these lines," Wilson said, "I don't think about who's going to say it or what it means. I don't think about emotions or ideas. It's just something to hear on a stage."[45] When Wilson says he does not think about the lines, he refers to psychology and semantics. But a good deal of thought goes into building a structure from sound, from which a psychological meaning always emerges on stage no matter how hard one tries to chase it away.

In reference to *I was sitting on my patio*, which uses language in a similar way, Wilson noted that "the text tells pieces of many little stories. It's like watching 500 different channels on television and flipping the channels constantly" (*Lear*). Postmodernism is a culture of fragments and quotations. Our age is an age of detritus. Wilson likes to crisscross texts with other texts, often from traditionally opposed discourses: Euripides' *Alcestis* with Müller's "Description of a Painting"; Ibsen's *When We Dead Awaken* with vaudeville songs; Shakespeare's *King Lear* with William Carlos Williams's "The Last Words of My English Grandmother." The Cologne Section of *the CIVILwarS* was an aural tapestry woven from fragments of Wilson, Müller, Frederick the Great, Shakespeare, Kafka, Hölderlin, Racine, Empedocles, Goethe, *et alia*. This tapestry of texts dramatizes Barthes's death-of-the-author theory: "We know now that a text is not a line of words releasing a single 'theological' meaning (the 'message' of the Author–God) but a multi-dimensional space in which a variety of writings, none of them original, blend and clash. The text is a tissue of quotations drawn from the innumerable centres of culture."[46] Wilson put together this "tissue of quotations" to create multiple perspectives on the theme of the work: civil strife. Bakhtin calls this polyphonic technique dialogism: "The unification of utterly heterogeneous and incompatible materials and the plurality of consciousness-centers which are not reduced to a common denominator . . . This persistent urge to see all things as being coexistent and to perceive and depict all things side by side and simultaneously as if in space rather than time . . ."[47] Wilson is a *bricoleur*. His texts are a palimpsest in which one reads traces of many other texts. He assembles bits and pieces yanked from a multitude of discourses; any one utterance is heard against many other utterances, setting up a radical relativity.

"To tell a story," Robbe-Grillet argues, "has become strictly impossible,"[48] and Lyotard characterizes the postmodern condition as the tumbling down of narrative.[49] The grand narratives have collapsed, and we are left with scraps of stories. From these scraps Wilson builds a new acoustical space where texts comment on each other. "Collage," writes Rosenberg, "is the form assumed by the ambiguities that have matured in our time concerning both art and the realities it has purported to represent . . . Twentieth-century fictions are rarely made up of whole cloth . . . Collage invites the spectator to respond with a multiple consciousness."[50]

Meticulously structured, Wilson's collages, like Picasso's, call into question not only the reality they represent, but their own means of representation. Like much avant-garde art, Wilson's theatre requires the spectator to suspend the search for meaning until the structure and principles of construction are understood. In collage, structure is meaning.[51]

Wilson's fragmentation of narrative and syntax is far from innocent. By violating the traffic rules of language, he reveals the arbitrary nature of all linguistic systems. And their fragility. Language, too, is mortal. Graver consequences accrue. By turning his back on syntax, Wilson's texts refuse to make assertions. "Syntax," Johnson notes, "is what makes it possible for us to treat as *known* anything that we do not *know* we do not know."[52] Wilson – his theatre is in the interrogative mode – dramatizes Montaigne's "What do I know?" Not only does he question perception and cognition by disrupting syntax and narrative, he also destabilizes our epistemological assumptions. At stake is knowledge and the legitimacy of what we think we know, for every narrative implies a teleology.[53] Univocal narration caves in under the weight of conflicting truths.

THE PLAY OF MEANING

Wilson's fourth strategy is to dramatize the play of meaning. Meaning is not an inert object the reader excavates from a text like Lord Carnarvon robbing Tutankhamen's tomb. Meaning is a process. It is a response produced by a receiving consciousness in relationship with a text[54] – a text capable of generating many other responses – what Barthes calls the plural text:

In this ideal text, the networks are many and interact, without any one of them being able to surpass the rest; this text is a galaxy of signifiers, not a structure of signifieds; it has no beginning; it is reversible; we gain access to it by several entrances, none of which can be authoritatively declared to be the main one; the codes it mobilizes extend *as far as the eye can reach*, they are indeterminable (meaning here is never subject to a principle of determination, unless by throwing dice); the systems of meaning can take over this absolutely plural text, but their number is never closed, based as it is on the infinity of language.[55]

Language, Lacan points out, can always "signify *something quite other* than what it says."[56] Jauss dubs this potential to generate plural readings "the successive unfolding of the potential for meaning that is embedded in a work and actualized in the stages of its historical reception."[57] *I was sitting on my patio* – composed of found language – demonstrates this "migration of meaning."[58]

The play takes place in a library – a prison cell of words. What better place to stage a play about the collapse of communication? Austerely elegant, the black and white set created a sense of oppressive solitude. Streams of light poured through three floor-to-ceiling windows. In act one Wilson, who directed himself, delivered a discontinuous, stream-of-consciousness monolog. (The program promised over "one hundred short story fragments.") The play dramatizes the way consciousness works, constantly slipping back and forth between different levels of reality – perhaps one should say levels of unreality: "I was sitting on my patio this guy appeared I thought I was hallucinating / I was walking in an alley / you are beginning to look a little strange to me / I'm going to meet them outside / have you been living here long . . ."[59] "The mind," Wilson says, "doesn't work the way language does" (*Quartet*).

In act two, Lucinda Childs, who directed herself, delivered the same monolog. The meanings and emotions generated by each actor contrasted sharply; audiences found it hard to believe they had heard the same monolog twice. Wilson was aloof, cold, precise. Periodically an outburst of violence shattered his control. Bach on the surface, *film noir* underground. Childs, a cross between Katherine Hepburn and Lucille Ball, brought screwball comedy to the fore, shading the lines with warmth and color. She playful, almost intimate with the audience; he, withdrawn, taut, on the edge. They emphasized different lines. When she said, with daffy charm, "I could be the best lifeguard on the beach if only I could swim," the house roared with laughter. When he said, "Ready, aim, *fire!*" he hurled the word "fire" into the theatre like a hand grenade. The audience ducked for cover. At the end, she stands, vertically triumphant, atop the chaise on which he had lounged horizontally (see figure 15). For the first time, the back wall lifts into space, and an exhilarating sense of freedom floods the stage. We have been liberated from the prison of language. Movements, gestures, tone of voice, music, lights, costumes – all these paralinguistic systems of communication shifted the semantic weight and destabilized the text's meaning. Meanings are not tethered to words like horses to hitching posts. With regard to this point, Wilson observes:

I'm an artist, not a philosopher. I don't make meanings. I make art. The responsibility of an artist is not to say what something means, but to ask "What does it mean?" The only reason to do a play is because you don't understand it. The moment you think you understand a work of art, it's dead for you. The last moment in any play must be a question. What happened? What was said? What is this? A play doesn't conclude. It should stay open ended. The last word must be a beginning, a door opening, not closing. A play is not a lecture in a classroom. I

15 *I was sitting on my patio* began with Wilson's recumbent horizontal and ended with Childs's triumphant vertical.

don't dictate meaning to the viewer. Theatre that imposes an interpretation is aesthetic fascism. By emptying out the meaning of a sentence, the text becomes full of meaning – or meanings. Actors, however, are trained to interpret; they feel it's their responsibility to color the text and situation for the audience. So they reduce the possibilities of meaning. But in my theatre, the audience puts it all together, and each person puts it together differently. And each night the play is different. The audience makes the meaning. I once told an actor to read the text as if he didn't understand language. There's so much going on in a line of Shakespeare, that if the actor colors the voice too much, the audience loses too many other colors. (*Lear*)

Knowles exerted one of the strongest influences on the formation of Wilson's aesthetic. Autistic children often speak as if they do not understand the meanings of the words they repeat. Their echoing voice carries little inflection, little affect.

Wilson's play of meaning and his insistence on end as beginning requires the audience to reassess the way it receives a theatrical event. Eco cites open-endedness as the hallmark of contemporary art,[60] and

Barthes notes that "an absence of meaning" is "full of meanings" since "this evictive state corresponds to a plenitude of virtualities."[61] Wilson's theatre desires the audience to complete it. Art, Jauss writes, is "a dialogue between work and audience."[62] The audience must take an active role in the production of meaning. By stressing the dialog between work and audience, Wilson encourages the spectator to expand the meaning and value of art. He forces spectators to make radical changes in their ideas concerning theatre – what to expect of it, how to interpret it. The relationship between spectator and play changes. No longer a passive recipient of pre-fabricated meaning, the spectator assumes a central and aggressive role in a dynamic exchange. As Gombrich notes:

The artist gives the beholder increasingly "more to do," he draws him into the magic circle of creation and allows him to experience something of the thrill of "making" which had once been the privilege of the artist. It is the turning point which leads to those visual conundrums of twentieth-century art that challenge our ingenuity and make us search our own minds for the unexpressed and inarticulate.[63]

THE DESTABILIZED SELF

By destabilizing the text and setting in motion a play of meaning, Wilson destabilizes the concept of self, closely bound up with language. To posit language as problematic is to posit self as problematic. Self must be interpreted to self, and language usually translates. Wilson's theatre wreaks havoc on the nineteenth-century view of psychology that informs Realism. "On or about December, 1910," Virginia Woolf jauntily notes, "human character changed."[64] It has continued to change. In fact, it has disappeared, relegated to the trash can of literary history, largely owing to its misalliance with language.[65] Sartre flatly denies a "transcendental I," and Goffman reduces self to a *coup de théâtre*, managed for theatrical effect.[66] "Language speaks us," Heidegger wrote, and more and more, theory is stressing the role language plays in constituting self.[67] "A life led is inseparable from a life told," Jerome Bruner asserts. "We see our lives as stories, and stories don't just happen. They're told. The remembered me is just narration."[68] We create an historical narration of our lives, and the medium of this narration is language. We identify with this fabricated discourse, which we accept as real. Consequently, one's sense of self is tied to the language one uses to refer to self. By disturbing language, Wilson undermines the moorings of a stable, coherent self. Just as Wilson's language destabilizes our epistemology, so too does it destabilize our ontology.

In Wilson's early plays, performers did not project a character. Usually they performed physical activities without talking. When Wilson began to scrutinize language with *A Letter for Queen Victoria*, lines were not assigned with an eye to psychology.[69] The fragmented language and autistic poetry had no desire to create the illusion of coherent character. Significantly, actors were given numbers, not names. On the first day of rehearsals for *The Golden Windows*, Wilson still had not decided "who would say what. Quite arbitrarily I went through the text and assigned lines, without thinking about what the words said. The actors had great difficulty because all they think about is the meanings of words and developing the psychology of a character."[70]

In recent stages of his career, the director has moved on to literary texts scripted by other authors. Here as well, Wilson has developed strategies to destabilize the self. In section II of *Hamletmachine*, a performer steps forward and pronounces: "I am Ophelia."[71] Until now, she has performed simple movements in street clothes, which reinforced her actual presence and "real" self rather than any fictional character she might be playing. Even in traditional, illusionistic theatre, which self is signified is problematic. When Olivier assumes the part of Othello, the audience is aware of the real person, the tax-payer who does TV commercials to pay his bills, who signifies a stage figure Othello, who refers to what? Words on a page that tumbled forth from Shakespeare's mind. The referent is just another word. As critics have pointed out, realistic productions try to hide the discontinuity between actor, stage figure, and imaginary referent.[72] Wilson draws attention to it. So when Jenny Rohn steps forward in T-shirt and ponytail to announce, "I am Ophelia," we do not lose sight of her as a beautiful, young undergraduate, but we also understand that she has turned herself into a signifier for Shakespeare's dramatis personae, Ophelia (see figure 16). But she immediately frustrates our expectations by continuing, "The one the river didn't keep." By redefining herself this way we begin to wonder who the referent is. Is there another Ophelia the river did keep? The actress seems to be trying to distance herself from Shakespeare's Ophelia. Is she the Ophelia in Rimbaud's poem or perhaps in Thomas's opera? Or perhaps she is Müller's? Or does she mean that Shakespeare's character was fished from the waves to receive a quasi-official burial in sanctified ground? In Müller's text the line appears once. In Wilson's production, the sentence is echoed by three other performers. The first "Ophelia" uses a flat voice, void of emotion. The second sounds like Mae West. The third like Scarlett O'Hara. The fourth pseudo-British. Who is Ophelia, and what is she? Clearly, not any one person or any one thing. Wilson uses the ambiguity of language to undermine the concept of a stable self.

16 *Hamletmachine*. Who is Ophelia (Jennifer Rohn on far right)? All four actresses who claim they are, and none of them. Identity is an elusive, evanescent construct. Self is a performance.

To complicate the situation further, in section V, Ophelia declares that she is Electra. Who is speaking? Who is spoken of? Who is this I? By distributing the narration of self among several speakers, Wilson dramatizes that self is both a subject speaking and a subject spoken of – two different entities that cannot be merged into one category.[73] He fragments self into a series of speakers who have no transcendental I but merely assume speaking positions in a pre-existing discourse whose referent is cast into doubt. In Wilson, self becomes a discontinuous signifier drifting away from an elusive signified.

In *Medea* Medea did not speak Medea's lines – her nurse and a soldier did. In *When We Dead Awaken* the director employed even more sophisticated techniques to shatter the unity of self. He divided the part of Irene between two performers, an African American and a blond Polish actress. The way they spoke, walked, and read their lines was antithetical. The former, cynical and cold. The latter warmer, more romantic. Self was revealed as other. At times they spoke together, now in unison, now out of sync. At times they divided the lines, sometimes switching speakers in mid-sentence or for just one phrase. Rubek dealt with both as Irene. In act II, Irene says to Rubek, "I obliterated myself forever." Wilson had the two Irenes repeat the word "forever" seven times, not to Rubek but to each other in internal debate. The first flat; second, questioning; third, aggressive; fourth, humorous; fifth, angry; sixth, mocking laugh; seventh, cool, final. By building this internal conflict into one of the strong points of the act, Wilson put in evidence not only the schizophrenia in every soul, but also the irreconcilable tension between the will to live and the will to die, the affirmation and the denial of life.

In addition, Wilson uses body language to refute the words that speak the self. In *When We Dead Awaken* Maya's gestures often contradict what she says. For example, she assures her husband that he has not offended her, but her hand – like an autonomous agent beyond her control – shatters a glass. The broken glass signifies the unconscious revulsion from her husband seeping up slowly from the depths of her being. What she says represents her social persona, a persona she still, to a degree, embraces.

Wilson also dramatizes the gaps and discontinuities in gender, an important part of identity. Early in his career, Wilson performed a female persona called Byrdwoman. Often he cross-casts sexually: women played Lear (*King Lear*), Frederick the Great (*the CIVILwarS*) and Franz Kafka (*Death Destruction & Detroit II*). Saint Sebastian – the part was doubled – was played by both a woman and a man. Orlando stumbles through the first half of her life as a man; the second half, as a woman. "*Orlando* is a fantasy all actresses have," says Isabelle Huppert, who played Orlando in Wilson's French-language production of Woolf's novel, "the fantasy to play both a male and a female. This desire touches something essential in the human story."[74] In *Quartet* Valmont and Merteuil switch gender by switching lines. "I believe I could get used to being a woman," Valmont confesses to Merteuil after his impersonation of Mme. Tourvel. "I wish I could," returns the Marquise. How much of gender, Wilson's production asked, is playing a part and speaking the right words?

Wilson works hard to empower actors to project a discontinuous personality. He often tells them the following story:

A famous psychologist in Paris had four thousand dollars in his drawer. Treating a patient one day, he had to step out of the room briefly. When he came back, the money had disappeared. The patient denied stealing it. The psychologist hypnotized him, and said "You're a detective. I've lost four thousand dollars. You must help me find it." The patient immediately told him where the money was. We're all thieves and detectives. Each person has many sides, many facets, many persons lurking inside. Look for Dr. Jekyll, he's in there too, and make sure you bring out all these contradictions when you perform. (*Quartet*)

THE COLLAPSE OF DIALOG

The fifth strategy Wilson uses to question language is the collapse of dialog. Language is a "social fact."[75] It is the glue that holds society together; through "language a child becomes integrated with a social community," and it "serves to maintain social interaction."[76] Since dialog is the primary vehicle of interpersonal relations – what Szondi calls the sphere of the between – it lords it over traditional theatre. "The absolute dominance of dialogue – that is, of interpersonal communication," continues Szondi, "reflects the fact that the Drama consists only of the reproduction of interpersonal relations, is only cognizant of what shines forth within this space."[77]

But Wilson attenuates this sphere. "Realistic dialog doesn't work for me," says Wilson. "What time is it? Five o'clock. How boring." During the rehearsals of *When We Dead Awaken* Wilson told two actors running through an Ibsen conversation not "to bounce diaglog back and forth like a ping-pong ball. Let the words fly past each other. Don't pick up each others' rhythms. Follow your own line. Each of you is lost in a separate world."

To decenter conventional dialog the director employs an arsenal of techniques. Often he suspends a sentence midair before it arrives at a conclusion. In act I of *When We Dead Awaken* Rubek asks his wife, "Have I offended the Frau Professor?" Instead of an answer an hypnotic dream sequence spills over the stage with bizarre images. Ten minutes later comes the answer, "No, not a bit." By the time the logical complement to a fragmented sentence or the answer to a question rolls round, the audience has forgotten the first part. Other techniques Wilson uses to turn dialog into monolog will be discussed in chapter 6.

By disturbing the flow of ordinary conversation, Wilson unravels the social fabric, disrupts interpersonal relations, and intensifies the mood of alienation. We communicate through systems of representation – language, pictures, gestures. All these systems are inadequate to the task. Dialog falters in Wilson because it depends on language, and language cannot bridge the gap between individuals. An awareness of self is an awareness of solitude; we are all locked into the solitary confinement of individual consciousness. "Communication," Heidegger observes, "is never anything like a conveying of experiences, such as opinions or wishes, from the interior of one subject into the interior of another."[78]

Language, a public convention, cannot capture the individual in all his particularity. A core of silence at the center of existence eludes words. "The individual absolutely cannot make himself intelligible to anybody," writes Kierkegaard. "Abraham keeps silent – but he *cannot* speak. Therein lies the distress and anguish. For if I when I speak am unable to make myself intelligible, then I am not speaking – even though I were to talk uninterruptedly day and night."[79]

In a Wilson production, even in a play choking on words like *When We Dead Awaken*, individuals despite all their chatter collapse into silence and solitude. Language cannot express the inner world. "The attempt to communicate where no communication is possible is merely a simian vulgarity, or horribly comic, like the madness that holds a conversation with the furniture," Beckett insists. "Friendship is a social expedient, like upholstery or the distribution of garbage buckets . . . There is no communication because there are no vehicles of communication."[80] By creating an atmosphere of alienation and by paring language down to Spartan austerity, Wilson's staging of *When We Dead Awaken* pulled the covers off Ibsen and Beckett sleeping together in the same bed of existential despair. Ibsen stands at the head of those great authors influenced by the philosophical tradition of Kierkegaard; Beckett, at the end. Wilson's production of the dour Scandinavian showed that Beckett's wasteland and Ibsen's velvet and mahogany parlour are, in reality, the same inferno. Wilson often expresses admiration for Beckett, and early in his career he wanted to direct *Happy Days*.

Further consequences flow from Wilson's disruption of dialog, character, and narrative (all compact with language). Traditionally, these three elements have been the backbone of Western theatre. Conventional drama has always stressed interpersonal relations and has shown people in action – in plots. By moving theatre closer to lyric poetry and painting, Wilson questions theatre as a genre. By pushing drama to its limits, he interrogates its means of representation. Combined with his disjunction of theatrical codes, Wilson's theatre, always metatheatrical, reflects on its own apparatus of communication. Reflecting on its own codes, it is "pure" theatre.

DECONTEXTUALIZATION

The sixth strategy Wilson uses to question language is decontextualization. Echolalia and context-deviant utterances characterize autistic language. Autistic children echo words, phrases, and sentences they heard earlier in a new situation in which the repeated language makes no sense.

Knowles, diagnosed as autistic, exerted the strongest influence on Wilson's theatrical use of language. Since language is ambiguous, meaning depends on context.[81] But language – spoken and written – can be replicated to infinity in contexts widely divergent from the original one. This decontextualization changes, confuses, and confounds the intention that generated the language. In *Einstein on the Beach* – knee play 2, for instance – the text written by Knowles would not seem strange in its original setting, as an advertisement for contact lenses heard on the radio (with the exception of the jokes played on language, such as "a Phonic" and "contactless lenses"):

So if you take your glasses off. They're easy to lose or break. Well New York a Phonic Center has the answer to your problem. Contactless lenses and the new soft lenses. The center gives you thirty days and see if you like them. So if you're tired of glasses. Go to New York a Phonic Center on Eleven West Forty-Second Street near Fifth Avenue for sight with no hassle.

However, when spoken by Lucinda Childs in the second knee play – sandwiched between the surrealistic circus of the trial scene and the mystical spaceship ballet – this ordinary language sounds demented.

Much of the language Wilson uses is found language, and decontextualization, which throws into relief the precariousness of meaning, is one of his most frequent devices. Using archaic language – *A Letter for Queen Victoria* serves as a good example – is another form of decontextualization Wilson employs to defamiliarize language and make it strange.

REDUCTIO AD ABSURDUM

The seventh strategy Wilson uses is a *reductio ad absurdum*. Act III of *A Letter for Queen Victoria* begins with the famous "Chitter Chatter" scene in which Wilson dramatizes the cocktail party syndrome. In a high-society café, elegant couples yammer away, setting up an incessant din of banalities (see figure 17). Against a chorus that repeats the words "chitter chatter," we pick up rags and patches of conversation: "it's such a charming place; how very touching; it's slipped my mind entirely; yes isn't it a shame; how dreadful." "Language," Flaubert sighed, "runs by itself." One by one, the ardent conversationalists are picked off by an invisible sniper, exasperated by their verbiage. Can language, Wilson wonders, rise above the trivial? Does it take a bullet to stop this ceaseless flow of verbal nonsense? We stitch together our crazy-quilt conversations with prefabricated formulas. Do we control language or does language control

17 *A Letter for Queen Victoria*, the "Chitter, Chatter" scene. The
cacophony and banality of everyday conversation. Sheryl Sutton
(middle, flanked on the left by Chris Knowles and on the right by
Andy de Groat) recalls that "we thought the performers in the café
scene were crickets at a tea party, chirping away." Pale gray costumes,
pale gray tables, pale gray drop. In this period black, white, and gray
dominated Wilson's minimalist palette.

us? James Joyce confessed that he had never written an original sentence
in his life. All we do is combine and recombine the clichés our language
gives us. Are we all autistic babblers, regurgitating found language? Has
everything always already been said? Is there nothing new under the linguistic sun? By questioning any original use of language, Wilson challenges the Romantic myth of originality in art.

This malaise with the *déja-entendu* aspect of language unlocks Wilson's
reinterpretation of the Don Juan myth. The title – *Don Juan último* –
implies that this avatar of Don Juan will be the last, and Wilson's seducer
is closer to Simone de Beauvoir's nihilist than to Kierkegaard's *bon
vivant*.[82] Wilson's Don Juan finds love ridiculous because he finds the language of love ridiculous.

The women in *Don Juan último* beg him to whisper sweet nothings in their ear, but Juan obliges reluctantly. He understands the strategic role words play in seduction: his retreat from language is in full *connaissance de cause*. Clichés nauseate him. Our language of love was invented by troubadours in twelfth-century Provence. After almost a millenium, one would expect this language to be worn out. But no. Each time we hear it, it sounds new-minted. We think that the language of love is the most personal language we speak. It speak us, however, and is the most impersonal, the least original language. When it comes to love, we can say nothing new. We cannot escape the prison of cliché. Wilson's Don Juan thirsts for originality. At the end, ironically, he becomes a statue. While Juan is turning into a museum piece, he says good-bye to language and good-bye to love:

But I've never managed to be a precursor. Perhaps I'm posthumous . . . Each new woman receives me knowing what I'm going to say: waiting for me to speak, imagining my words as if she'd heard them before, mouthing them before I've opened my lips, checking them against her memories . . . Am I condemned to repeat what I wasn't the first to say? What I whisper as I lean on a woman's breast comes from the mouth of other women . . . Words desert me at the key moment, tired of the limited number of permutations I permit them, always identical, always successful. I know they'd sometimes like to have a lower success rate.[83]

The last Don Juan turns out to be a romantic Existentialist who recently has been leafing through Barthes, Foucault, and Lacan. Don Juan says good-bye to the language of love because of its inauthenticity. The language of love is not a transparent window on the soul; it is a debauch of platitudes, an abject surrender to the trite. Don Juan flees this embalmed language. Until he can say "I love you" and cease hearing the echo of everyone else including himself who has ever whispered this phrase, he prefers to withdraw into a pure and chaste silence. His libido, like his language, is exhausted. Ennui, not love, conquers all.

JAMMING

The eighth strategy is jamming. Since language is a physical signal – waves floating through air – many disturbances interfere with its emission, transmission, and reception. Noise can drown language out, making it unintelligible. In *When We Dead Awaken* loud industrial sounds and overlapping dialog often threw the semantic freight of language overboard. During the ritual scene in *Alcestis*, language started out clearly and distinctly. Soon, however, it began to sound like a bad connection on a transatlantic phone call. As the ritual progressed, so many overlapping recorded voices were added that language evaporated in a cloud of sonic dust. Words vaporized into the unknown, leaving in their wake an ecstasy of cackling, hissing, howling. Now and then an electronic voice, screaming from some far-off wilderness, tried urgently to communicate, but the message faded away, dying inaudibly in the distant hills. Wilson is fascinated by that mysterious frontier where inchoate noise forms articulate language and articulate language collapses into noise. How, Wilson's theatre asks following linguistic theory, does our mind turn "a stream of sounds into meaning?"[84]

Hans-Peter Kuhn, who built the soundscape of *Alcestis*, refers to the ritual as

vocal disorientation. Confusion is a normal part of life. The ritual was a taped collage of voices. I used eighteen speakers. Everyone recorded one word, so every nineteenth word was said by the same person. The soundstructure was based, not on the text but on an acoustic curve: a symphony of vocal sounds. When the ritual started you could follow the words, but it got more and more dense, and in the end it was pure noise.[85]

LANGUAGE AS PURE SOUND

The ninth strategy to question language is playing with the sounds of words. Wilson is acutely sensitive to sound and often uses an anti-realistic *Sprachgesang*. In rehearsal he spends an extraordinary amount of time working with the actors' voices to get the color, pitch, duration, and accent he wants. Wilson loves the music of words. At times he will run an entire scene with his eyes closed, listening intently to the sounds of language, and he frequently berates actors for swallowing consonants or mumbling. Wilson composes the vocal score of his productions with an almost Mozartian sense of classical composition. In *Quartet* during the seduction of the niece, Wilson had Childs sing "When the Saints Go Marching In" while Valmont spoke his dense, elliptical, religioerotic text. I mentioned to the director that the scene might be confusing because one could not process simultaneously the different sound tracks. "It's much richer this way," Wilson replied, "it's like a duet in opera. Listen to the music."

Wilson toys with words to pulverize meaning into sound. In *Hamletmachine* the line "butchered a peasant" was repeated five times; each time "butchered" and "peasant" become increasingly strung out in a melismatic riff, turning word into melody. In *Quartet* Wilson had Childs stammer repeatedly over the "b" in blood until the sound became an onomatopoetic gurgle, representing spurts of blood. Similarly, Wilson had

Maya hiss out the "s" in house until it became a dagger through her husband's heart. In *A Letter for Queen Victoria* Wilson was primarily interested in setting one actor's voice off against another's to create patterns of sound.[86]

Wilson's exploration of sound dramatizes that language conveys more than abstract semantic meaning. Children respond to voices long before they understand language, and the way words are spoken expresses more than their content. The pleasure of language involves the sensuous experience of sound. Much of what the voice communicates is not verbal, and tone often contradicts word. Wilson exploits all these levels.

THE MAGIC OF LANGUAGE

Wilson's tenth strategy to inquire into language is to release the magic of words. In the beginning, according to Freud, words and magic were one.[87] Wilson's theatre restores to language its primitive power to make visible the invisible, to reach beyond ordinary experience into extraordinary realms of consciousness where the spirit, instinct with godhead, establishes contact with the divine. Much of the energy of ritual derives from verbal magic. Dominated by a special phonology, sing-song rhythms, repetition, metaphor, formulaic phrases spoken in parallels, and words whose meanings have vanished into the mists of time – ritual language sounds weird to the ear of common day.[88] Ritual language, stylized and formal, pushes the expressive qualities of speech to the limit. Soaring towards the transcendent, ritual language becomes ecstatic, incantatory. In the presence of ritual, the idle chatter of every day falls silent. In ritual, language recuperates its magic: words can conjure up a new heaven and a new earth. The force of ritual reorders experience.[89]

Words form a central part of religious rituals – in prayers and songs, in blessings and cursings. Ritual language stresses the sounds of words and heightens language as a sensuous and emotional experience. Often unintelligible, ritual language is associated with the holy and with the authority of divine revelation. Hebrew, Latin, Arabic, and Sanskrit – all ritual languages – are closely related to sacred texts. Not all ritual language is meant to be understood by the participants. The intelligibility of ritual language is not the critical factor. The purpose is not communication among humans. The purpose is to establish contact with the transcendent. Ritual language performs a speech act. It does something. It transforms the psychic state of the participants. Anthropologist Annette Weiner contends that some social tensions can be resolved only through the power of ritual.[90] Ritual heals wounds that can only be cured through the magic of words. In ritual the semantic meaning of words matters little. What matters is their magical power.[91]

The epilog to act IV of *the CIVILwarS* shows how Wilson turns language into ritual. Leading up to it, we have seen blood-drenched scenes of violence spanning families and nation states. The death drive of the species, destructive and self-destructive, seems to have strangled the will to live. The script is fashioned from fragments of well-known, one might even say, canonical texts: the Bible, Shakespeare, the Brothers Grimm. Coming from distant and disparate times and places – long ago and far away – these texts establish multiple frames of reference to look at one theme: the slaughter of the innocents.

The epilog begins in a mysterious half-light. Slowly, as the stage brightens imperceptibly, we glimpse a giant white bird – a Snow Owl – perched aloft a black branch. On the ground of a deserted battlefield, Mary Todd Lincoln as mourning Earth Mother holds her empty arms forward, caressing the corpse of an invisible child. In a *basso profondo*, she intones fairy tales about child murder: "Coo-coo, coo-coo. Blood in the shoe . . . O Falladah there thou hang'st." Rather than telling the familiar stories, her voice creates a mysterious web of sound studded with images of violence. The Snow Owl chants a Hopi prayer for peace in the original language: "yaw itam quw yaykyalaqu yaw." To the audience it sounds like a strange, incomprehensible plea. The sky has brightened into that dazzling blue only Wilson's lights can paint. Into this storybook land stumbles a faltering King Lear, coiffed with a paper crown, robed in a blanket, cradling crumpled newspapers.[92] He begins his lamentation over Cordelia: "Howl, howl, howl, howl! O you are men of stone. A plague upon you murderers . . . Now she's gone forever." The papers unroll. He realizes his daughter is never more. Abraham Lincoln – a gigantic floor-to-ceiling puppet – crosses the stage slowly, reciting *Ecclesiastes* in Latin: "*Omnia tempus habent . . . Tempus nascendi, et tempus moriendi . . . Tempus belli, et tempus pacis.*" Most do not understand, but his words – sonorous, dignified, plangent – cast a magic spell. Lincoln topples over. His body levitates off stage. Lear drops to the ground. As darkness falls, a crystal mountain rises from the earth, glowing like a promise from heaven.

An emotional tidal wave washes over the audience. Conflicts built up during the preceding scenes of destruction resolve into harmony.[93] Anger against a blood-drunk race descended from Cain yields to pity and terror. Language as prayer has worked its magic. Through language we reach out to God in supplication and to each other in compassion. Far from diminishing language, as many claim, Wilson's theatre reveals language in all its power, glory, and mystery. "Poetically man dwells."[94] Language is not only – as Heidegger points out – our house of being, it is also our temple.

Another scene from *the CIVILwarS* dramatizes Wilson's concern for language. At various moments, Black Scribes write in the air with long, black quills. This gesture of futility – all that effort comes to naught; the wind carries away our words – sets off the scene with the White Scribe. In act IV, scene A, section 2, a White Scribe, dressed in yards and yards of masking tape with a pencil stuck through her back like a sword, walks slowly up and down the *hanamichi*, reciting: "Always the same rock always up the same hill. The weight of the rock increasing, the manpower decreasing with the incline. Stalemate before the top . . . Hope and disappointment." The circular text repeats over and over. Given the name and costume of the speaker and the allusions in the text to Sisyphus, we can take this scene as Wilson's and Müller's portrait of the writer as absurd hero. For Camus, the experience of the absurd results from the split between our longing for meaning and clarity and the indifference of the universe. Lost in a confusing world, we can transcend the futility of life by a revolt against the absurd. Through revolt we impose human values on an inhuman cosmos. Trying to create meaning and beauty from the resistant rock of language, pushing it up the mountain to see it fall crashing into nonsense, we must, none the less, imagine the writer, like Sisyphus, happy. The struggle toward the heights is an absurd victory.[95]

3 Alchemy of the eye

See in nature the cylinder, the sphere, and the cone.
Paul Cézanne, a letter to Emile Bernard dated 15 April 1904

VISUAL THINKING

Leafing through any anthology of drama criticism from Aristotle to the present, what does one find? A history dominated by visual illiterates – puritans who excommunicate sight, "the most magical" of senses.[1] In two thousand years of philosophizing, moralizing, and arguing about drama, theatre has dwindled into a written text. The sensuous component of theatre is swept under the rug like dirt. Mistrusting the senses, criticism rates thinking higher than perception, not realizing that perception is thinking. "Sight . . . is the most efficient organ of human cognition . . . Vision is the primary medium of thought."[2]

Language, Wilson's theatre dramatizes, often breaks down, unable to communicate. "What words don't express," Kandinsky avers, "is the kernel of existence."[3] Language is not the key to the theatre's power. Theatre withers on a page. Like film, it transcends literature. Ingmar Bergman contends:

Film has nothing to do with literature; the character and substance of the two art forms are usually in conflict. This probably has something to do with the receptive process of the mind. The written word is read and assimilated by a conscious act of the will in alliance with the intellect; little by little it affects the imagination and the emotions. The process is different with a motion picture. When we experience a film, we consciously prime ourselves for illusion. Putting aside will and intellect, we make way for it in our imagination. The sequence of pictures plays directly on our feelings. Music works in the same fashion . . . Both affect our emotions directly . . . And film is mainly rhythm . . . I often experience a film or play musically.[4]

Bergman suggests that theatre, like film and music, is processed differently by the mind than literature. Wilson's great gift to us all is to have ripped the blindfold off Melpomene and given the Muse eyes.[5] Wilson challenges the dominant tradition of western drama, grounded in idolatry of the word. Wilson changed the way theatre looks and sounds. Few artists make that kind of difference. By refusing to flirt with the corpse of

Naturalism – tied to ordinary language – Wilson wakes the audience from its stupor. But to appreciate his dramaturgy, one must learn to read images.

During the first three days of the *King Lear* workshop in Frankfurt, Wilson seemed to be playing for time. Over and over he rehearsed the prolog, based on William Carlos Williams's poet about his dying grandmother. The actors, none of whom had worked with Wilson before, grew restless. "We're getting nowhere," they grumbled. Meanwhile, Wilson drew incessantly. "I think with a pencil," he explained. "This is my way of analyzing the play." On the third day, Wilson, inspired by a portrait of Dame Sybil Thorndike as Lady Macbeth, fashioned an octagonal crown for Marianne Hoppe, his Lear. During the division of the kingdom, the director told her to take the crown off. But he was not sure what to do with it. Wilson, who creates with a hands-on approach in rehearsal, tried various solutions. First he had the crown destroyed. He did not like that. Then he had Goneril and Regan pull the crown apart. He did not like that. Then he asked Lear to place it on the ground. The director stared for several minutes in total silence. The actors fidgeted. Wilson released them for the rest of the day and continued to stare at the tiny crown on the enormous stage for over an hour. Without saying a word to anyone, he left, lost in thought.

Next day, grinning like the Cheshire cat, he strode into rehearsals with a giant scroll under his arms. Gathering the actors round, he ceremoniously unrolled the four-by-twenty-four foot sheet: "This is our production," he announced. The scroll – Wilson calls it a story board – contained a picture for each of the parts he had divided the play into (see figure 18). He proceeded to describe how the stage space would change for each part. Wilson explained:

I'm a visual artist, I think spatially. Most directors would have been analyzing the text with you, discussing what it means. If you want that kind of chatter, go to the library and read a book. Listening to schoolteachers babble away about what they think Shakespeare means bores me. I don't work that way. I have no sense of direction until I have a sense of space. Architectural structure is crucial in my work. If I don't know where I'm going, I can't get there. The crown was the visual key that unlocked the play for me. It became a tiny wall in this enormous space, and I started thinking of the stage as a dialog between empty space and walls that fly in from time to time to change the space.

The director spent the next two hours explaining how the space would continually define and redefine itself. No psychology. No metaphysics. Nothing about British history. Nothing about Shakespeare's concept of monarchy. A lecture on walls.

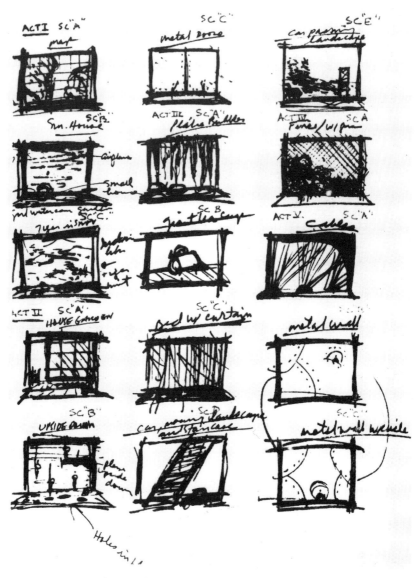

18 An early story board, outlining *the CIVILwarS*. After dividing a play into sections, Wilson finds a visual motif for each section.

A primordial influence on Wilson's theatre was Raymond Andrews, a deaf-mute. "I knew Raymond was intelligent," Wilson recounts (*Quartet*). "But he didn't know any words. I thought I thought in words, so I wondered how he could think without words. He made drawings to communicate with me, and I realized he thought in images. This experience proved to me how much the mind depends on visual thinking."[6]

Although Wilson rarely refers to literature, he often talks about artists, Cézanne in particular:

Cézanne is my favorite painter. My work is closer to him than to any other artist. My production of *Hamletmachine* is like a Cézanne painting in its architecture. Cézanne simplified and purified forms to reveal classical structure and composition. I learned everything from Cézanne, his use of color, light, the diagonal, and space – how to use the center and the edges. His images are not framed by the boundaries. (*Lear*)

From Cézanne Wilson imbibed monumentality; the dynamics of architectural form in terms of the pictorial plane; the interplay of "activating and balancing forces";[7] the use of warm and cold light to heighten plasticity; the importance of linear rhythm; unity through repetition; hierarchical composition; spatial tension; the dialog between depth and flatness; and the creation of mystery through abstraction.[8] From the master of Provence, the director also learned the importance of negative space – the empty space around objects. In Wilson one often sees the blue of Cézanne's Mediterranean sky and the ochre of his sun-baked earth.

An analysis of Cézanne's *Mont Sainte-Victoire* lays bare the principles of composition underlying Wilson's stage design (see figure 19). A tall tree – abstracted to one long vertical line – dominates the canvas, dead center. To the left, a clump of trees reinforces this vertical through repetition. A diagonal traced by the road divides the rectangle of parched earth into two triangles. Bisecting the dominant vertical and thereby emphasizing it, the horizontal viaduct, abstracted to a long white line speeding through space like the Mediterranean express, cuts the tree in half. The canvas seems almost empty; the negative space emphasizes the dominant vertical. The trees cling to the picture plane, making the viewer aware of its flat surface. Simultaneously, and setting up spatial tension, Mont Sainte-Victoire pulls the eye into the distance, creating a sense of depth. The use of light makes the vertical trees leap out from the ground toward the viewer. The composition spills over the edge of the frame; the open form makes us aware of the space beyond. Nature, abstracted into architecture, haunts us with the mysterious beauty of primary form.

Cézanne, the most architectural of painters, profoundly influenced

19 *Mont Sainte-Victoire*. "Tel qu'en lui-même enfin l'éternité le change" (Mallarmé, "Le tombeau d'Edgar Poe"): Underneath the perishable surface of nature, Cézanne saw the eternal forms of geometry – verticals, horizontals, diagonals.

Wilson, the most architectural of directors. Architecture, the most abstract and geometric of the arts, creates space. Space is not given by nature, it is made by man. Wilson refers to his theatre as "constructions in time and space." Space speaks. To understand the geometry of Wilsonland, one must begin where he begins, with the articulation of space. To survey a Wilson work and chart a map means to study the relationship between vertical, horizontal, diagonal; to see how these three lines create space; to track how this space changes through time as the relationship between vertical, horizontal, and diagonal changes (see figure 20). When analyzing a Wilson work, in addition to space, one must also pay close attention to all aspects of visual perception: balance, shape, form, light, color, movement, dynamics, and the expression embedded in structure.

To see is to see relationships; to grasp a Wilson work is to grasp the forms that structure space. The vertical line provides the dominant axis, but the vertical is "defined only by its contast with the horizontal."[9]

20 Wilson's drawing for the prolog to the Rome Section of *the*
CIVILwarS shows how the director organizes space by contrasting
lines: horizontals, verticals, diagonals. Note the precise notation of
time indicated at the bottom, demonstrating that theatre for Wilson is a
construction in space and time.

Wilson loves lines – long lines, strong lines. Perhaps the best introduction
to his visual world is "Poles," a sculpture he created by sticking 678 tele-
phone poles in a wheat field (see figure 21). Like much hard-edged minimalist art, "Poles" – built from found industrial objects – is austerely
abstract. The minimalist aesthetic derives from reductionism. By eliminating decorative details and expressive emotion, it emphasizes structural logic, primary shapes, clarity of style. Like most minimalist
sculpture in the sixties, "Poles" denies metaphysical implications, stressing the immediacy and primacy of perception – the pure phenomenology
of vision. Repudiating the psychological emoting of the abstract expres-
sionists, the hard-edged minimalism of Frank Stella, Kenneth Noland,
David Smith, Carl Andre, and Donald Judd was emotionally cool, like a
Balanchine dancer or a Wilson actor. When Wilson incorporates this aesthetic into a theatrical context, however, it may acquire symbolic and
metaphysical resonances, similar to the paintings of Mark Rothko, Ad
Reinhardt, and Agnes Martin, who use minimalist techniques to reveal

21   The entrance to "Poles," a site-specific, environmental sculpture. Through the modular repetition of a strong, simple contour (the rectangle), Wilson emphasizes the contrast between vertical and horizontal and gives prominence to architectural structure. The repetition of primary geometric forms shapes the minimalist aesthetic. Note the metal hooks that add visual texture and draw the eye to the top.

the transcendental.[10] Despite the rustic setting and materials, "Poles" is severely elegant. Frankly, simply, beautiful lines (see figure 22).

Because Wilson likes to see lines moving in space, he often gives actors long poles to carry. In *When We Dead Awaken* Maya's alpenstock became a long silver spear. Asked why he had given her a spear, Wilson answered: "It creates a nice line moving in space." True enough, but in the context of the play, this weapon directed at the husband dramatized the ferocious battle of the sexes. At other times, the long poles Wilson gives actors are simply lines drawing interesting geometric patterns. In the second knee play of *The Forest*, four men dressed in white trousers and long jackets – half-Oriental pajamas, half-hospital robes – go through a series of bio-mechanical exercises with long white poles that form, deform, and reform: verticals, horizontals, diagonals, reverse diagonals, the letters x and v, triangles, batons twirling in circles (see figure 23). Here, rather than projecting any symbolic meaning, the lines moving in space are lines

22 The grandeur of simplicity. Wilson's set for the palace in *Alceste* is an elegant, refined version of "Poles." By reducing the height of the receding columns, the director forces the perspective. Wilsonland is rectilinear.

moving in space, a ballet of sticks reminiscent of a Bauhaus performance. At times Wilson's theatre is symbolic, at times pure phenomenology.

The power of lines, mere lines, to generate meaning can be seen by looking closely at the epilogue to *the CIVILwarS* act IV. Dominating the stage, a long, black, horizontal tree branch stands out sharply against the serene blue sky.[11] Slowly, slowly a tall, black, vertical line (a seventeen-foot puppet of Abraham Lincoln) enters stage left.[12] As the vertical line inches its way toward the horizontal, dynamic tension, the essence of drama, floods the stage. At the climax, the two lines meet, and the branch becomes a sword, thrust through the heart of Lincoln. Simultaneously, the two lines form a cross, symbol of martyrdom and appropriate emblem on this blood-soaked field of Gettysburg. Unexpectedly, the Lincoln puppet, the tall vertical line, topples over, becoming a long horizontal, echoing visually the horizontal branch and figuring death. An unforgettable *coup de théâtre*, rich in meaning and emotion, conjured up by the energy of two simple lines.

23 During a knee play from *The Forest*, performers articulated space
and formed geometric configurations with long white sticks.

Mise-en-espace opens the sesame of Wilson's theatre. "When I make a
play, I start with a form, even before I know the subject matter. I start with
a visual structure, and in the form I know the content. The form tells me
what to do. I begin to fill in the form. I can diagram all my plays" (*Quartet*).
In Wilson's vocabulary form and structure mean architecture. When
designing a production, Wilson begins by organizing space through the
field of forces generated by the tension between vertical and horizontal,
between striving and stability. Infinite is the variety he rings by varying
these two fundamental axes of architecture, and unlike his more intuitive
behavior in other periods of the creative process, when he carves out the
basic linear relations that will shape the stage space – the blueprint of the
production – he is extraordinarily rational and analytical, often placing
pencils on his drawing paper like tinker toys to visualize better the vectors
and increase the counterpoint between horizontal and vertical. If his
images – surreal and anti-rational – bubble up from the subconscious, his
articulation of space is pure Euclidean geometry: the rational ordering of
space. The director constructs his works with the monumental symmetry
of classical architecture and a visual logic strictly Aristotelian. The secret

of Wilson's creativity is contradiction. His mind runs on contrasts. The power of his theatre springs from the unity of antagonistic forces, a *complexus oppositorum*: vertical, horizontal; silence, sound; light, dark; fast, slow; cold light, warm light; minimalism, maximalism; realism, abstraction; rational, irrational; comedy, tragedy; sublime, grotesque.

Understanding the visual patterns that Wilson uses to structure space takes one a long way toward understanding his work: *A Letter for Queen Victoria* was based on a diagonal; *the CIVILwarS* on a triangle. After a performance of *Quartet*, an audience member buttonholed the director. "Mr. Wilson, your show is beautiful, but I don't get it. What's the subject?" "Space," Wilson replied laconically. "Space?" queried the befuddled spectator. "What does it say about space?" "It doesn't say anything," the director answered wearily. "It takes place in a 540-square-foot trapezoid." But spatial composition is not empty formalism in Wilson; rather, form in Wilson conveys content, and often the simpler the form, the greater the complexity of connotation. In addition to the pure sensory pleasure visual composition offers, it always and on many levels generates signifying chains: "The simplest line expresses visible meaning and is therefore symbolic. All shape is semantic. In great works of art the deepest significance is transmitted to the eye with powerful directness by the perceptual characteristics of the compositional pattern."[13] In Wilson, the structure of space is the plot.

Wilson's design for *When We Dead Awaken* illustrates the symbolic aspects of design. Using Ibsen's stage directions as a point of departure, but moving, as he usually does, from realism to abstraction (the river in act II became a ribbon of blue fluorescence, cutting the stage diagonally), Wilson created a visual composition that communicated the spiritual journey of the play in terms of visual composition: in act I a black mountain plunged diagonally into the sea from left to right against a poison green sky; in act II a black canyon rent by a vertical cleft shut out most of the light; in act III a snow-covered white mountain rose from left to right into the glistening heights of a clear, blue heaven (audiences in the West read images from left to right). Diagonal contrasting with vertical contrasting with reversed diagonal. Elegantly simple, simply elegant. By itself the design conveyed the idea of a fall into the abyss and a spiritual rebirth. The stage grew increasingly dark; the mountain in act II closed off even more sky than act I. Act III ended in a blaze of light that dissolved matter in a radiance of white. Much of the iconography Wilson used came from his perusal of Doré's illustrations for Dante. Visually, Wilson traced Rubek's descent into the inferno of the heart – the solitude he discovers in love – and his waking to new life in death. The three sets forged an allegory of the struggle between light and dark, despair and transcendence, spiritual death and the necessity of killing the old self to be born anew. Design told the story.

Critics crab that Wilson's works are pretty but vapid. The Pulitzer Prize Board vetoed the American Repertory Theatre's version of *the CIVILwarS* after the nominating jury had chosen it unanimously. The board claimed the work was not theatre because it had no text. In fact it does have texts by Wilson and Müller. It also has long Wilsonian silences that speak with a golden tongue, and haunting images. Wilson's drawings were the genesis of *Einstein on the Beach*; the rest of the production – music, text, staging – was built around them. The music and the images inform each other to such a degree that Glass will not let any other director stage the opera.[14] Nevertheless, three times the Library of Congress refused to copyright the visual portion of the work, saying that *Einstein on the Beach* was a suite of drawings, not theatre. "The art of seeing," Marguerite Duras asserts in *Hiroshima mon amour*, "has to be learned."[15] Not everyone has the discipline or the visual acuity to learn to look.

SOURCES OF THE IMAGES

The sources of Wilson's images are manifold. He guzzles images rapaciously, an artistic magpie who, like Shakespeare, takes his material where he finds it, and he finds it everywhere – in newspapers, magazines, museums, books, pop culture, photographs, in rehearsal, on the street, and from the depths of memory, desire, and dream. He liked the way Marianne Hoppe, exhausted, slumped her head over a wall to rest. It became part of *King Lear*. In the Stuttgart art museum, he saw a neo-classical statue of a woman riding a panther. It became part of *Quartet*. On a back street in Hamburg, he saw a thief hold a gun to his temple to blackmail the police. It became part of *Quartet*. He saw a tree ripped asunder by a storm in Frankfurt. It became part of *King Lear*. He saw a photograph of a terrorist behind an iron fence in *The Herald-Tribune*. It became part of *Doktor Faustus*. At the *Doktor Faustus* rehearsal I asked Wilson what the source was of an arresting image – pens hovering in the air like hummingbirds around Adrian Leverkühn as he tried to compose. "From a dream I had last night," he answered. During workshops Wilson turns the walls into a gigantic bulletin board and invites actors to bring in any picture or text they think resonates with the play. Any image that strikes his fancy Wilson recasts in his aesthetic. Weaving them together in an architectonic unity, he makes them inalienably his.

The text Wilson works with also suggests images, though the untutored eye might miss the connection. In Woolf's *Orlando* the oak tree functions as a central, organizing symbol. In Wilson's production, the oak, abstracted into a towering black vertical, dominates the stage. *When We Dead Awaken* also illustrates the point. Each set for the three acts – how remote they seem at first from Grieg and Ibsen's Norway – is a meticulous translation of the stage directions into an abstract idiom, down to the stream and rocks of act II. Wilson took the naturalistic stage directions and nudged them away from realism towards stylization. For example, in act III Ibsen calls for "an old, half-tumbled-in hut." In Wilson's production the hut becomes an abstract black portal, more Chinese calligraphy than alpine shelter (Wilson had been thumbing through a book of photographs on the Alps) (see figure 24).

The luminous dream sequence from *When We Dead Awaken* further proves the point: seven women float slowly across the stage in a trance. They wear identical Victorian gowns of gray china silk (serial repetition is a key element in Wilson's visual grammar). Gray tulle pouffes swathe their ghost-white faces. Who are they? Maya's alter egos? They echo her words. They appear when Rubek asks his wife, "Have I offended the Frau Professor?"[16] The original stage directions read as follows: "Guests at the spa, mostly ladies, begin coming alone or in groups from the right, across the park and out, left."[17] How did Wilson get from Ibsen's naturalistic description to this surrealistic hallucination? Since the production had been rather spare until now, the director wanted a big moment, "a mass of people." He decided to have only female guests ("It's stranger with only one sex," he mused). He put them in identical dresses to create a "wall of women" (Wilson always thinks in architectural terms). Then he veiled the faces to make the guests more mysterious. The turn-of-the-century costume (Wilson wanted historically accurate clothes to counter the abstract sets) was a simplified version of a late Victorian fashion Wilson has used frequently since *Deafman Glance*: a high, tight neck; a closely fitted bodice; a full-length, A-line skirt; pared-down, leg-of-mutton sleeves; primitive pleating. "It's the most beautiful dress in the world," Wilson claims, "because the line is so severe" (*When We Dead Awaken*). Wilson made the line even more severe – longer, stronger – by lengthening the sleeves past the fingers and pulling the collar "as high and tight as it can go, until the actors choke." During a fitting, Wilson insisted that the costumes be "more sculptural. The only thing I want the audience to see on this dress is the line." To achieve the architectural form he wanted, Wilson weighted the bottom of the dresses so they would hold their line when the actresses moved. Frequently he adds a layer of heavy weight muslin underneath for the same reason. He also corseted

24 *When We Dead Awaken*, act III, American Repertory Theatre. Wilson scrutinized a photograph of an alpine hut and then abstracted it to its primary architectural shape. Since the silhouette created an interesting frame, Wilson directed Rubek to stand in it. From left to right: Irene (Elzbieta Czyzewska), Ulfheim (Mario Arrambide), Rubek (Alvin Epstein), and Maya (Stephanie Roth).

the chorus tightly to get rid of surface details like secondary sex characteristics that might detract from the line.

The World's Tallest Woman with a dwarf (William the Silent) on her outstretched palm – a striking tableau from the CIVILwarS – also exemplifies Wilson's concern with line and shows how he transmutes a found image – the lead of realism – into the burnished gold of stage magic.[18] The director ran across a Matthew Brady photograph of the giant Anna Swann with the Lilliputian King – two sideshow freaks (Wilson has a penchant for freaks) (see figure 25). Wilson enlarged the difference in scale between big woman, little man, and by eliminating surface details turned the hulking female into a stark geometric shape (see figure 26). "Simple forms," notes the director, "are more interesting than romantic bric-a-brac" (When We Dead Awaken). Always, the director emphasizes the silhouette of costume for two reasons. First, he likes the architecture of long lines. Second, with backlighting, humans become inscrutable – enigmatic forms moving in the dark. Wilson's eye metamorphoses objects and people into primary shapes – abstract, mysterious.

Preparing a new production, the director conducts a staggering amount of research – visual and historical. (An acute historical sensitivity runs throughout Wilson's work.) Wilson is an inveterate workaholic. At the party following the premiere of King Lear, when most artists would have relaxed and chatted with the actors and stage hands, Wilson sat down at table next to Heiner Müller, who was drinking away and bantering cheerfully. Wilson started to draw scenes for his production of The Magic Flute, which premiered in Paris a year later. The visual research for the CIVILwarS crams seven large boxes and includes stills from Melies's movies; photos of astronauts, rockets, and planets; pictures of animals – owls, giraffes, horses, sharks; antique automobiles; army uniforms; natural disasters – floods, avalanches, volcanoes, fires, storms; photographs of bridges; paintings of Frederick the Great and his dogs royal; illustrations from Jules Vernes's fantastic voyages; photographs of the American Civil War, including the ruins of Richmond and piles of bodies at Cold Harbor (images of cruelty we prefer to suppress); photographs of Mary Todd Lincoln's dresses, whose opulence set the tongues of Washington wagging; a picture book entitled The Marvellous World of Trees. The file on Lincoln contains over twenty contemporary political cartoons of Honest Abe, all emphasizing his string-bean silhouette, a strong vertical line that would play such an important part in the CIVILwarS.

Audience members will not be aware of the origins of many of Wilson's images. As with allusions in any work of art, the wider one's

25 Matthew Brady's portrait of Anna Swann with the Lilliputian King
provided Wilson with material for one of the most arresting images in
the CIVILwarS.

26 The World's Tallest Woman (a giant puppet with Sutton inside).
When a picture stimulates Wilson's imagination, such as the Brady
photograph, he transmutes it into an image unmistakably his own.

frames of reference, the richer one's response. The more images one rec-
ognizes and puts back into their original context, the more echoes one
hears in one's head, the deeper one's interpretation will be. However,
since these images are brought together in a new work of art, they
signify independently of their origins. Without a program note and
photograph, virtually no one would recognize Barnum's "sensational
'Nova Scotia Giantess' Anna Swann"[19] as the visual source for Wilson's
Big Woman – a symbol of royalty – in the Dutch section of *the
CIVILwarS*. It does not matter. It will still be obvious that the play deals
with the theatrical ritual regimes need to cloak themselves in an aura of
legitimacy and with the symbols political power deploys to fabricate its
grandeur while concealing its strategies of repression. Another layer of
grotesque irony is added if one sees in this emblem of European royalty
a conflation of the Dutch monarchy with sideshow freaks exhibited to
entertain a naive public. The House of Orange is one of the wealthiest in
the world, but like the land it rules – despite public relations images of
tulips, plump Gouda cheeses, and Hans Brinker's gliding across frozen
canals on silver skates – it grew fat off a ruthless colonial subjugation of
non-Europeans in Asia, Africa, and Latin America. Casting an African
American in this role reverberated with Holland's complicity in the
slave trade. The work, after all, is called *the CIVILwarS*, and one of the
officially proclaimed causes of the Civil War was slavery. A black
woman who embodies an icon of European royalty sets spinning a
whole series of painful questions about the distribution of power and
wealth and racial tensions. But to miss these cross-references – the more
virulent in their aggression by their smiling innocence – does not dimin-
ish the immediate, sensuous pleasure one gets from the startling image,
nor the other potential meanings Wilson invites spectators to generate
for themselves. The figure itself fascinates because it elicits conflicting
emotions. It is both comic and sinister – a swollen body capped by a
diminutive head. Wilson does, however, appreciate theatres that put
together intelligent programs with background information and copious
illustrations of both his own drawings and visual material that stimulated his images. Wilson works closely with dramaturgs on these programs, some of which, especially in the German theatres, grow into
tomes, opulently illustrated, diligently researched. But on every level
Wilson's theatre militates against the imposition of a single, theological
interpretation. Wilson's theatre dramatizes the coexistence of different
and opposed meanings.

SIMULTANEITY AND MONTAGE

Two other concepts help to explain Wilson's *mise-en-scène*: simultaneity and montage. Ever since Cubism, simultaneity has been the war cry of the avant-garde. By juxtaposing heterogeneous elements, simultaneity rejects a single point of view to explore an object from multiple angles. Jung's synchronicity, Einstein's relativity, Heisenberg's uncertainty – our age is the age of doubt. By telescoping space and time, by yoking together a kaleidoscope of clashing perspectives, simultaneity enables an artist to create a new aesthetic unity without denying the contradictions and chaos of experience.[20] Picasso's *Girl Before a Mirror* reveals conflicting facets of the same woman, yet the painting itself transcends these conflicts by creating a new structural unity.

Wilson's imagination works the same way. The opening scene in the ART's production of *the CIVILwarS* (act III scene E) shows how simultaneity functions in his theatre. Unhurriedly the morning sun rises over a camp of Confederate soldiers. The young men, roused from slumber, drowsily go about the routines of waking: stretching, shaving, washing, dressing, cooking. They ready themselves for death; the guard in the background, rifle cocked and ready to shoot, reminds us that all this life – flesh is as grass – will vanish into the smoke of canons, like ashes scattered in the wind. *Lachrymae rerum*. Tenderness for the trivial beauty of daily life suffuses the scene. "Hold that cup in your hands as if you knew it's the last time you will ever smell coffee," the director reproached a nonchalant soldier. "Caress it." As the soldiers slowly line up to march off to war, a vaudeville dancer sashays across the stage, followed hard behind by an antique motor car, *circa* 1910, filled with a group of narcoleptic bourgeois out for a joy ride, sporting goggles, broad-brimmed bonnets, floor-length dust coats (see figure 27). As they hum "In My Merry Oldsmobile," Frederick the Great, in the back seat, stands up, looks round, and brandishes his cane at phantoms in the air.

What does all this mean? As T. S. Eliot observed, analyzing St.-John Perse's epic *Anabasis*,

Any obscurity of the poem is due to the suppression of "links in the chain," of explanatory and connecting matter, and not to incoherence, or to the love of cryptogram. The justification of such abbreviation of method is that the sequence of images coincides and concentrates into one intense impression of barbaric civilization. The reader has to allow the images to fall into his memory successively without questioning the reasonableness of each at the moment; so that, at the end, a total effect is produced. Such selection of a sequence of images and ideas has nothing chaotic about it. There is a logic of the imagination as well as a

27 The American Repertory Theatre's production of the Cologne
Section of *the CIVILwarS* began with an elegy to the young soldiers
about to perish as canon fodder in the American Civil War. Wilson
often dramatizes the fragility of life.

logic of concepts. People who do not appreciate poetry always find it difficult to
distinguish between order and chaos in the arrangement of images; and even
those who are capable of appreciating poetry cannot depend upon first impressions. I was not convinced of Mr. Perse's imaginative order until I had read the
poem five or six times. And if, as I suggest, such an arrangement of imagery
requires just as much "fundamental brainwork" as the arrangement of an argument, it is to be expected that the reader of a poem should take at least as much
trouble as a barrister reading an important decision on a complicated case . . . But
Anabase is poetry. Its sequences, its logic of imagery, are those of poetry and not of
prose.[21]

Eliot might just as well have been explicating *The Waste Land* or *the
CIVILwarS*. Condensation, displacement, ellipsis, syncretism, and the
construction of an epic–tragic vision of history through shards and fragments hallmark the style of both Wilson and Eliot.[22] Wilson's theatre is
poetry, not prose; connotative, not denotative.

It took five or six readings before Eliot – no common reader – under-stood the imaginative order behind *Anabase*. Like any difficult work of art, Wilson's productions can strike viewers, especially those unfamiliar with or antagonistic to his vision, as obscure. Some critics blast his works as boring, vapid, and pretentious. But obscurity in Wilson is not obfusca-tion; his theatre deals with complex and psychologically disturbing material.

Difficulty characterizes much of the greatest art of the twentieth century. Writing about the novel, John Barth notes:

James Joyce & Co. set very high standards of artistry . . . On the other hand, we have their famous relative difficulty of access, inherent in their anti-linearity, their aversion to conventional characterization and cause-and-effect dramaturgy, their celebration of private, subjective experience over public experience, their general inclination to "metaphoric" as against "metonymic" means . . . If we need a guide, or a guidebook, to steer us through Homer or Aeschylus, it is because the world of the text is so distant from our own, as it presumably was not from Aeschylus's and Homer's original audiences. But with *Finnegans Wake* or Ezra Pound's *Cantos*, we need a guide because of the inherent and immediate difficulty of the text.[23]

Returning to the opening scene from the ART production of *the CIVILwarS* and to the technique of simultaneity, we see that Wilson has telescoped time and space: eighteenth-century Prussia; a Civil War battle-field; a rambunctious America on the brink of becoming a world power in the bloodbath of World War I (a war fought for many reasons, including the race among European powers for colonies). The mark of Cain – brother murder – links all these disparate elements. "History," Voltaire sneered, "is little else than a picture of human crimes and calamities." The soldiers marching steadfastly off to doom wear Dixie gray. They could just as easily be wearing Prussian blue or English red. Throughout *the CIVILwarS* images of predators – bears, eagles, humans – suggest that violence lurks in DNA, a basic component of our genetic baggage. "Considered biologically," William James noted, "man is the most formidable of all the beasts of prey, and, truly, the only one who systemat-ically devours his own species." The key term here is "systematically." We alone have the intelligence to elaborate complex engines of war. The Oldsmobile, rolling merrily over the consecrated ground of Gettysburg with its cargo of oblivious bourgeois, dramatizes the wanton destruction of the agricultural South by a brutal, industrialized North, intent on dic-tating economic policies and using abolition as an excuse. The sword of Frederick the Great, not the spirit of Abraham Lincoln, keeps the mili-tary–industrial engine achugging. Into this phantasmagoria of death and destruction dances a clown. Why? First, he adds necessary comic relief. He checks the pathos of the slaughter of the innocents: the nameless, faceless footsoldiers who never understand the economic forces sacrificing them to Moloch. Wilson refuses to let his theatre become maudlin; he often uses comedy to offset tragedy. Second, the clown embodies the folly of human history, an eternal return of the same sins, the same tragedies. Through simultaneity Wilson dramatizes history as a vicious circle.

Simultaneity enables Wilson to layer different zones of time and space against each other. Act II, scene iv of *Doktor Faustus* takes place in a villa in the German countryside. During the design workshop Wilson asked an assistant to read aloud the description from Thomas Mann's novel. The director then drew a floor plan, dividing the space into six separate zones – five rooms and a yard. Wilson wanted different activities in each space. "I want to see different things going on in the different rooms simultaneously, but they can also be different time periods." The composer objected. "I want a whole house," he pleaded, "and realistic so the audience can identify where they are. We must show them a real Bavarian house and a real Bavarian landscape, not just slices of rooms." "That doesn't matter," Wilson shot back. "This is more interesting architecturally. I want to layer different planes of reality."

Wilson's production of Richard Strauss's *Salome* at La Scala also shows how the director uses simultaneity to tell the same story from different points of view. Central to Wilson's vision is the realization that relative and diametrically opposed truths criss-cross any human interaction. He divided the stage into three major zones: a downstage platform for singers, a *hanamichi* stage left for actors who mimed the roles the singers sang, and an upstage space dominated by a young actress who represented Salome as Alice in Wonderland while Montserrat Caballe sang her music. Multilayering is essential in Wilsonian texture; here it captured the contradictions of this naive *femme fatale* who exploits her sexual power without knowing anything about sex. The schizoid stage dramatized the guilt of this innocent necrophiliac. The *mise-en-espace* presented, simultaneously, three different psychological realities. If, for instance, Herodias was singing on the platform, on the *hanamichi* the focus shifted to Herod to show what was going on in his mind. Upstage the audience saw Salome's interior reaction to her mother. On the downstage platform, the singers acted out the external drama. In the two other zones, actors played out a theatre of the soul. The superimposition of internal truth set against external gesture conveyed the complexity of social interaction. Wilson's stage made palpable the split between inner and outer: humans live their lives on two levels – one directed toward action in the exterior world, one lost in the shadows of fantasy. We are all, under the skin, sisters of Madame Bovary. In theatre no one has captured this tragicomic schism with the brilliance of Wilson. Marvin Carlson cites "psychic polyphony" – the ability to "allow simultaneous statements to be made by a variety of presences" – as one of the theatre's most potent weapons.[24] Wilson takes this weapon to its lethal conclusion.

During rehearsals Wilson often tells actors about the psychological studies of mothers and infants conducted by Dr. Daniel Stern at Columbia University.

In the sixties I saw films of over 300 mothers picking up crying babies. Seen at a normal rate of projection, the mothers would reach for the baby and comfort it. Stern slowed the films down. In eight out of ten cases the initial reaction of the mother was irritation or anger. Mother lunged at child; child retreated. The body moves faster than the mind, and the body doesn't lie. The body says things that have nothing to do with what the tongue is saying. When the mothers saw the films in slow motion, they were horrified. "But I love my baby," they protested. They could not admit their ambivalence toward their children. What happens between humans in one second is complicated and contractory. When Romeo tells Juliet "I love you," that love, like all love, is complex. You must bring that complexity to the part you're playing. (*Lear*)

To dramatize this complexity Wilson layers his productions: movements, words, lights, colors – all theatrical codes tell a different story. "What the audience hears and what it sees shouldn't be the same," the director explains. "At first this disjunction may seem arbitrary, but it isn't. It fits into an overall structure. This is not a rational way of working, it's intuitive. Slowly the pieces fall together and add up. More meanings emerge in my theatre because more than one thing is going on at the same time" (*WWDA*).

Simultaneity explains how Wilson structures a scene visually; montage explains how he links one scene to another. Like the great formalist directors of Soviet cinema – Eisenstein, Pudovkin, Vertov – Wilson builds the visual architecture of a work rhythmically through montage, a dialectical process of free association that creates meaning not by narration or discursive logic but by the juxtaposition of two often seemingly unrelated scenes. In contrast to smooth transitions based on cause and effect, montage creates a dialog among disparate realities. The meaning lies not only in each individual scene but also in the juxtaposition of scenes, which creates emotional climates, reveals psychological insights, and generates abstract themes. Montage destroys the "real" time and "real" place cherished by naturalism to emphasize the dynamic collision of opposites. Not only is conflict the subject of *the CIVILwarS*, it is also its technique – visually, verbally, aurally, structurally. For Eisenstein montage is a "creative remolding of nature . . . the unexpected junction found at polar extremes . . . a qualitative leap," rather than the plodding, quantitative accumulation of prose realism.[25] The polyphonic structure built up through montage is greater and more powerful than the sum of its parts.

Two scenes from *the CIVILwarS* demonstrate how Wilson works montage. In act IV, scene A, section 9, entitled "Frederick and Katte," Frederick takes on the role of Phaedra; Katte – Frederick's homosexual lover – the role of Hippolytus. Since women play both men, audience members unfamiliar with the details of Fredericks's biography would still feel emotionally the tension generated by a scene that transgresses erotic tabus. Together they play out act II, scene V, of Racine's tragedy, the most poignant explosion of guilty love in the canon. Phaedra, despite herself, pours out her longing to her stepson, the forbidden object of desire. Embarrassment, guilt, lust, anger, fear of rejection, exaltation, pride, timidity, tenderness – all whirl through Phaedra's soul: "Yes, Prince, I suffer, I burn." In the Cologne production the two actresses repeated this line twenty times in a litany of sexual frustration. Frederick's father, concerned over his son's masculinity, had Katte executed before Frederick's eyes. Many moments in *the CIVILwarS* explore the brutal father–son relationship. (The *American Repertory Theatre News*, mailed out in advance, provided audiences with the necessary historical background.)

In the next part (act IV, scene A, section 10), (see figure 28) Frederick – old, stoop-shouldered – crosses the stage slowly in a straight line parallel to the proscenium; turning at a right angle, he approaches a large black dog; pauses; stares; pauses; raises hand above dog's head; pauses; touches dog tenderly; dog barks; Frederick starts; dog stands on hind legs; Frederick caresses dog's face; embraces dog; buries head in dog's chest; dog growls; Frederick backs off; walks back on a straight line; turns at right angle; crosses stage; reaches edge of stage; stops; long pause; spins rapidly round; holds arm out full length; shoots dog – coldly, cruelly; freeze frame; light on dog off. Frederick strides off, walking like a man, as impassive as the faces carved on Mt. Rushmore. Wilson cites this scene as the most important in the entire twelve-hour epic: the turning point. Seemingly unrelated to the fragment from *Phaedra* that precedes it, the juxtaposition of these dialectical scenes generates a synthesis, suggesting that Frederick became the monster history abhors because his father succeeded only too well in making a man of him, the very model of a modern German general, who ordered thousands of his subjects to spill

28 *the CIVILwarS*, American Repertory Theatre. The dynamics of love:
First Frederick the Great (Priscilla Smith) caresses his favorite dog
(Thomas Derrah). Then he shoots him. In Wilson, as in Racine, love is
often a game of executioner and executed. A scene from *Phaedra* had
immediately preceded.

their guts on a battlefield while he composed a flute concerto. By destroying his son's ability to love, Frederick's father set loose on the world the
demons of Prussian militarism that leads in an unbroken chain of "blood
and iron" to Hitler. The executed becomes the executioner; the victim, the
victimizer. The lack of emotion on Frederick's face when he destroys
what he loves most – his dog – offers a glimpse into the living soul of evil.

FUNCTIONS OF THE IMAGES

Wilson's visual images perform many functions. Through repetition,
they create structural unity in diversity; they generate atmosphere,
provide humor, suggest psychological insights, and, heightened to
symbol and allegory, convey the director's urgent thematic concerns.[26]

the CIVILwarS pulls together so much heterogeneous material – the
entire history of the human race is telescoped into the epic – it constantly

threatens to fall apart. What keeps it together? Visual syntax. By reiterating visual leitmotifs, Wilson's tectonic structure triumphs over the centrifugal, disparate elements. Wilson says that *the CIVILwarS* is a play about triangles; the repetition of this visual shape – sail boats, shark fins, tents, pilgrims' capes – is the silken thread on which Wilson strings his pearls. *Hamletmachine* also demonstrates how Wilson uses visual repetition to create clear structural unity. In the director's silent prolog to Müller's play, Wilson establishes a visual vocabulary for the audience: backdrop stage right; real tree upstage right; long table with three chairs behind and one chair in front set on a diagonal center stage. Through an additive process, the actors go through a series of strange, autonomous gestures, building to a climax. This visual structure is repeated five times – always from a different angle, always with a different text. (In part two, the backdrop has shifted to the back wall; the diagonal is now dialectically opposed to the first diagonal; the tree is upstage left. The fifth repetition brings everything back to its original position.)

In addition to providing structural unity, Wilson also uses visual images to create atmosphere. The sets he designed for Chekhov's *Swan Song* and the final scene of the D'Annunzio–Debussy ballet–mystery–oratorio – *Le Martyre de Saint Sébastien* demonstrate how the director's eye transmutes realistic knickknacks into abstract metaphors that communicate with a fierce beauty. Chekhov's stage directions read as follows: "The empty stage of a second-rate provincial theatre, littered with the remains of the evening's scenery and various backstage tools and equipment. There is a stool, upside down, in the centre of the stage. It is night, and dark."[27] The subject of *Swan Song*, as the title suggests, is death: the death of an old trouper. With comic swings of mood, he first blames the theatre for ruining his life and then, antithetically, seeks in the theatre consolation for the stupidity of life. Like all Chekhov, it is an amalgam of pathos and ridicule, compassion and tough lucidity.

Nothing is quite as forlorn as a dark, empty theatre, which moments before buzzed with the boisterous joy of performance. A row of empty chairs face Wilson's grim stage – a dark gray, stark box that feels like a mausoleum with black holes in the walls like coffins (see figure 29). Chekhov's "litter" has been reduced to a Corinthian column and a ladder against the backwall (two tall verticals summing up the history of theatre from Aeschylus to Wilson), a dressing table, the upside-down stool, a low horizontal table and bench, and, of course, the ubiquitous bottle of vodka on the floor. Wilson's desolate space – it feels as warm as a snow squall in Antarctica – creates the loneliness of death. As the curtain rises, gusts of wind howl through the theatre, chilling the marrow of the bone. An old,

29 Functioning like a *Stimmungsdichtung*, the set for *Swan Song* evoked a mood in which one fell "half in love with easeful death."

emaciated man – more wraith than flesh – runs round the room, frantic. He screams – a shrill, throttled cackle like a chicken choking in its own blood. He disappears into a black hole in the wall. On this bare stage, walking shadows will strut and fret their hour, playing out the last scene of all, giving Chekhov's little farce a dark resonance.

In contrast to this rendezvous with death, the last scene of *Le Martyre de Saint Sébastien*, entitled "Paradise," creates an atmosphere of pure, unsullied joy (see figure 30). This act presents a director with an impossible conundrum to solve: how to concretize paradise, the most spiritual of concepts, in the theatre, the most physical of arts. No previous production has successfully navigated between this Scylla and Charybdis,[28] and D'Annunzio's feverish stage directions, redolent of fin-de-siècle decadence, do not help. Any attempt to stage his neo-Byzantine icon of paradise – burning forever with a hard, gem-like flame, scented with lavender and opium – would sink any production.[29] Wilson creates his own vision of heaven, which seduces the eye and tickles the soul.

Instead of the fire and diamonds dreamt by D'Annunzio, Wilson's paradise recalls American folk-painting: innocent, child-like, naive. Paradise is a garden of light, bathed in unearthly, numinous glow (provided by

30 *Le Martyre de Saint Sébastien.* Paradise as an eternal romp with stuffed animals that have sprung to life off the pages of a child's story book. Left, Saint Sébastien (Sylvie Guillem) and right, Saint Sébastien II (Michael Denard).

HMI's, the strongest source of light available in theatres).[30] This ultra-bright light dissolves matter in a halo of radiance. The set – plants, animals, people – shimmered: white on white on white. White fronds, white animals, white sky. Paradise for Wilson is nature transfigured by art. Hence a garden where polar bears clap their paws, snow monkeys play with magic wands, and a towering white heron dandles in the air an invisible cup of Earl Grey tea. Reminiscent of the early Renaissance paintings that depict paradise as a courtly stroll through a garden,[31] the two saints, in the whitest of white robes, go awandering and awondering through this enchanted forest. For contrast (it enables us to appreciate the blaze of whiteness), one blood-red angel – red face, red robe, red wings – floats across the stage, frozen in a stigmata of ecstasy. Wilson's startling mix of sophistication and naivete transports the spectator to beatitude.

Through visual images, Wilson also creates humor, a crucial aspect of his work. "Never," Wilson counsels his actors, "do a play without humor. The darker the tragedy, the brighter the humor. You can deal with serious themes, but you must never let a play get heavy and sad and weepy" (*Lear*). "Beardance" from *the CIVILwarS* (act IV, scene A, section 4) shows how Wilson creates humor through visual magic. On a backdrop, a film depicts a volcano's erupting; waves of hot lava cascade down like Niagara Falls on fire. Two bears – a white polar, a black grizzly – lumber out. Clumsy, they clamber around the small downstage platform, sniff each other, stare at the audience, poke their faces into the first row. Frederick the Great – in full military regalia – comes out and starts playing his rococo flute concerto, white gloves scudding up and down an imaginary flute. Light and bright and sparkling. Smiling, the two bears rub each other's noses, slap each other's back, hug. Their heads bob with the lilting cadences of the music, twinkling with joy. Frederick somer-saults over to the bears, bows profoundly with a courtly gesture, starts to minuet. The bears peer at him, peer at each other, stand up on their hind legs, and imitate Frederick's elegant capers. The three twirl, dip, pirou-ette in a fantastic *pas de trois* – gossamer arabesques from unlikely syl-phides. Frederick – old Fritz – embraces the grizzly and invites him to gavotte. They take a few steps together. Bear whacks King across fore-head. King tumbles to floor. Grizzly runs off, rejoins polar. The two exit with a hesitation crawl – pausing rhythmically with the rear right leg extended. A courtier enters with a gold Louis-Quinze throne. He places it atop Frederick, still lolling on the floor. The King crawls on all fours like a child, juggling the chair on his back. The emblem of his authority crushes him: he feels inadequate to assume the throne of his father. The light-hearted joy he shared with the bears evaporates like morning mist at high noon. Remembering this scene or the giant frog swilling down martinis in *Deafman Glance* or the butler dashing plates against the banquet table in *Alcestis*, one smiles again. The child-like whimsy that runs through Wilson's humor disarms the adult.

Wilson also uses images for characterization. Ulfheim in *When We Dead Awaken* shows how the director elaborates a persona visually. Until he enters, the spa, where Rubek and Maya bicker away, has been elegant – a world of white linen and starch. The conversation has run on such topics as should an artist follow a new vision, which triggers misunderstanding and hostility, or should he satiate the vulgar and stupid with facile, worn-out forms that insure critical and commercial success. Into this rarefied world of wealth, refinement, and intellect, storm the barbarians: Ulfheim and his dogs, howling for raw meat. Ulfheims's visual appearance, even before he utters a syllable, clashes with the world he has roared into (see figure 31). Chalk-white skin, blood-red lips and a black diagonal streaking across his forehead, his Expressionist face looks like a devil escaped from Kabuki. His black hair curls up in a bride-of-Frankenstein coiffure that suggests two horns sprouting out of his skull. He sports an ankle-length leather overcoat – jungle green and open to the belly button to flaunt his hairy chest. On one foot a snakeskin boot with a spur that jingle jangles. On the other a cloven hoof.

This high fantastical attire was suggested by Maya's description of Ulfheim in Ibsen's text: "Do you know what you remind me of, Squire Ulfheim? You remind me of a satyr . . . An ugly, lecherous creature with cleft feet and the beard of a goat. Yes, and horns, too."[32] Wilson literalized the metaphors visually, a technique he often uses. Ulfheim's get-up characterizes him not only as a man of flesh, blood, and testosterone, it also establishes – immediately, directly, powerfully – his opposition to everything Rubek stands for. The play hinges on this diametrical contrast. Ulfheim will play Pappageno to Rubek's aging Tamino, the sensuous man who thinks with his penis, pitted against the alienated artist desperately trying to keep faith with art. Ulfheim's vulgarity – charming in its simplicity – also provides the necessary touch of humor to undercut the gravity of the preceding scenes and prick the balloon of Rubek's pretentious jabbering about art. There is more than a hint of playful self-mockery in Wilson's portrait of the artist as a "big, overgrown baby."[33]

Wilson heightens his visual images to the level of symbol, making them resonate to the depths of consciousness and beyond. "It is not surprising," Jung writes, "when an archetypal situation occurs, we suddenly feel an extraordinary sense of release, as though transported, or caught up by an overwhelming power. At such moments we are no longer individuals, but the race; the voice of all mankind resounds in us."[34] Many such moments occur in Wilson's mythopoetic universe. Through archetypes, Wilson's theatre suggests more than it states. *Quartet* provides multiple examples. Müller's text deals with the longest war in history: the battle of the sexes. "Man survives earthquakes, epidemics, famines," wrote Tolstoy, "but the most poignant tragedy was, is, and ever shall be the tragedy of the bedroom." It is the tragedy no one survives. Müller knew this tragedy firsthand, and many of the images from Valmont's last speech derive from the suicide of Müller's wife Inge: "I shall open my veins as I would an unread book. You will learn how to read it, Valmont, after me . . . Green and bloated with poison I shall walk through your sleep. Swinging from a rope I shall dance for you. My face will be a blue mask. The tongue protruding."[35]

Wilson's set design dramatizes visually the agony between male and

31 *When We Dead Awaken*, American Repertory Theatre. Ulfheim's expressionistic make-up, as well as his outrageous get-up and behavior, opposes the elegant refinement of the spa. Ulfheim (Mario Arrambide) and Maya (Stephanie Roth).

female. A diagonal line bisects the trapezoid performance space, creating two triangles. A floor-to-ceiling gauze curtain echoes this diagonal. An upright phallic chair dominates the upstage triangle, associated with the male (Valmont). A black chaise-longue, whose graceful curve was suggested by the arm of a neo-classical nude, dominates the downstage triangle, associated with the female (Merteuil). Two triangles, eternally united, eternally opposed. But the opposition is more apparent than real; from time to time the gauze curtain is drawn back to recreate a unified square, hinting that male and female may not be the binary opposites defined by our culture. But, in a world of the play, this binary opposition leads to a struggle unto death.

Wilson undermines the male–female opposition through gender role playing: the Marquise de Merteuil assumes the part of a ruthless Don Juan who wantonly destroys women; Valmont, the part of his sexual victims. Female plays male beautifully; male, female. The play suggests that we are all gender impersonators. Wilson insinuates this visually throughout his production; the scene entitled "The Annihilation of the Niece" illustrates how. A large disk dominates the stage. On one side a male nude reminiscent of da Vinci; on the other, a Membrace Amerindian pot – ritually pierced in the center, symbolizing the female.[36] The disk begins to spin; male and female blur. Around the gyrating disk, Merteuil and Valmont whirl. She – mature, worldly wise, cynical – plays a naive virgin who, in a mystico-erotic frenzy, mistakes semen for an effusion of the Holy Ghost, a rococo Marilyn Monroe, playing dumb to increase the testosterone level of her lover. He – a rotting hulk of a man, world-weary, impotent – gets down on all fours to play, one last time, the lion in love. Gender, the visual metaphors imply, is performance: socially constructed, not biologically determined; sex, a willing suspension of disbelief; love, the greatest weapon of destruction. Around and around the disk they go, pursuing, not each other, but phantoms of their own desire. Sex is pretext. What each wants is power, power over the other. The scene ends with the death of the female. Wilson reveals sex as *wille-zur-macht*. After reading Strindberg's *Father*, Nietzsche exclaimed: "My own conception of love – with war as its means and the deathly hatred of the sexes its fundamental law." In Wilson's production, the inequality between men and women results in a battle where the enemy may be destroyed, but no victory is won. Malignant and far-reaching are the psychological and political ramifications of this inequality. "In our society there exists a thoroughly realistic basis for conflict: men and women are irrationally defined as unequal . . . All relationships that are irrationally unequal (*e.g.*, blacks and whites, women and men) share characteristics that lead to profound psychological results . . . Mutually enhancing interaction is not probable between unequals . . ."[37] Taking on the identity of a woman who killed herself for him, Valmont kills himself, leaving Merteuil alone and defeated in triumph. In his death is his victory. She lives on, caressed by bitterness.

OBSESSIVE IMAGES

Reiterated images – images repeated from work to work – provide important clues about any artist's vision. Freud suggests that obsessive visual images vent the unconscious. These obsessive images reveal the urgent concerns that seek expression in the artist's work. Becoming conversant with these key images takes one far into Wilson's imagination. Five major clusters of images figure prominently in Wilson: nature, the outcast, the family, the voyage, the apocalypse.

Nature provides Wilson with some of his most striking images, especially trees and animals. Marvellous and unforgettable was the parade of trees from the end of *the CIVILwarS* or the convocation of beasts in *Life and Times of Sigmund Freud*, reminiscent of Edward Hick's "The Peaceable Kingdom". Wilson's animal fables carry the same utopian dream as Hick's painting, inspired by Isaiah 11: "The wolf also shall dwell with the lamb, and the leopard shall lie down with the kid; and the calf and the young lion and the fatling together; and a little child shall lead them."

As a child of the twentieth century, Wilson problematizes Hick's naive vision with Freudian conflicts between id and superego. In Wilson, harmony depends on a marriage of man's mind to nature. In his notebooks from the *Deafman Glance* workshop in Iowa, Wilson wrote, "Nature helps one's spiritual side . . . We should not offend the earth or it will break us." When he discusses his theatre, Wilson often mentions the formative influence on him of nature: "I was born in Texas. That landscape is still in my head."[38] Nature in the Southwest – its immensity and grandeur, its silence and solitude – overwhelms. Heiner Müller claims that he never understood Wilson until he saw the endless horizons of Texas.

During the early years, the director desperately wanted to buy a track of wilderness in Texas or Canada as a spiritual haven for his company, and in 1973 the Byrd Hoffman Foundation, the institution Wilson established to support his work, bought land in British Columbia. Later Wilson would buy land in Water Mill, Long Island, to workshop projects and renew his contact with nature. "Water Mill can be something free, something that takes place in a natural environment, outdoors. I want to spend more time working that way. I've spent most of my life in indoor spaces in theatres. I'd like to work more outside."[39]

In Wilson's works, communion with nature cleanses the mildew of the soul. But this communion has been disrupted by a civilization steeped in an intellectual arrogance that sets man apart from, and above, nature. *The Forest* – the title carries its own commentary – can be read as an allegory of the fall into civilization. In it, Wilson superimposes two time frames: the transition from hunting and gathering to agriculture, represented by Gilgamesh and the city–state; and the transition from agriculture to industry, based on exploiting nature and workers, represented by the nineteenth arms factory of Krupp – wealth for the few based on death and destruction for the many. The evolution of Enkidu from noble, nude savage to effete, overdressed bourgeois, ashamed of his body, tells the age-old tale of civilization and its discontents: something vital gets lost in the process of socialization. By curbing instincts, civilization inflicts an eternal malaise. Frequently in Wilson one sees a Victorian world of repression blown up by the forces of nature.

For the prison scene in *Danton's Death*, Wilson used a realistically painted mountain (it is unusual for him to be so literal) in the distance to contrast with the abstract prison cell – a shower of golden strings. Awaiting the guillotine, a vision of this far-away landscape haunts Danton's inner eye. The mountain symbolizes a natural Eden of freedom and innocence from which man, the political animal, has been forever banished.

Act v of *The Forest* takes place in the opulently appointed library of the Krupp villa. Gilgamesh and Enkidu, dressed in the redingotes of nineteenth-century robber barons, wander around, idly. A forest of pine trees enters, and a chorus of men crawls on the floor. *The Forest* takes place simultaneously in Babylon and in nineteenth-century Europe in the throes of industrialization. It pits images of nature against images of the machine age. This invasion of nature into a temple of greed, guilt, and intellect shows that "The world is too much with us; late and soon, / Getting and spending, we lay waste our powers." Wordsworth's poetry, one of the first cultural responses to industrialization, attacks the brutality of an age that cut us off from nature. Throughout Wilson runs the urgent need to heal the breach between man and nature.

Another image Wilson often repeats is the outcast, usually an old man, a young child, or a disabled boy. Einstein fiddling away on a solitary beach; Raymond Andrews, the deaf-mute, silently watching *Deafman Glance*, aloft and alone; Chris Knowls, the autistic poet, flying through the air in *A Letter for Queen Victoria*; Adrian Leverkühn, who sells his soul to the demon of art in *Doktor Faustus* and winds up crazed; Lewis Carroll, who created a fantasy world that unmasks the brutality of adults and the confusions of growing up. Different though these outcasts be, they share many traits in common: their inner vision cuts them off from others; their superior gifts alienate them from society. To other men they seem insane because they see what others cannot see. Dreamers all, they search for the Holy Grail, and if their quest touches madness, these holy fools are, in the Baudelairean sense, artistic beacons, whose creations reveal the divine within.[40] They dare to dream and follow their dreams, even into the abyss. Rejected by the common herd for being different, these deviants, none the less, nudge humanity onward and upward.

Wilson named his foundation after Byrd Hoffman because she was an artistic outcast among the Philistines of Waco – the buckle on the Southern Baptist Bible Belt. Contrary to the widely circulated but erroneous myth, Hoffman was never Wilson's teacher. His sister's ballet teacher, she was an occasional dinner guest at the Wilson home and was a beacon for the young Wilson. The director remembers her fondly:

People in Waco had narrow and peculiar ideas about propriety. Byrd never fit in. She had great style. She dyed her hair a bright, carrot red and piled on lots of white powder with heavy eye shadow. She wore organdy dresses soaked in sweet-smelling perfume and shoes with high, plastic heels. She loved white, and everything she had was white, including her dogs. The last time I caught a glimpse of her through her front door she was an old woman standing on her head. What a wonderful image! The Waco community considered her bizarre and out of place. Since she was the first artist I knew, I named my foundation after her. (*Faustus*)

Like the outcast, the image of the family turns up again and again in Wilson. *KA MOUNTAIN AND GUARDenia TERRACE* is subtitled: "a story about a family and some people changing." Families play a central role in many Wilson works, including *Deafman Glance, The Life and Times of Joseph Stalin, the CIVILwarS, Media, Salome, Alcestis, Orlando, Hamlet, King Lear,* and *The Magic Flute.* Wilson's mother, whose own family had been tragically disrupted by the death of her father, stressed over and over to her two children the importance of family. Frequently she hosted large dinners to gather it together. When talking about his childhood, Wilson often refers to the importance of this ritual of the family at table. "I hated these formal dinners," the director reminisces (*Lear*).

The dining room is a privileged site to study tribal behavior – psychologically, sociologically, semiotically. Ray Birdwhistell, one of the pioneers of kinesics, elucidates this phenomenon:

Children in both American and British society escape from the family table with delight. While there are exceptions in both societies, interviews with children and with adults are revealing as to the extent of resentment and emotional tension engendered by the experience . . . One thing is evident from the observation of families at mealtime or interviews in depth about the family table: much more goes on than is evident from reading a script of the vocalizations at the table . . .

A series of tapes of vocal families reveals little variation from meal to meal. In a highly organized manner the vocalists play their roles, exchange statements and even break into quarrels with such regularity that the observer can only conclude that this is a ritual. It sounds almost as though each member of the family has learned his lines, knows his cues, and synchronizes in the family drama . . .

The audio-verbal channel may carry the "official" behavior of the family. It can serve as a screen behind which the family members can covertly go about the remainder of their communication . . . These vocalic interchanges may function as a public performance which in its very stereotypy serves to instruct the membership to look elsewhere in the communicative system for significant information.[41]

The elsewhere, in life as in Wilson's theatre, is visual, which almost always contradicts the official verbal message.

"Family at Table" the CIVILwarS (act IV, scene A, section 1), presents the archetypal Wilson family going about the archetypal ritual. From behind a backstage screen, Frederick the Great watches in silence as an American family solemnly congregates around a table. In its sleek modernity, the table, created by strong, simple lines, contrasts sharply with the old-fashioned wardrobe of the family, part Amish, part Quaker, part Pilgrim.[42] Since the Father was played by an African American, the scene represented *all* our forefathers who "brought forth on this continent a new nation conceived in liberty and dedicated to the proposition that all men are created equal."

With a vertical white line bisecting his face, Father enters stage right, crosses in a straight line parallel to the proscenium, pauses in the upper corner of a large platform, stage left. He then proceeds to the dining-room table in the middle of the platform. He stations himself at the head of the table. Pauses. Sits down. Mother, Boy, Young Woman, Aunt, Young Man – each takes his place at table, following the same formal pattern which turns dinner into a highly structured ritual with strict protocol. Then Grandfather enters, pauses, continues to a chair set apart from the table. Father stands up. Grandfather sits down. Father sits down. Grandfather has Voltaire's *Candide* in hand and starts reading the celebrated auto-da-fé chapter. The phrase "langsam verbrennen," which captures the exquisite sadism of the religious ceremony, tickles his funnybone.[43] He repeats the phrase over and over, chuckling in delight and wondering how the

University of Coimbra decided how slowly the human kindling should burn. The joy of violence as a basic strand in our DNA is a major theme of *the CIVILwarS*. What do we live for if not to make life a little more difficult for each other?

Watching this family share a meal disconcerts – if one can call it sharing. They go about their business like robots overdosed on Valium: the coldness of steel, the control of a machine. Nothing is said. Faces betray no emotion. They have no joy in each other's presence; they take no pleasure in physical closeness. Because of the silence and emotional distance, tension fills the air. No signs of affection. Little interaction takes place, each member of the tribe lost in a private world. Only in the bosom of family does one feel truly alone. Young Man places head on table. Boy bounces ball on table, loudly, rudely, disruptively, begging for attention. Aunt grabs ball from Boy. Throws it away. Grandfather continues chuckling over Voltaire's depiction of human brutality in *Candide*. Father reads a letter Frederick the Great received from his father:

Thy headstrong wicked will, which loves not thy father! For if one does all – if one loves one's father over all – then all is done to please him, not only when standing over you, but when he turns his back. Furthermore, thou knowest well I cannot stomach an effeminate fellow without manly inclination, blushing like a girl, who cannot ride nor shoot, and at the same time cuts an awkward figure – hair brushed like a fool's, not properly groomed – and I have reprimanded you a thousand times upon the subject, but in vain, no improvement seems forthcoming. What's more – haughty, stubbornly proud . . . screwing up his face as if he were a fool, never bowing to my will when not prompted to do so by force – never out of love! – no desire at all but the following of his own whims; and the result? It will come to naught.

"Never out of love!" is repeated six times. Love is the greatest weapon of coercion ever invented. Behind the screen, Frederick the Great crouches down, upstage, looking over his shoulder in fear, quaking in his boots at the phantom of his father.

Young Man stands up. Young Woman stands up. They form a pair. Mother stands up, walks over to Father. She touches Father's shoulder. They form a pair. A film of a blue, blue ocean is projected over the family, dissolving it in time, gathering it to eternity. Aunt walks to stage middle. Young Woman runs to Aunt. Young Man walks to Young Woman. Mother walks away from Father, first slow, then fast. She hesitates center stage at the family group, but continues walking off stage. Father walks past group, stops. Grandfather beckons little boy to come to him. Boy crawls under table. Family group center stage laughs, mockingly. One by one they walk off. Frederick the Great continues to watch, impassive. Boy

32 *the CIVILwarS.* Wilson's drawing for the underwater turtle, a film,
and the departure of the family, bound together despite themselves.

remains under table, head in arms in fetal position. On film, a giant,
primeval turtle swims underwater (see figure 32). White Scribe enters,
begins monolog (discussed in chapter 1, p. 75). Men in black carry off
table and chairs. More men in black enter with long white poles. Wave
poles to create giant x's in the air. Little boy builds a sculpture out of
blocks, a post and lintel structure similar to the entrance to "Poles." Boy,
absorbed in this architectural task, is insensible to all else. Grandfather
stands up, pauses. White Scribe coughs. Grandfather looks frightened.
Grandfather scurries out, knocking over Boy's construction. White Scribe
shrieks like a banshee. Boy gets up, walks out. Rocket flies across top of
stage. Turtle continues to swim, as he has for centuries, serenely. Our
reptilian granddaddy will survive us all.

The image of the turtle assumes many functions. First, from the mirror
of eternity, the turtle mocks the petty human drama played out beneath
it. Second, it offers a Darwinian perspective on *homo sapiens*, linking us to
our origins in the slime. Third, it stresses the evolution through time of
the family and the race (as does Wilson's simultaneous layering of time
zones), fusing the story of the individual with the history of the species.
Fourth, through humor it keeps the scene from becoming heavy-handed
or sentimental.

To prepare *the CIVILwarS*, Wilson researched over fifty famous fami-
lies, including the brothers Karamazov and Marx, the Borgias and the
Bachs, the Bonapartes and the Bourbons, the Fords and the Fondas, the
Medici and the Ming, and Donald Duck, not to mention the Atrides of
Mycenae and the Wilsons of Waco. The family at table represents the
entire species, and the family comes across not as a warm hearth

forging from generation to generation the humane virtues of loving and caring and friendship, but rather as a breeding ground of neurosis, paranoia, and sadism. This dysfunctional family – unable to communicate openly and freely – trains its wrath on the most helpless member: the boy.

How many sons have heard from how many fathers for how many centuries the same sermon Frederick's father crammed down his throat? For Lacan the phallus symbolizes paternal authority; the penis, a biological organ. In this Œdipal war of sexual jealousy, the father's message to the son is blunt: you may have a penis, but you will never have a phallus. You will never have the male potency I have. Symbolically I castrate you and cut you off from authority, power, and sex. The grandfather knocks over the blocks, the boy's only creative act and source of self-esteem. Self-esteem, Erik Erikson writes, is essential to identity formation, and "in the jungle of human existence there is no feeling of being alive without a sense of identity."[44] The older males want to destroy the younger male before he can rival or replace them. They do not want him to develop an autonomous sense of self. *the CIVILwarS*, which also deals with the difficult relationship between Kafka and his patriarch, might have borne the subtitle "Fathers and Sons."

The theme of the abused child recurs over and over in *the CIVILwarS* and throughout Wilson, and the image of the mother as murderer often graces his stage – from the prolog to *Deafman Glance* through various versions of *Medea* to *When We Dead Awaken*, where Wilson stresses the theme of child murder. In the operatic version of *Medea* he wrote with Gavin Bryars, as Medea leads her children off, the company, now in contemporary dress, come out and read newspaper articles about mothers who have recently murdered their children and other cases of child abuse. After finishing the articles that document how widespread the problem is, they talk with the audience about its repercussions. The dialog comes to an end when, off stage, screams of children pierce the hall. Medea, Wilson's favorite mom, has done it.

We now know how destructive child abuse is, and this abuse takes many forms: emotional, physical, sexual. Many forms of love are forms of abuse, especially if, as Alice Miller writes, the parents lavish their affection not on a real child with desires different from the parents' but on a convenient fantasy child the parents need to fill their own emotional needs. The parents find in "their child's 'false self' the confirmation they were looking for, a substitute for their own missing structures."[45] Alienated from his inner world, the child of flesh and bone learns to distrust his own feelings. The psychological devastation strikes deep.

Child abuse – often wearing the smiling face of love – is an everlasting cycle responsible for much of the violence drowning us: "An adult perpetuates the destructive treatment he endured as a child . . . To combat cruelty, a person must first be able to perceive it as such. When someone has been exposed throughout childhood to nothing but harshness, coldness, coercion, and the rigid wielding of power, as Hitler and his closest followers were, when any sign of softness, tenderness, creativity, or vitality is scorned, then the person against whom that violence is directed accepts it as perfectly justified."[46]

No artist since Dickens has spoken up quite so eloquently as Wilson for the wounded child. In Wilson the abused child is often associated with an artist in embryo whose creativity and individuality are menaced by the family. The evil father is often associated with a businessman, as in *Medea*. Whereas the others wore antique garb, Jason strutted about in a gray flannel suit, cut from good Republican cloth.

In *Alice* the abuse is sexual as well as emotional. In the musical we see Alice through the pedophiliac lens of Charles Dodgson, who wrote under the pseudonym Lewis Carroll. During the prolog the entire cast, dressed as Dodgson in black leather coats, comes out and taps the soles of its shoes. Immediately after, a large nineteenth-century camera, covered with the traditional black cloth, pops out on the left. Slowly, mysteriously, it creeps across the stage, growing like Pinocchio's nose. Dodgson slithers out from underneath. Removing the lens, which turns out to be the glass bottom of a whiskey bottle, he pours himself a good, stiff drink. He proceeds to take photographs of Alice that explore her face lovingly. We now know that Dodgson was one of the finest Victorian pornographers. With their fusion of sensuality and innocence, the photos he took of little girls in various stages of undress still startle, still disconcert. "I'm a perfect Anglo-Saxon, aren't you?" Alice says. "That will do, Mr. Dodgson, that will do!"[47] The same actor played Dodgson, the White Rabbit, and the White Knight. Having one person assume such contradictory roles dramatized how Alice's encounter with Dodgson complicated her relationship with men: the same man offers adventure, safety, and abuse.

Alice's encounter with the caterpillar brings the house down. As the decadent worm lounges atop the magic mushroom, languidly sniffing his hookah, he sings a soft-shoe shuffle: "Tabletop Joe." A Coney Island sideshow freak inspired the song. As Mr. Caterpillar sings to Alice, the sweet aroma of hashish intoxicates her. As his tumescent tail grows and grows and grows, it chases the little girl around the stage.

In only one scene does Alice speak in her own voice. In a scarlet forest that, like Georgia O'Keefe's flowers, oozes sex, an aging and alcoholic Alice Liddell – the real-life prototype of Alice in Wonderland – pours out her long-repressed rage against Dodgson in a martini-dry tirade to her cat. Dodgson had imposed on her a sexual role she did not want to play, a role that responded to his needs, not hers.

Stations explores the themes of child abuse in great detail. Telling its tale without words, the video – a stream of images – concerns a sensitive, willful child who, feeling his parents ignore him, withdraws into a private fantasy world. The parents, obsessed with the humdrum chores of daily life, do not understand the child, who would like the parents to acknowledge and appreciate his fantasies. They do not, and he dreams the universal dream of children: kill the parent.[48] In his mind's eye, one catastrophe after another befalls the sourpusses. They go up in flames. Extraterrestrial beings invade. A giant octopus ties them up. The child looks on with no emotion. In one poignant scene, he crawls up to the mother at the kitchen sink. She turns away. Much of the action takes place at table. The mother, clasping a butcher knife, turns slowly to the husband and points the knife at his back. One expects her to stab him, but no. Slowly, she points the knife at the child, who first is terrified, then smiles gleefully. The inscrutable mother throws everyone off guard emotionally. The child has a will of iron and eventually forces the ogres to enter his dreamland. Few and far between, there are signs of affection. When the child is sick, the father sits by his bed and feeds him. At the end, a flood sweeps the home away. Mother and father thrash about in the water. Like Maggie and Tom on the last page of The Mill on the Floss, the flood reunites the family. They embrace in an eternal bond of love and hate. The psychopathology of civilization begins at home.

In all these scenes in Wilson what is at stake is the identity of the child, his ability to individuate and create an autonomous self based on his own needs, not the narcissistic needs of the parents. By their refusal to share in their son's fantasy world, the parents in Stations deny their child his identity; they refuse to see or love what he really is. As Margaret Mahler has shown, the psychological birth of the infant – the slow unfolding of an independent self in touch with inner emotions – is a difficult task characterized by the child's conflicting urges to cling to mother and push away.[49] The desire to merge, the fear of fusion – this conflict reverberates throughout the life cycle. The children in the CIVILwarS and Stations fear psychic annihilation. If parents shove their official version of reality down a child's throat and forbid him from constructing his own version, they prevent individuation. Severe psychological disturbances ensue:

"The child . . . blocked from individuation may eventually become schizophrenic."[50] Schizoid characters appear often in Wilson's work, and, as discussed in chapter 2 (pp. 65–67), Wilson encourages actors to project the sense of multiple personalities. Only if parents respect the child as the person he is, only if they can tune into his inner feelings, only then will he be able to create a vital, authentic personality. The alternative is self-alienation. But not all parents encourage growth towards independence and self-fulfillment. "The biggest defect our mother had," says Suzanne Lambert, "was her inability to let go. She clung to her children and wanted to be a big part of their lives. There came a moment when Bob simply had to break away from her."

Kafka, whose stormy relationship with his father presents a case study in the damage done by the lack of paternal understanding, plays an important part in both *Death Destruction & Detroit II* and *the CIVILwarS*. In the latter Kafka's *Letter to His Father* is quoted at length: "I don't recall your directly hurling verbal abuses at me. It wasn't necessary, you had so many other means at your disposal . . ."[51] In contrast to narcissistic parents, who use children for their own needs, parents who empathize with their child recognize in him a separate individual with independent ideas, feelings, desires. A lack of this empathy leads to severe psychological wounds.[52]

In 1966 Wilson had a nervous breakdown, tried to commit suicide, and spent several months in a mental institution. In all his public lectures Wilson speaks about his family. The family member he talks about the most is his deceased mother, Loree.[53] He portrays her an unemotional and controlling woman whom everyone, even the father, feared. Rarely does Wilson fail to mention that the only time his mother touched him was the day he left for college. That day she hugged him.

We now know how vital the sense of touch is for psychological and physical health. Touch, one of our strongest instincts – overshadows nursing in the development of infant affection. Without something to cling to – even a surrogate mother concocted of wire mesh and terry cloth will do – baby rhesus monkeys fail to thrive. "Contact . . . is . . . of overwhelming importance. The baby, human or monkey, if it is to survive, must clutch at more than a straw."[54] Deprived of touch, the infant undergoes bereavement. "Grief and mourning occur in infancy whenever the responses mediating attachment behavior are activated and the mother figure continues to be unavailable." This process of infant mourning is an event of "high pathogenic potential."[55] Given Wilson's description of his mother, it surprises not that loneliness, the lack of touch, and the slaughter of innocent children are overriding themes in his work.

About his deceased father, Diuguid, a former city manager of Waco, Wilson often says "He was a curious man." The anecdotes Wilson tells depict a distant, successful lawyer, punctual to a fault. The figure in the trial scene of *Einstein on the Beach* hypnotized by their wristwatches mimic Wilson's father in his most characteristic tic. In contrast, Wilson always arrives late. "My tardiness irritated my father," Wilson says, smiling like a cherub. Never close, their relationship became particularly strained when Wilson, who had been studying business administration at the University of Texas, Austin, to please his father, resolved to pursue a career in the arts in New York. A recurrent motif in *the CIVILwarS* is the cruelty of castrating fathers. After his father had seen one of Wilson's productions, he told the director, "Son, not only is it sick, it's abnormal" (*Lear*).

One must be wary, however, of seeing in any work of art a straightforward representation of an artist's biography. Great art works through metaphor, and the families in Wilson's work are not documentary photographs of his family.

Another image Wilson returns to often is that of the voyage. Travelling through space or time figures prominently in *Einstein on the Beach*; *KA MOUNTAIN AND GUARDenia TERRACE*; *Medea*; *Alcestis*; *Parzival*; *Orlando*; *King Lear*; *The Forest*; *When We Dead Awaken*; *The Magic Flute*; *Alice* and *the CIVILwarS*, peopled by boats, cars, submarines, and rockets. One of the oldest archetypes in literature, the physical voyage parallels a mental voyage, a process of discovery. The journey transports the spectator to a new realm of experience, often symbolized in Wilson by a magic forest. Wordsworth's image of Newton "with his prism and silent face, / The marble index of a mind for ever / Voyaging through strange seas of Thought, alone" sums up the Wilsonian voyage of the imagination, always seeking, always searching. In Wilson the wanderer is the artist, who through the power of imagination quests for spiritual truth in a world suffocated by materialism. The imagination is the spirit, and the purpose of art, Kandinsky says, is to wake up souls who have fallen asleep.[56] Some souls need electroshock. Wilson administers it. The Wilsonian voyage, epic in scope, like Baudelaire takes the wanderer "to the bottom of the unknown, to find something new."[57]

The last key image in Wilsonland is the apocalypse. Images of catastrophe – natural and manmade – haunt his work like the specter of Armageddon. *KA MOUNTAIN AND GUARDenia TERRACE*, Wilson's seven-day play that took place on seven mountains near Shiraz, Iran, encapsulated the entire history of man, more or less. On the seventh day, at midnight, Wilson wanted to dynamite the top of the seventh mountain, but local authorities withheld permission. Instead, a giant *Tyrannosaurus rex* belched forth the sulfurous flames of hell. *Einstein on the Beach* and *Alcestis* climax with a nuclear holocaust. *When We Dead Awaken* ends with an avalanche; *Doktor Faustus*, with the threat of World War II. In *King Lear*, the storm became a war of the worlds; suns, moons, and stars crashed into each other, bursting into an intergalactic Fourth of July. Floods, volcanoes, blizzards – images of natural disasters dot *the CIVILwarS*, counterpointing the horrors of war. In the "Smilers" sequence (act IV, scene A, section 12), twenty actors, including Frederick, march on stage single file and position themselves on the platform stage left. This additive process – first an empty space, then one by one actors filling it up – is one of Wilson's basic strategies. (Frequently he clears the stage, as he does in "Smilers," with the inverse process of subtraction one by one to let the energy out of the space gradually.) Projected behind the actors, a film shows one skyscraper after another smashing to the ground in a whirlwind of dust. Pedal to floorboard, Glass's pounding music accelerates the heartbeat and sends a hit of adrenalin through the body. Suddenly across the actors' faces creep beatific grins. The spectacle of mass destruction delights their souls. The joy of destroying is as necessary to us as the air we breathe. We are more than half in love with death, and violence has entertained humans since the dawn of time. "Man is a wolf to man. Who, in the face of all his experience of life and of history, will have the courage to dispute this assertion?"[58] And the most sinister part of the rage to destroy is the desire not merely to hurt one's neighbor but to see the whole world consumed by flame, including the self. Freud concludes *Civilization and Its Discontents* by musing whether eros – the will to live and love – or thanatos – the will to death and destruction – will triumph. The book ends with a question mark.

Always in Wilson, the apocalypse exhilarates, singing an irresistible siren song. Riveting in its diabolical energy, the dance of death inside the Einstein spaceship burns forever in one's memory, as does the stage of *Alcestis* flooded with a red, radioactive glow. A Wilsonian apocalypse is always sublime. "In *Alcestis, the CIVILwarS*, and *Einstein on the Beach*," the director says, "I was concerned with the biological instinct for destruction and self-destruction. It's a real possibility that we may blow ourselves up. The terror of war is its beauty. To shock people back to sanity," he adds, smiling like Buddha, "you have to make the death drive as seductive as possible" (*Alcestis*).[59]

Many of Wilson's recurrent images – nature, the outcast, the child as seer, the voyage into the imagination – play a central role in English

Romantic poetry, as does the shift from a poetry of discourse to a poetry of symbol. The word "romantic," invented by Humpty Dumpty, means anything anybody wants. Wilson uses the term pejoratively to refer to the sentimental, middlebrow theatre that flourishes on Broadway (*When We Dead Awaken*). To stipulate my meaning as precisely as possible, when I call Wilson's vision Romantic, I refer specifically to techniques and themes in the poetry of Wordsworth and Coleridge, Shelley and Keats, which for generations formed the bedrock of literary education in American schools. Paradoxically – and paradox pervades Wilson's work – the director uses an abstract, minimalist, industrial visual grammar to set off the motifs of nature, the child, and the poet as dreamer who sees the heavens open. Through contrast, geometry and nature emphasize each other. But a deeper paradox haunts Wilson's vision. On the one hand, his layering against each other of multiple, dissonant, and simultaneous realities dramatizes the Kantian split between object and subject. We can never penetrate the thing in itself; we are locked into individual perceptions and subjective interpretations. The perceiving subject is radically distinct from the perceived object. On the other hand, Wilson's *naturphilosophie* (the origins of this tradition go back to Schelling) belies the hope to merge with nature, transcending this breach between subject and object. The knowledge of separation brings with it the nostalgia for union.

Moving away from traditional theatre and closer to lyric poetry, Wilson's stage – a stage of suggestion, not statement – relies on recurrent visual images to call forth from the spectator urgent, imaginative responses. This reliance on symbolic expression can be traced back to English Romantic poetry, and it derives from the Romantics' uneasiness with language. In Shelley, for example, the poem

attempts to express the ineffable. No single image or metaphor could begin to hold what the speaker has in mind or the emotions felt with respect to it. Thus it is approached through many metaphors, and the hope seems to be that in the mixture of ingredients an explosion will take place, that the reader will somehow pass beyond the veil of words to an intuitive apprehension. Such a passage, then, may suggest a certain distrust of language.[60]

What Shelly longed to achieve in poetry was simultaneity and montage. Visual images give Wilson more resources to circumnavigate the limits of language than are available to poets like Shelley, imprisoned by words. Consequently, the opportunities for explosions of "intuitive apprehension" that take us "beyond the veil of words" are far greater on a stage than in a sonnet.

One grand arc of European culture stretches from the Romantics through the Symbolists to the Surrealists. One cannot understand Wilson, latter-day incarnation of this tradition, without understanding how it questions the dominant culture of the West – the positivist, rational culture that expresses itself in newspapers, locomotives, and realistic drama.

4　The deep surface

The depth is on the surface.
Robert Wilson, personal interview, March 1993

THE MIRACLE OF LIGHT

Art depends on technique. One reason Wilson is a great director is because he is a great technician. Like a shoemaker cobbling boots or a woodworker carving marquetry, Wilson is a mastercraftsman who has honed the skills of lighting, sculpting, and movement to perfection. During rehearsals Wilson never looks quite so joyous as when he is tinkering around in a storeroom, improvising makeshift props. He loves visiting workshops and hunkers down with the stage hands to help paint a drop or chisel a sculpture. "In my next life," the directors sighs, "I want to be a potter, sitting at a wheel, molding clay all day."[1]

In creating stage images, the crucial element in Wilson's alchemy of the eye is light. Wilson loves light. The director insists:

Light is the most important part of theatre. It brings everything together, and everything depends on it. From the beginning I was concerned with light, how it reveals objects, how objects change when light changes, how light creates space, how space changes when light changes. Light determines what you see and how you see it. If you know how to light, you can make shit look like gold. I paint, I build, I compose with light. Light is a magic wand. (*Faustus*)

Light gives Wilson's images their distinctive character.[2]

Wilson's drama is a drama of light, and the director's analogies – painting, building, composing – explain how he uses it. Painting suggests light as a device to organize stage pictures, and light is Wilson's main resource for visual composition. "A set for Wilson," says Tom Kamm, who designed the scenery for *the CIVILwarS*, "is a canvas for the light to hit like paint."[3] Through dominant and subsidiary contrasts, Wilson creates a hierarchical visual structure. The eye goes immediately to a bright spot, especially if it contrasts with a darker surrounding area. By exploiting this physiological reflex, Wilson gives his stage pictures a strong focus, guiding the eye and letting it take in the composition. Wilson avoids visual confusion by allowing the spectator sufficient time to explore his images.

121

Through light Wilson enables the eye to perceive the formal elements of composition as a harmonious whole. These formal elements, of course, always reveal inner states: design and theme merge; form is content. "Form," confesses Wilson, pontiff supreme of formalism, "bores me. It's a means to get you somewhere. How you fill the form in is what counts. At bottom, formalism and realism are similar. Underneath the stylistic differences, both grapple with the same eternal conflicts, the same eternal truths" (March, 1993, during a workshop for Jean Genet's *The Balcony*).

Building suggests the articulation of space, and watching Wilson carve out space with light reveals how his imagination works. The same space on the same stage with the same set keeps defining and redefining itself as the light alters. Light constructs our sense of space: "Light alone can create the effect of enclosed space. A campfire on a dark night forms a cave of light circumscribed by a wall of darkness . . . It follows, therefore, that if you wish to create an effect of openness you cannot employ concentrated light. Early in his career Frank Lloyd Wright recognized this. In his houses . . . you find walls and partitions which do not go all the way to the ceiling but leave space for openings at the top. This not only gives an open feeling to the room but it admits extra light."[4] The parallel contrasting scenes in *The Life and Times of Joseph Stalin* of the cave (a small circle of light surrounded by dark) and the temple (light creating a sense of openness) demonstrate this principle. In *Danton's Death*, the shifting play of light across the same bare stage suggested, now a claustrophobic garret, now a broad Parisian boulevard. "Theatre doesn't live in words," Wilson holds. "It lives in space. A director works with space. Light lets you see the architecture of the space. Other directors pore over the text. I draw space. I always start with light. Without light there is no space. With light you create many different kinds of spaces. A different space is a different reality" (*Balcony*).

Composing suggests the rhythmic element in Wilson's lighting. Wilson's lights are fluid, constantly changing and changing constantly our perceptions. The genius of Wilson's lighting – in the profession he is considered the greatest light artist of our time and the only major director to get billing as a lighting designer – can only be understood through time. Whereas conventional directors turn the lights on and leave them on with relatively few changes during the course of an act, Wilson's lights cast their spell through subtle shifts. *Quartet*, which ran ninety minutes, had 400 light cues. It is Wilson's ability to *durchkomponieren* – to through-compose a complex structure with lights – that leaves other lighting designers agog. Steven Strawbridge, a lighting designer who has frequently worked with Wilson, observes:

Wilson's lighting is like a musical score. I know the techniques of lighting. I know how to get objects and actors to look the way I want. But Wilson uses lights like phrases in an orchestral tone poem. The movement of the lights follows a line through time. What amazes me about him is the overall shape, how all those cues add up to a total composition. He works lights in unexpected ways that catch you off guard, and you don't understand what he's up to until the first runthrough. Then everything falls into place.

Watching Wilson's lights unfold is like watching a visual Ninth Symphony. Beethoven astounds, not because of the individual notes he uses or the melodies he writes – Tchaikovsky tossed off seductive melodies too – but because of the colossal architectural structure. The individual moments in Wilson are astonishing, but even more astonishing is how they fit together into a monumental cathedral of light.

Wilson's lights give his productions an unmistakable look. The two most characteristic aspects of this look are the dense, palpable textures – one can feel, taste, smell the light in Wilson – and the way people and objects leap out from the background. The director deploys various strategies to achieve the boldness of these effects. According to Binkley, "Wilson uses the full realm of what lighting is about. He goes through the whole sphere of moods from one extreme to the other because he understands what light is and how it works." One reason lighting designers hold Wilson in such awe is he knows the instruments and techniques needed to create the look he wants. Most directors do not. And unlike most directors, for whom lights are an afterthought tacked on at the end of the creative process, lights are on Wilson's mind from the start. They form an integral part of his original thinking about any work. The first preliminary sketch he makes of the stage space already indicates the source and kind of light he wants. Lights are breathed into the production from its conception. Wilson may be a wild-eyed visionary who picks mushrooms on the dark side of the moon, but his visions are grounded in meticulous craft.

During the design workshop for *When We Dead Awaken* at the ART – the first stage of the creative process – Wilson called the technical director of the theatre in and said, "I need tons of light in the back." He continued with the following specifications for the upstage area: five feet of stage depth to put strips of light on the floor and ceiling (one strip of green, one of blue, one of clear, top and bottom; one strip of fluorescents on the floor); a bounce behind the lights to reflect them (the striplights are beamed at the bounce, which softens and diffuses them, creating a more even distribution); a translucent RP (rear projection) in front of the striplights (the translucent RP adds depth, texture, and atmosphere to the light). In addition, Wilson frequently hangs a white screen in front of the RP. This setup typifies a Wilson production, and when the director begins to tech the lights, he starts with the background. He often uses this wall of light upstage to backlight actors or objects and emphasize the silhouette (line and primary shape reign supreme in Wilson's aesthetic). This RP is a work of art in itself. In *Orlando* it transformed itself into a series of abstract, minimalist squares (inspired by Woolf's descriptions of the windows in Orlando's manor house). In *King Lear* projections turned the RP into cosmic fireworks as the storm exploded on the blasted heath. The sense of depth that the light creates behind the translucent RP – it gives the illusion of infinite space – is important to the director. Although Wilson has worked in many different kinds of spaces – Great Jones Alley in Soho; the mountains of Shiraz; the bare, black box of a student theatre at New York University – he has a penchant for the proscenium arch. His compositions may not stop at the frame, but he uses it as a compositional device to organize the stage picture. "I prefer a proscenium for many reasons," notes the director (*Faustus*). "I like its form. I like the tension it sets up between two and three dimensions. I like the distance it creates between stage and audience. And I like what it lets me do with lights." The picture-frame stage, by emphasizing the dominant dimensions of width (the horizontal) and height (the vertical), tends to flatten depth. To increase the sense of depth, Wilson not only uses the translucent RP and wings, but also divides the floor into horizontal zones of light parallel to the picture frame. By lighting the zones alternatively with warm (yellow) and cold (blue) light, he increases the sense of depth. Like Cézanne, Wilson sets up tension between depth and flatness.

Wilson also uses massive sidelights (camouflaged by the wings). Since his sidelight originates behind wings and disappears into opposite wings, it does not hit the floor. Spots on the floor distract from the director's primary compositional focus, and they drive him berserk. Light travels in a straight line, and if a spot lights an actor's face, chances are it will hit the floor like spilled milk. Wilson spends hours and hours and hours mopping spots up off the floor (sometimes by lightening the floor if nothing else works). Sidelights eliminate this problem. (Actors often complain that Wilson's banks of intense sidelights blind them.) Also, sidelights – typical of dance companies – enhance the plasticity of the body, especially as it moves through space. Since a Wilson actor frequently speaks with his limbs, not his tongue, sidelight works magic by heightening the dimensional quality of the actors' movements while separating them from the background. To pull the actor or object (it might be a table or chair) further out from the ground, Wilson lights each one separately, creating the palpable texture that characterizes his lighting. "Wilson would really be happy," says Kamm, "if he could put two or three light bulbs inside each actor's body to separate it even more from the field."

Another device the director uses to make objects jump out from the ground is to play warm (yellow) light off against cold (blue). Color temperature plays a key role in his lighting. Incandescent light turns increasingly yellow as the intensity decreases. To counter this tendency – I call it the bluing technique, familiar to anyone who has tried to get a yellowed white shirt white again – Wilson uses a special blue gel (a Lee 201) over the lights he wants cold. This device creates a freezing, steel-cold beam that chisels a hard edge. Since the eye is drawn naturally to the brightest spot of light, Wilson sets warm against cold to direct the gaze where he wants it. Thus, an actor's face or hands (the parts of the body Wilson tends to emphasize with special lights), are hit with a cold light, the body with a warm one. Furthermore, he usually whitens and lightens the face and hands with makeup he calls "the porcelain look." Because of the dominant contrast, the eye goes first to the face. If an actor is wearing a white shirt lighter than the face, the director has it tinted down, usually with a gray wash. In *Quartet* Wilson at times lit one half of Lucinda Childs's body with warm light, the other half with cold. This chiaroscuro effect sculpted the body; and the actress, detached from the surrounding environment, seemed to float in space. The director uses many tightly focused, bright specials to iris in and highlight a hand, a face, a foot, or an object as the rest of the stage darkens. Wilson calls it a zoom and compares it with a cinematic close-up (the director often uses cinematic terms to describe his theatre). Good examples occur in act I of *When We Dead Awaken* (Maya's champagne glass, which she will shatter in unconscious rage) and *Danton's Death* (the spot on Danton's hand in prison, insisting that responsibility be accepted for one's political acts).

Wilson works patiently to sensitize new actors to light so they are in the right place at the right time to be hit by a special (counting steps and time is essential). The day he began lighting *Quartet* he cautioned: "Learn my vocabulary of lights. Take notes in your scripts. If you don't understand how light works, you can't perform in my work." Wilson trains actors to feel light and shadow with the skin so they can move back into the light if something is out of sync. The director tells with relish an anecdote about the notoriously difficult Spanish prima donna Monserrat Caballé, who was singing his *Salome* at La Scala. He asked her on a count of forty-five to raise her arm at a thirty-degree angle, where a special would zoom in on her hand and make it the center of the visual composition. "Do you think you can do that?" the director asked gingerly, worried she would walk off the set and sink the production. "Mr. Wilson," the Spanish diva replied, "I have been searching for the light all my life. If the spot is there, I'll find it." Wilson always warns actors that if, as they enter or leave a stage, they knock a sidelight to alert the stage crew at once. Because of his precise lighting design, if a light has been nudged even half an inch off, disaster results.

Wilson's lighting – sophisticated and refined, subtle and beautiful – depends on his impeccable eye, craft, and resourcefulness, not on expensive technology. He loves the state-of-the-art equipment theatres in Germany put at his disposal, but even in the poverty-stricken regional theatres of America with their primitive lighting systems, he creates magic. All he needs to produce extraordinary effects is a Roscoe 78 (a dark blue gel), a Lee 201 (a lighter blue for cold light), and clear white (that yellows and warms the lower it gets). "I can do anything with those three lights" (*Quartet*). On occasion, he adds red and green, but what leaves one lost in admiration is how rich and dense and complex his lighting design is, based on such simple means. The violets and oranges, the grays and azures – the whole dazzling array of colors he used in *Quartet* – who could guess that he pulled them out of his magic hat, starting with almost nothing? This palette was unusual for him. The director dedicated the production to Andy Warhol, who had passed away the year Wilson created the work. "I was moved by Andy's death. I felt the color temperament of Müller's language was close to Andy's. Andy used colors in the strangest combinations. I'd never used color like this before" (*Quartet*).

If Wilson works miracles with relatively simple equipment, one thing he does need is time, and plenty of it. A Wilson production costs a pretty penny because he requires aeons to tech lights (with a full crew present to make necessary adjustments). Few theatres can afford to leave their house dark for two weeks to fidget with lighting cues. But Wilson insists on taking the time to get it right. He spent two days lighting the prolog of *Quartet*, which ran fifteen minutes. Easily he can spend three hours lighting one hand gesture. For *When We Dead Awaken* he used sixty hours of tech just to fix the lights (and this was fast for Wilson). By contrast, an average production in a regional theatre would get thirty-six hours to tech everything, including a runthrough and dress rehearsal.

To watch Wilson slave away over lights is to understand the craft, discipline, precision, stamina, and obstinacy needed to create great theatre. First Wilson tells everyone to shut up. "Absolutely no talking," he admonishes. "Doing lights requires enormous concentration. I have to keep eight to ten different numbers in my mind at once to balance the lights, so no whispering, no munching carrot sticks, no giggling." During the *Quartet* tech a young woman sat in the last row of the theatre, quietly reading a book. When she turned the first page, Wilson wheeled round. "Out!" he screamed. "Stop making noise. This is a theatre, not a library. In a theatre you have to be quiet." Abashed, the girl slunk out.

To start, Wilson checks all the lighting channels and equipment. Lights which are supposed to be the same often vary, and he wants to see all the lights at all intensities to make adjustments (the lights are on dimmers so one can go from zero to a hundred in one percent increments). Wilson teching lights sounds like a frantic day on Wall Street: a ragout of mysterious numbers barked out that make or break the dealer. "Twenty at one hundred, ninety-nine, ninety-eight, ninety seven . . . Hold it for fifteen." The formula – punched into a computer – refers to a lighting channel that controls, usually, one light, at various intensities held for a precise number of minutes before shifting to another intensity or going out. Most people cannot tell the difference between ninety-eight and ninety-seven, but to Wilson a mistake of one percent can destroy a composition. "I want a brighter, tighter spot on that face, pull it out more," echoes again and again during tech, as does "What's wrong with these lights? Why aren't they balanced? That's supposed to be a cold, white light. Why is it warm? If that's cold, we're in Equatorial Africa."

And the result of this concentrated frenzy? The greatest light show this side of the aurora borealis. Photographs do not do justice to the quality of Wilson's lighting since no film stock is sensitive enough to capture its subtlety and refinement. Even people who do not fathom Wilson's theatre concede the point. When it comes to lights, no one can touch him. Priscilla Smith, who played Frederick in *the CIVILwarS*, sums it up: "He doesn't know what to do with actors, but no one ever doubted his ability to work with lights."[5]

Light in Wilson creates its own formal structure. At times this structure runs parallel to the text without doubling it; at times, it contradicts the text; at rare times it illustrates the text. Lights work subliminally on our feelings. They are one of the theatre's strongest weapons to create emotional climate. Wilson is a master of generating atmosphere through lights. Maya's crossing the river in act II of *When We Dead Awaken* demonstrates this beautifully, although when one tries to describe in words how light works, one crashes into a concrete wall: the incompetence of language. By crossing the river, Maya resolves to leave her prune-faced husband and take back her life. The physical river represents a psychological boundary she has feared to cross. When she does pass over, finally, the downstage triangle (the diagonal river bisects the stage into two triangles) is lit for the first time. Until now darkness covered it. Previously the production has been cold, cruel, and emotionally distant. Suddenly, a fearful tenderness takes hold – as if an axe had struck a frozen sea: the waters begin to flow. In this thoughtful, quiet, lonely moment Maya, albeit frightened, takes responsibility for herself and her sexuality. During this *rite de passage*, a little girl trembles into womanhood. The downstage triangle – a new, wonderful space for her to explore – glows warm and golden, like the sands of the Sahara. Often in Wilson (*Quartet* is a perfect example), light expresses the unconscious – thoughts and feelings hiding just beneath the skin. These emotions can never be heaved into the mouth; language cannot speak them. Light whispers them. In sum, "light," says Wilson, "is the most important actor on stage" (*Quartet*).

SCULPTURE/FURNITURE

Wilson the craftsman takes as much care with props as with lights. Not only does he design the props he uses, he also drops by the shop frequently to check the construction and lend a hand with the sculpting and painting. His obsession with perfection explains his insistence on a *Bauprobe*, a German ritual he imported to America. Usually during the second workshop of a production, Wilson has full-size mockups made of all the props so he can look at them on the stage he will be using. Most directors are satisfied with a small-scale model, but Wilson knows that models – approximations at best – deceive. He demands a *Bauprobe* to check proportion, balance, and visual relationships before any props are built.

After the props are built, he is renowned for sending them back again and again and again until they satisfy him. The revolving disk from *Quartet* with a Membrace Amerindian pot on one side and a male nude on the other went back to the shop to be repainted a dozen times. Each day the tech staff would show him the disk. Each day he would shake his head, "No, that's not quite right." Painters are expensive – then about $200 a day – so by the time he accepted the disk, it had become a pricey piece of scenery. Wilson changed the crocodile in *Alcestis* at least twenty times; slowly it metamorphosed into a dinosaur.

Jeff Muscovin, former technical director of American Repertory Theatre, remarks:

Wilson is a great director because he's a stickler for details. No other director I've worked with has such a strong visual sense. Other directors have only vague idea about what they want. They will say "I need a fish tank in this act" and leave it at that. For *Quartet* Wilson gave us the exact measurement of the tank he wanted, the kind of glass, and the curve of the metal molding. He not only knows what he wants, he knows how to build it, and it had better be right, or it will go back.

I saw a mockup of the chairs he had designed for *Quartet*, and I was worried about their structural integrity. Wilson wanted them built by a skilled cabinet-maker of smooth, clear wood with no visible knots or joints and no hardware at all – no nails, no plates, no cracks in the joints. Fine furniture, but they were tall and thin, and I didn't know if the structure would support the actors' weight. Often they had to sit on the edge. At one point, the young girl jumped up and down on her chair; at another point, the young boy falls over in his chair. I asked Wilson if we could weld the chairs out of aluminium and skin them with wood. They would look like wood to the audience but be stronger. He thought about it for a moment, then said, "No, Jeff, I want wood chairs. If we make them out of alumin-ium, they won't sound right when they fall over and hit the floor. They'll sound like metal, not wood. It will sound false. Just make sure you get strong wood. And no knots."

Wilson wanted fine furniture and fine furniture he got. His props are so fine, in fact, that they have found their way into major museums and private collections. Curators regard them as sculpture, not props.[6] Everyone has his own favorites, so I might as well talk about mine. Rubek's chair from act II of *When We Dead Awaken*. It looks like a giant Giacometti candle, tall and thin, melting down in waves of black angst. When the light played across the surface, it was beautiful and sinister – a perfect visual metaphor for the bent-but-not-bowed misery of the ego-centric artist. The tiny copper door from *Orlando*. Jutta Lampa's contem-plating this Alice-in-Wonderland peephole captures all the delight and mystery of the play. Enigmatically, the door sprouted up from the floor. Burnished like red gold and beckoning like a siren, it seemed to contain the riddle of the universe, if only one could crawl through it like a camel through the eye of a needle. This piece of art would have felt perfectly at home at the Whitney Museum's exhibit of recent American sculpture.[7] Also at home at the Whitney would have been the pavilion from *When We Dead Awaken*, a stunning triumph of minimalist strength and beauty. The quiet repetition of a simple geometric form – the square – fashioned from steel tubes reassured and, simultaneously, threatened (it suggested both a cage and a playground). Lit from inside with thin strips of neon, the pavilion gave off a weird, otherworldly luminance. The giant light bulb from *Death Destruction & Detroit* – pop art with bite, mocking and eerie (see figure 33). The beach chairs for *Death Destruction & Detroit* – austere yet sensuous; pristine and cruel, long slats shining like blades of chrome desire. From *Doktor Faustus*, Esmeralda's red lacquer chaise-longue:

33 The giant light bulb in *Death Destruction & Detroit*: the miracle of
light, the miracle of sight.

sleek, simple – a Bauhaus bullet streaking through the air, the bed of a
virgin whore.

The *Parzival Chair* with shadow shows how Wilson's props work
dramatically, formally, symbolically (see figure 34). Simple and sophisticated, it is beautiful to look at. The strong, basic lines create a complex
system of space. The black shadow dogging the bleached birch is playful
and sinister, suggesting the struggle between good and evil at the heart of
Parzifal. But if I had to pick one, just one, of the many beautiful pieces
Wilson has made, it would have to be *Mme. Curie's Chair* from *De Materie*
(see figure 35). Like his set design, Wilson's sculpture/furniture is about
proportion, balance, symmetry. *Mme. Curie's Chair* is really an anti-chair,
matter dematerialized (what more appropriate symbol for the pioneer of

34 *The Parzival Chair*: the contrast of light and dark. Wilson's mind runs on contrasts.

35 *Die Materie. Marie Curie Chair.*

radium?). Made of industrial materials – safety glass and threaded steel evaporating into a flicker of neon – the chair articulates space by a graceful interplay of lines. The pure, rectilinear silhouette of the chair contrasts ironically with the dangling electrical wires plugged into the battery clump on the floor. Poised for flight like a Brancusi bird, yet rooted in the ground, Wilson's sculpture creates a witty Socratic dialogue between the reality of a chair and its Platonic idea. All these objects functioned originally as dramatic props, but as the Museum of Fine Arts' show demonstrated, they have a glorious afterlife as sculpture.

THE RHETORIC OF MOVEMENT

The last crucial element to take into account when analyzing Wilson's alchemy of the eye is movement.

When I arrived in New York in the early sixties to study architecture, I went to Broadway to see plays. I hated them and still do. Then I saw the work of George Balanchine and the New York City Ballet. I liked that very much and still do. The first major influence on my work was Balanchine's choreography. I was fascinated by his abstract ballets – no story, just the visual rhythms of bodies moving through space. I liked the architectural patterns. I even liked his story ballets because the performers maintained a distance. The best dancers danced for themselves, not for the audience; their interpretations were for themselves. So the audience had more space to think about what it was experiencing. In contrast, the actors on Broadway overinterpreted their roles. Later I saw the ballets of Merce Cunningham. I liked them very much and still do. They were abstract constructions of time and space. (*Quartet*)

During these early years in New York, David Denby, America's most distinguished dance critic, was Wilson's mentor, and anyone interested in understanding Wilson should look at Denby's writings on Balanchine and Cunningham.[8]

When Wilson speaks of distance in Balanchine's ballets, he means that neither the choreographer nor the dancer dictated a single, univocal meaning of the dance; consequently, spectators felt more freedom to generate sundry interpretations. Balanchine's style is often dubbed cold and unemotional (epithets also hurled at Wilson). Accentuating movement as movement, Balanchine and Cunningham choreographed ballets that turned their back on conventional narrative, psychology, and expressive intent. Structure became content, content structure. Bodies – beams and bricks – build architecture. Whereas Balanchine emphasized formal, classical beauty and music,[9] Cunningham stressed stillness, the unexpected quirk, and the disassociation of theatrical codes. Cunningham put the movements together without any knowledge of the music. Often the dancers heard the music for the first time on opening night. Cunningham expounds on his approach in the following way:

The different elements are made independently of each other. One doesn't support the other. They are brought together at the moment of performance. The separate elements coexist. One is going on, and the other is going on. They can jar or not jar, depending on the individual response of each member of the audience. When these elements which were made separately are brought together in performance, they produce something unexpected, something we didn't know about. Performance is a discovery, not something you have already figured out. But nothing is improvised in performance. Absolutely not. It's complex, and it's rehearsed a good deal.[10]

Cunningham's choreography escorted Einstein's theory of relativity onto the dance floor. Space became process; time structure. Rejecting Freud as well as Newton, his ballets threw narrative, character, and emotion overboard. "Movement became important not for what it meant, but for what it was. The ego and the id were of less consequence than the arm and the leg. The subject of dance became dancing."[11] One need not search far to see how all these qualities found their way into Wilson's work. Ever since the Symbolists, the poet has dreamt of pure poetry, the painter of pure painting. Wilson is the first to make pure theatre – theatre that explores its own essence.

Not by coincidence does Wilson cite dance – a genre that renders words superfluous – as the primary influence on his theatre.[12] The subject matter of dance, Denby reminds us, is too big for language, and language can neither describe movement accurately nor analyze it deeply. "Bob didn't talk at all in the early days," recalls Sutton, who has collaborated with Wilson for a more extended period of time and in more works than any other actor.

When we created Deafman Glance, we didn't have one conversation about what we were doing. He gave people specific directions about how to walk, where to walk, how slow to walk. He never discussed a scene. We didn't have to talk. Communication was based on movement, inside and outside the theatre. We didn't miss words. We didn't need them. We shared a physical vocabulary. We spent hours and hours and hours together dancing. We got to know each other through movement. We learned to listen to each other's body. And these dance sessions were not only a warm-up for the work, they were the work, the source of material we would use.

Not surprisingly, ballet forms an integral part of many early works – *The Life and Times of Joseph Stalin*, *A Letter for Queen Victoria*, and *Einstein on the*

Beach; and movement is the basis of all Wilson's theatre. Anyone who cannot read movement will go astray in Wilsonland.

Many anthropologists and linguists believe speech arose from body movement; the honey dance – a signal code that sheds light on the origins of language – enables bees to transmit and receive complex messages.[13] Theatre derives from dance. "The early playwrights were actually called dancers,"[14] and the ecstatic rituals in honor of Dionysus united dance, music, and poetry in a chorus, the heartbeat of tragedy. "The theatre presents to us an art-form in which movement of living actors is the first and necessary attribute," claims Allardyce Nicoll, "and any theatre which refuses to make use of this element is clearly falsifying its essential purpose."[15] Western theatre, by letting language ride roughshod over all, has castrated movement into an afterthought – like so many commas, semi-colons, and apostrophes scribbled atop a sentence to clarify verbal meaning. Not so in Wilson, and the way he works explains the primal importance he accords movement.

Currently, Wilson's typical creative process takes place in three stages, separated by long stretches of time – two to six months: workshop A (design); B (movement); and C (text and tech).

The workshop process lets me get my arms around a piece. Through the workshops I find a direction. Only by living with a work for a long period of time do you get a perspective on it. A complex work needs time to grow inside. I used to think more about a play before the workshop. Now I think it's better not to think about it so much, not to come in with preconceived ideas. It's better to look at the room and the people in the room you're working with and make it happen with them. When I look at an actor I have to think about not only the character he's playing but also the person breathing in front of me. I don't like thinking in the abstract. I have to see something to know what I'm doing. (*WWDA*)

Wilson's extreme sensitivity to actors – his instinctive knowledge of their strengths and weaknesses – helps account for his success as director. He always tailors his conception to the individual standing before him. In one production he wanted an actress to run across the stage; unfortunately, the actress "looked like a dumpling" when she moved quickly. The director replaced the run with a slow, elegant stride. In his remounting of *Quartet* in America, the actor playing Valmont was afraid to be hung upside down, swinging in the air with a rope attached to one ankle. The moment – stunning in the German production – was an important thematic and structural climax. Learning of the actor's trepidation, Wilson immediately worked out a new sequence. Wilson has an infallible eye for actors. He sums them up quickly and knows what they can do, what they cannot do, when to push, when to accommodate. And he knows how to manipulate actors to get what he wants – a necessary talent in any director.

The director compares the workshop process to "peeling an onion." The early workshops start out rather free and enable him to explore a play with actors and experiment with various approaches. During the early period, Wilson is open to improvisation and suggestions. The later rehearsals become much more precise. The movement patterns – and by movement I include all gestures and spatial relations among actors with each other and the stage – are sketched out in workshop B. By this time Wilson may not have read the text (Müller's *the CIVILwarS*); he may have a passing acquaintance with the text (*Quartet*); he may know the text extremely well (*King Lear*). In any event, when he starts mapping out the movement, he puts the text aside.

He explained to the actors in *When We Dead Awaken*:

I do the movement separate from the text. I do movement before we work on the text. Later we'll put text and movement together. I do movement first to make sure it's strong enough to stand on its own two feet without words. The movement must have a rhythm and structure of its own. It must not follow the text. It can reinforce the text without illustrating it. What you hear and what you see are two different layers. When you put them together, they create another texture. It's not a chance operation like Cage and Cunningham. I'm much more interested in structure than they are. It may seem arbitrary at first, but later the different layers add up. There will be an architecture. Meanings will emerge. My way of working is not rational. I'm intuitive.

When auditioning actors, Wilson often does an elaborate movement sequence. He asks the actor to repeat it. Most cannot. Wilson is looking for a good eye, a good visual memory, and a body that knows how to move. Only after the actor has passed the movement test does Wilson ask him to read a section from the play. When asked during rehearsals for *the CIVILwarS* at the American Repertory Theatre what he required in actors, Wilson answered: "All an actor has to be able to do is walk and count." Wilson's attitude towards actors has evolved over the years, and he would never, today, make such a statement. In the early days, he preferred unprofessional performers – people he picked up off the street or in Grand Central Station because their look captivated him – or the Byrds, people who had worked on movement with him at the Byrd Hoffman Institute. But after working with some of Germany's leading actors – *Death Destruction & Detroit* was his first piece with primarily professional actors – his attitude to professionals changed, as did his method of working with them. In terms of physical types, the director prefers polar opposites: either the classically beautiful (like Lucinda Childs and Sheryl Sutton) or the weirdo. He also has a penchant for bodies tall and thin and prefers a well-groomed look. During rehearsals of *When We Dead Awaken* he fired an actress who appeared with disheveled hair. "An unkempt actor doesn't respect the profession. People think of artists as bohemians – bedraggled, besmirched. When I was a student at Pratt, I attended class in coat and tie. When you come to my rehearsals, you come clean, neat, and combed."

Auditioning for Wilson can be a trauma. Thomas Derrah, who worked with Wilson on *the CIVILwarS* at the American Repertory Theatre, recollects:

I didn't know much about Wilson except that he was *très* avant-garde. We were all waiting outside the rehearsal room. One by one the actors staggered out. We quizzed them on what he had asked them to do. The first said "I had to walk across the room in a straight line on a count of 10, sit down on a count of 21, put my hand to my forehead on a count of 13." The second said "I had to walk across the room in a straight line on a count of 26, sit down on a count of 42, put my hand to my forehead on a count of 18." By the time the tenth actor stumbled out, we were petrified. When I went in, he asked me to walk across the room on a count of 31, sit down on a count 7, put my hand to my forehead on a count of 59. I was mystified by the whole process. I didn't have a clue about what I was doing or why I was doing it. But I did it. As soon as I finished, he jumped up, clapped his hands, and shouted, "Bravo. You're the first actor today who can count." I left the room confused. Was that a compliment? It's the first time someone had praised me for counting since kindergarten. But I was intrigued, and by the end of the rehearsal process, I loved his way of working. It's all about precision of movement. He demands meticulous attention to detail, down to the angle of the fingers and the eyes.[16]

Seth Goldstein, who played the child in *the CIVILwarS*, recounts that "every movement from the moment I walked onto the platform until I left was choreographed to the second. During the scene at table all I did was count movements. All I thought about was timing. Bob didn't talk about family dynamics or subtext. Nevertheless, from all these different actors counting different movements, a highly emotional portrait of a family emerged that was never explicitly discussed by the director."[17]

Actors, especially those who like to analyze language and psychology, find working with Wilson less than exhilarating. During the rehearsals of *King Lear*, Marianne Hoppe sighed,

This Wilson can't fool me. I started out at the Deutsches Theater with Max Rheinhardt. I know what a director is. Wilson is not a director. He's a lighting designer. A Wilson actor runs here or there only because there's a change in the lights. On a Wilson stage, light pushes the actors around. Light is important, but in Shakespeare, language is also important. I can speak these lines the way he wants, but I don't believe Shakespeare wrote the part of Lear to be recited by an autistic child.[18]

Actors who have studied dance find it easier to adjust to Wilson than those who have studied the method. "I'm used to sitting at table and analyzing character and subtext before getting up to block it," noted Stephanie Roth, who played Maya in *When We Dead Awaken*. "It was difficult to work with Wilson until I stopped thinking about it as theatre and started thinking about it as dance. I studied ballet for many years, and for Wilson I learn my part the way I learned a *pas de deux*."[19]

Since Wilson's movement patterns are so complex and precise, he breaks them down into numbered sequences to help actors learn them – the way one learns a tap dance routine. "I feel right at home in this rehearsal room," said Honni Coles, the renowned hoofer Wilson recruited to perform the knee plays in *When We Dead Awaken*. "It's just like vaudeville. It's all about practice, precision, rhythm, and timing."[20] The number of movement sequences in a scene can easily run over five hundred. "Look at my script," sniffed Elzbieta Czyzewska, who played Irene. "There are so many numbers and notes in the margins that when the production ends, I'm donating it to the Smithsonian."[21]

Isabelle Huppert, the film star who acted in Wilson's French-language production of *Orlando* made the following observations about her collaboration with the director:

Usually I prefer the screen. The camera zooms in for a close-up, and like a microscope it sees into your soul. In theatre you have to be much more exterior, projecting to a large auditorium. But Bob has found a way to capture interiority on stage. By breaking the conventions of all that exaggerated emoting, Bob has created a new way of acting, a new way of inhabiting the stage that for the first time enabled me to reach the same level of sensitivity and interiority as in film.

At first learning all those precisely choreographed movements was difficult, but when I had them down pat and understood how they express Virginia Woolf's novel on a deep level, a big surprise came. After melting myself into Bob's highly formalistic universe, I discovered complete liberty. That formalism became a support, carving out a space where I could express myself. Never on a stage have I been so free, so much myself. I felt like a child, playing at home in an attic, all alone. When you think no one is looking, you do the most extravagant things. Bob gives you permission to do this. But to get to that playful state of mind, you must discipline yourself mentally and physically to master those complex movements. Nothing is improvised on a Wilson stage. Structure in Bob creates freedom.[22]

Depending on circumstances, including how much time he has, Wilson works out his movement sequences in one of two ways (see figure 36). He may get up and do the movements himself, asking the actors to watch carefully and imitate him. Wilson is a marvellous performer, and the basis of much of his direction is this ability. As he works out a movement sequence by doing it – the act of performing becomes the act of directing – a videotape is made which actors can later study. Also, the assistant director takes elaborate notes, paying attention not only to who walks where on a count of how long, but also to gestures and angles of head, arms, hands, fingers, eyes, and when the weight should shift.[23] The stage manager, stopwatch in hand to clock movements, and the actors take their own notes. Or Wilson may let the actors improvise, taking the movements he likes and building them into a structure.

After the basic movement pattern has been roughed in, Wilson turns his attention to the words. One of his primary concerns is to leave enough "space around a text" to let the audience take it in. By now the actors have learned the movement sequence by numbers. ("Memory," the director says, "is in the muscles. There's no substitute for rehearsing. You can't rehearse my plays too much.") Wilson calls out the numbers, the actors do the movements, and Wilson reads the text where he wants it placed. The process is intuitive. If asked why he put a chunk of text with a particular movement, he'll respond, "Because it feels right." Or the director may have the actors read the text and call out the movement numbers when they "feel right." During this stage Wilson frequently interrupts a scene: "Come over here, actors. Something is wrong. We have to check your scripts to see if you put the numbers in the right place." Pace and rhythm are crucial to Wilson, and he wants to make sure that the rhythm of the movements does not pick up the rhythm of the text or the rhythm of the other actors. Each marches to the sound of a different drummer, except on those rare occasions, to contradict himself, he lets them hook up. One of the hardest things for actors to master in the Wilsonian style is to speak and move at two different rhythms. The body – browbeaten by language – has been trained to follow the tongue and, automatically, falls into line. "I know it's hell to separate text and movement and maintain two different rhythms. It takes time to train yourself to keep tongue and body working against each other. But things happen with the body that have nothing to do with what we say. It's more interesting if the mind and the body are in two different places, occupying different zones of reality," the director tells actors (Lear). Wilson is extremely sensitive to visual rhythms and to the contrast between slow and fast movements. Watching him build these movements into an architectural structure is to learn the

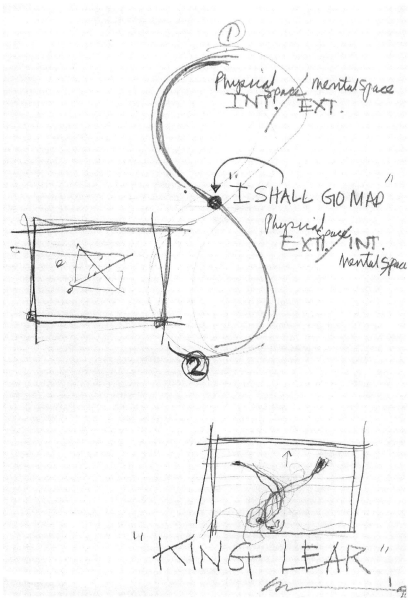

36 Wilson's drawings for a movement sequence in *King Lear* (Act II, scene iv, line 281), demonstrating how a formal pattern of movement may concretize psychology, often reflecting the unconscious.

importance of counting. "Timing is essential," he alerts actors. "Think of my gestures as choreography" (*WWDA*).

The body in Wilson speaks eloquently. Movement generates meaning. How and what it means, however, can never be satisfactorily answered because our answers are always words, and words are impotent to describe movement, let alone explain it. But this quandary does not give us license to shrug our shoulders and duck the attempt. Movement generates meaning in many ways: a ballerina, Mallarmé suggested, is not a girl dancing but a metaphor that dances.[24] In Wilson the reverse is also true: a body moving in space may be just a body moving in space, nothing more. But that nothing is something. In Wilson's theatre, movement, in and of itself, is interesting and important. On the other hand, an individual movement may set off ripples of signification that in the context of a theatrical structure acquire meaning. The parallels with postmodern dance should not be overlooked. When Wilson arrived in New York, he saw postmodern dance and later collaborated with leading postmodern choreographers who wielded a crucial influence on his style – Lucinda Childs, Andy de Groat, Kenneth King, Meredith Monk.

In postmodern dance movement becomes both the medium and the message. Postmodern dance interrogates itself, puzzling over the nature and function of movement. Like Wilson's theatre, it wrestles with the mysteries of perception and cognition. In *Terpsichore in Sneakers* Sally Banes separates postmodern dance into two periods: analytic in the seventies and metaphoric in the eighties. The evolution of Wilson's career parallels this development. In the analytic period, postmodern choreographers repeated simple, everyday movements. They emphasized choreographic structure, "foregrounding movement *per se*. Their program was to make dance as such the locus of audience attention by making dances in which all the audience was given to see was structure and movement . . . movement without overtly expressive or illusionistic effects or reference." In the metaphoric period, virtuosity of movement returned as well as a bemused exploration of narrative and language. "These dances are different from modern dance, however, because in important ways they *present* the non-dance information (i.e., plot, character, situation), rather than *represent* it. They are not seamless theatrical illusions, productions of fictional worlds (à la Martha Graham or Doris Humphrey). The movement vocabulary is only partially expressive; it also remains partly abstract and it resists definitive interpretation. The emotional or narrative content remains elusive and fragmented, and the meaning of the dance is played out in several, not always corresponding, dimensions."[25] Analytic postmodern dance corresponds roughly to the first half of Wilson's career; metaphoric, to the second half when the director turns his attention to literary texts.

Movement is "part of the calculus of meaning . . . [It] appeals to many sensory modalities simultaneously."[26] Movement makes meaning through various modes of representation, from imitation through exemplification (the physical property of the dance exemplifies what it means).[27] Movement communicates emotions "inaccessible to verbal or intellectual expression."[28] In daily life, "probably no more than 30 to 35 percent of the social meaning of a conversation or an interaction is carried by the words."[29] The rest is conveyed by movement, which for biological reasons always attracts our attention. With movement, as with all forms of visual communication, one must pay close attention to the pattern of visual forces and the tension they create.[30] In *Reading Dance*, Susan Foster offers the following roadmap for choreographic meaning: "(1) the frame – the way the dance sets itself apart as a unique event; (2) the mode of representation – the way the dance refers to the world; (3) the style – the way the dance achieves an individual identity in . . . its genre; (4) the vocabulary – the basic . . . moves from which the dance is made; and (5) the syntax – the rules governing the selection and combinations of moves."[31] Although Wilson's movement is not balletic, these criteria still obtain.

Like his lights, Wilson's movement has an overall structural development. His form includes statement, repetition, contrast, reversal. His style, which has evolved over the years toward greater stylization, tends to emphasize a long, elegant line traced by the body moving slowly through space. Usually the spine remains centered over the heels, creating a balanced body and precisely controlled posture. The weight does not shift – this would create jagged lines – it rotates. Actors are drilled to transfer the weight before beginning to move to avoid jerky starts. From time to time an abrupt, angular, or quirky movement throws the body off center, but only incidentally. Before long the spine returns to its axis, and the body resumes tracing the long paths that form the clear geometric patterns used in classical ballet. These patterns – Wilson heightens them with lights – reveal best the body in movement: horizontal lines parallel to the picture plane (Wilson's path of choice); diagonal lines for dynamic contrast; straight lines directly toward or away from the audience; and, from time to time, a circle.

In the early days, the horizontal pattern dominated almost completely, creating a theatre of ceremonial procession. At that time he divided the stage into horizontal zones parallel to the proscenium arch; people moved across the stage horizontally and usually stayed in their zone.

37 *The Forest*. Movement generates meaning. Wilson calls the lines
bodies trace as they move through space "fields of force." The slow
walk of Enkidu towards the prostitute on a straight line parallel to the
proscenium created unbearable erotic tension. With her kiss Enkidu
falls into civilization.

Turns in this rectilinear world were at right angles, executed with military precision. Only after *Einstein on the Beach* and *the CIVILwarS* did
Wilson begin to explode the space as much front to back as side to side.

   Not only are the paths people and objects trace through space one of
the major structural elements in Wilson, they also forge one of the major
links in his chain of theatrical signification (see figure 37). "The nature of
the pathway that a moving object produces may often have highly significant communicative value. An automobile may proceed in a straight line
or may weave in and out of traffic. A drunk may sway, flounder, or
stagger from one side to another. Often the informative value is conveyed
principally by those body parts that move the most and those that move
the least."[32] As with any movement structure, one must pay close attention not only to the pathway, but also the point of origin, the destination,

the speed. Who is moving where and away from whom has the greatest significance in Wilson. One of the first questions to ask about a Wilson work is who walked where.

Wilson's vocabulary of movement is eclectic. Some gestures he picked up from Raymond Andrews (deaf-mutes rely heavily on the body for communication); some from Chris Knowles (Wilson loved the autistic child's sense of highly structured spatial patterns); some from the loonies he scrutinizes, strolling through urban blight: a person writing in the air, an obsessively recurring image in Wilson, comes from a mad-woman he observed at a bus station in Iowa. Suzushi Hanayagi, the Japanese dancer and choreographer, has also influenced his movement, nudging it toward more formalization and abstraction. Trained in both Noh and Kabuki as well as in postmodern American dance, Suzushi has worked with Wilson on many of his big projects, giving the actors work-shops in the morning (based on Japanese training) and devising chore-ography and gestures with Wilson in rehearsal. Some gestures – Alceste's hand held before her face in mourning – come directly from Noh.[33] The slow, controlled, elegant movement of traditional Japanese theatre appeals, naturally, to Wilson's sensibility, as does its fluid back-and-forth modulation between referential and abstract movement. Sometimes Wilson's movement refers to the world and relates to what the actors are saying; usually, however, a gesture that began naturalisti-cally metamorphoses into an abstract line. In *Quartet*, based on Laclos's epistolary novel *Les Liaisons dangereuses*, Childs tore up a letter. At first the movement imitated ripping a sheet of paper. Before the rehearsals finished, however, the gesture had transmogrified into an elegant move-ment of the hands in space; no one who had not seen the process could have guessed its origin. It became a mysterious and beautiful expression of the rage to destroy.

During the *King Lear* rehearsals, Wilson gathered the actors together. "Suzushi," he said, "do something with your feet. Western actors always forget their feet. When they think about gestures, they think about hands. Watch Suzushi." Off came her shoes, off came her socks. She wiggled her toes. Then she slapped her big toe as if it were the serpent in the Garden of Eden. Next she pulled her toe, as if to yank it off her body. Then she rubbed the toe, now fast, now slow. Asking the actors to take off their shoes, the director continued:

Look at your feet. Examine the heel. The body is connected. Hear with your eyes. See with your ears. Move the toes. Feel the ear wiggle. When I walk I feel it in my fingers, in my hair, in my elbows. Feet are the most beautiful part of the body and a major means of expression. They are as expressive as the hands. With the foot, one makes contact with the ground. The Japanese believe the gods live in the floor. Through the foot you connect with the divine.

Wilson heaves his towering frame up in a bold leap, lands roundly on the floor, and challenges an invisible samurai to a duel, feet pressing down against the ground, like the Colossus of Rhodes.

Now the floor supports me. The floor pushes up against my foot, my foot pushes down against the floor. The weight is all over the foot, not just on the sides. If your weight and balance are off, you can't walk right, speak right, or sing right. Try singing Wagner on your toes. The way you stand makes a difference in how you sound. If you want to sing Isolde, your two feet had better be firmly on the ground. If you want to act, if you want to speak, if you want to sing, you must start with the body. The body is your instrument. Learn to play it. You can count the actors and singers on one hand who know how to walk.

With this introduction, Wilson launched his celebrated lecture on feet and walking – a sermon preached at least once during every movement workshop:

This isn't a fashion show. You're walking as if you're on a runway being photographed for *Vogue*. The movement is too exterior, too aggressive. The movement must be interior. Don't perform to the audience. Let the audience come to you. I anticipate all your movements. I see you preparing them mentally. You must always surprise the audience. Never let them know what you're going to do, where you're going to go. If you're going to turn left, prepare mentally to turn right. Now you're turning your head in the direction you're going to move to, like a gate swinging open. Your eyes anticipate the direction you're moving to. Stop them. They should move with the head, not before it.

You totter with every step you take. You must learn to walk all over again. You're not secure, you're not balanced. Children are nervous when they learn to walk. They're afraid to put one foot in the air before the other. Adults have never overcome this fear. One foot off the ground in the air still terrifies us. The body quivers and quakes. You must break the strategies you used to cope with walking as a child. If you stand on one foot correctly, if your body is balanced, you can swing the other foot anywhere and maintain an elegant line. Practice it. Do it slowly. Most people slam their feet on the ground because they're afraid of being on only one foot. Get over that fear. Learn to be centered and secure so that you control the line your body is tracing through space. Think of your body as a pencil drawing beautiful lines in the air. Don't wobble. You must move smoothly. Only after you can move smoothly, can you wobble. Then wobbling makes sense, depending. You need a larger vocabulary of movement. Smooth when you want, off balance when you want. Feel the foot. Feel it lift into the air. Really feel what it means to walk. Shut your eyes so you're more aware of the foot and movement. It's not an intellectual exercise. It's physical. It's a sensuous experience. The foot is very sensitive, very sensual. Practice these movements over and over until you don't have to think about what you're doing. Experience each second. Only when you're in complete control are you free.

Then come gentle remonstrances:

You're taking the foot off the ground slow and putting it down fast. Don't. Maintain the same speed throughout. When you stop, your head bounces back. It shouldn't. It should stop with your body. Stop means stop, not stop, start. You stand still, but the movement should continue. There is never no movement. Maintain the concentration. Then when you start to walk again, it's not a new start but a continuation. I don't want to see the movement start. Shift the weight to the right foot before you have to move the left. Don't jerk. Don't break that line. Your walk is constipated. Unless you break the movement down and know when to transfer your weight, you will never control the line. Break it down, and practice, practice, practice. Only then, when you don't have to think about it, are you free.

Space helps us see. The more space around an object, the better we see. Leave more space around your head and between your arms and body. Open the body more to the audience. Think of your body as a piece of living sculpture. Don't crowd yourself. Don't lock the limbs in so tight. It's more elegant when you stretch them out. Keep that head up, more space between chin and neck, open those eyes wider. Make that line with your arm longer. You will never be a good actor until you and your spine become friends. You must control the spine. The body is the actor's most important resource. All theatre is dance.

Stalking up behind a slouching actor, Wilson yanks him up by his bangs.

You're not walking on a street. A street is a street; a stage is a stage. The stage is an artificial space. What happens on a stage is different from what happens on a street. Don't use everyday, casual movement. The line you're drawing in space is not functional. It's formal. Every time you're on stage, remember: I'm behind you pulling you up tall by the hair on your head. Stand straight. Think of your body as a spotlight. That light can be beamed in any direction. Focus that energy. Every movement, every gesture – even walking off stage – must have direction and focus. When you leave the stage don't be in such a hurry. You're not running to catch a bus. (*Faustus*)

Space is the canvas on which Wilson paints his movement patterns. "Nothing is more beautiful than empty space. It's like fresh air in the theatre," Wilson sighed during the *Doktor Faustus* workshop in Milan. The night before he had seen Franco Zefferelli's *Turandot* at La Scala. "Zefferelli heaped so much garbage on that stage it looked like the city dump. At the end the hordes littering the set took out big white handkerchiefs and started waving them in time with the music. With that chaos, the eye sees nothing, the ear hears nothing." If music accompanies movement in Wilson, he makes sure the two neither start nor stop at the same time and that the rhythm of the movement does not pick up the rhythm of the music.

Several important points emerge from Wilson's critique of Zefferelli. First, Wilson gravitates toward relatively spare sets. Clutter would interfere with the long lines of movement that sweep across the stage (as well as with the sidelights that heighten the plasticity of the body in motion). Second, the minimalist stage design contrasts with the baroque, surrealistic images that haunt the space. Third, a spare stage enables Wilson to emphasize primary shapes, both in design and movement patterns. Fourth, the infinite, lonely horizons of Texas forged Wilson's epic sense of space. Fifth, negative space is crucial to Wilson's aesthetic. "We must give the audience time to think and space to see," he repeats. During the *King Lear* rehearsals, to press his point, he made two drawings (at rehearsals a neat pile of white sheets stands and waits for the master's hand, accompanied by a stalwart band of freshly sharpened pencils). On one drawing a melee of lines squiggling wildly in every direction, filling the page with a confused swirl. On the other, one tiny black dot slightly off center. The director then asked actors:

Which mark do you see? Which mark is more important? If you have two spaces that are the same, and if you put a large scribble in one, and a tiny dot in the other, the tiny dot is bigger because there's more space around it. Often on stage, the person standing still is the focus. When I directed *Medea*, the lead singer was upset. I had her stand still on stage while everybody else moved around her. She complained that if I didn't give her movements, no one would notice her. I told her if she knew how to stand, everyone would watch her. I told her to stand like a marble statue of a goddess who had been standing in the same spot for a thousand years.

After seeing a production of *The Marriage of Figaro*, Wilson sighed, "There's a lot of frantic horseplay going on. I felt like telling the director it isn't necessary to put together on the same stage an opera, a circus, and Disneyland. Calm down. Listen to the music."

Wilson works for hours with actors on how to flick a finger, how to cock a head. In the main, the direction is technical, with little or no discussion of text or psychology. Bodies are treated as vectors, lines of force moving through space. "I have a spatial way of thinking. You must translate all that psychology into tension in the space. A playwright can't write space. He writes a text. But space is also a text." The visual effect comes first, but, in the context of a play, psychological implications follow. "Get the effect first," says Wilson, "a million causes can be found later" (*WWDA*).

Rehearsing the entrances of Lear's daughters for the division of the kingdom, Wilson strove to achieve high contrast in the rhythms and walks of Goneril, Regan, and Cordelia. Wilson performed each walk and asked the performers to imitate him, but the actresses weren't delivering the qualities he wanted. "Your walk is your character," he cajoled. "I can't explain it, but I can draw it." Grabbing a sheet of paper from the pile sitting loyally on the table – Wilson thinks and communicates through pictures – the director drew three long lines on the page: a strong, straight arrow, shooting boldly through space (Goneril); a kinky knot of zigs, zagging their way through space (Regan); and a graceful curve, flowing through space (Cordelia).

For Kent's entrance into Goneril's house (act I, scene iv), Wilson went over the movement sequence with the actor again and again.

How does Kent walk? Find the character through the walk. The others will be quick, but you must enter slow. Walk in backwards. This must be a strange moment. You're entering a different space. You must indicate that your body is experiencing a change of space. Walk in a straight line. I said straight. A quick turn there, an attack in space. Now put your hand up to your face. Slowly pull the fingers down around the nose, and feel your face. Put your fingers on your eyes. Do not exteriorize your pain. Keep the pain inside. Less exterior emotion, more interior. Don't project an emotion to the audience. Reflect it to yourself.

Before a rehearsal for the CIVILwarS at ART, Wilson slipped over to an actor limbering up with calisthenics. "Stop all that jumping around this minute," Wilson ordered. "That's not how you prepare for my work. Go into a quiet corner, face the wall, breathe deeply, meditate."

"Don't jerk your eyes around," Wilson continued to direct Kent. "Every time you move your hand you duplicate that movement with your eyes and head. Don't. Hands and eyes must move separately. It creates more tension if the hand moves independently. Now cover your entire face with your hand, turn your head, and walk fast because all this has been slow."

In production, Kent's entrance – weird and disturbing – communicated a great sense of dislocation, a world out of joint, a world that makes no sense. Kent seemed to be walking in his sleep, held captive by a nightmare he could not wake up from. Now disguised as the servant Caius, he has become a stranger in a strange land, palpating his face as if it had turned into a malevolent pumpkin. Kent does not like this strange, new world he has walked backwards into, but the loyalty and stoicism that gain the upper hand (some of the gestures against the face seem like masochistic self-torture) are sadly beautiful. "Wilson gives you the gestures and the walk," says Richy Müller, who played Edmund in *King Lear.* "From those you create the character. It's a paradox. You're completely mechanical. You're completely free." The mechanical part is clear: the precisely paced movement Wilson demands. The freedom comes from Wilson's encouraging actors to "fill out the line." By "filling out the line," Wilson means that actors can invent whatever subtext they want to resonate with or against the movement.

It's not important for me to know your subtext, but it helps you fill in the line. A thousand ballerinas have danced *Giselle.* To dance this ballet you need technique and absolute control, but technique doesn't make you a great ballerina. It's your inner feeling about what you're doing that makes it special. The subtext can change every night. In that sense every performance is an improvisation. As you master the movement sequences, I hope you'll fill in the form. Make up your own story. Think about anything, or think about nothing. What you think can be in character or not. You can think "Tonight I'm an actress on stage playing Goneril," or you can remember "When I was a little girl my mother told me to button my dress. I didn't want to, but I had to." (*Lear*)

In Wilson the body speaks, and almost always it contradicts the voice. The director's movements often dramatize the unconscious: repressed emotions tingling across the surface of the skin, too ambiguous, too transient, too dangerous to dawn into consciousness. Frequently, they contradict the dialog, revealing what the characters feel, not what they say. Maya's trance sequence from *When We Dead Awaken* illustrates this use of movement.

Showing a keen interest in one of the female guests at the spa, Maya's husband queries the manager about her identity, "Who was that woman?" Maya's dialog reveals the typical wifely reaction: jealousy. At this point Wilson inserted a trance sequence to explore Maya's unconscious conflicts. After tapping her champagne flute three times with her knife and pointing it at her husband, she rises slowly, like a somnambulist, knife extended as a weapon. The two Irenes (her husband's former lover) enter the pavilion like the shadows of ghosts. Maya turns, and sticks a piece of toast into her mouth. Suddenly she hoists the knife into the air in a paroxysm of anger. During rehearsal, to get the right tension in the gesture, Wilson strode up to the actress and put his arm high over her. "When you raise the knife, hit my hand hard, as if you want to hurt me. It must be cruel." (See figure 38.) The two Irenes (Wilson split the character between two actresses) come out of the pavilion. The three women form a unit, like sculpted figurines twirling around an ormolu clock. As Maya raises the knife, Irene turns with extended arm. Strangely, the movement

38 *When We Dead Awaken.* Stephanie Roth (Maya), rehearsing the stab.
Toast gags her mouth. When a character falls silent, the truth comes
out. "Words lie," Martha Graham said, "but the body tells the truth."
(Personal interview, February 1987).

patterns and gestures of the three women – theme and variation – bind
them into a whole. Rather than rivals, are they three aspects of one
woman? Does Rubek always fall in love with the same figment of his
imagination, not a woman but a false image in his mind that he projects
onto the flesh and blood creature in front of him – Stendhal called it
"crystallization"? Welling up from her unconscious, Maya's hatred of her
husband explodes in this trance, a hatred she is not ready to admit to
herself consciously. She points the knife – castration and murder –
directly at her husband at the beginning and end of the trance. Waking up
from this descent into her unconscious, Maya wobbles as if drunk, sits
down slowly, and proceeds to smother her toast with caviar. "Make this

scene big, strange, and off balance," Wilson instructed. "When you come
to, it's as if someone had thrown a bucket of ice-cold water on your face.
You don't know what happened. It's as if you were waking up from a
dream." Movements in this sequence functioned as a visual soliloquy.
Less precise, more ambiguous than language, movement speaks the
unconscious more potently.

The last scene of *The Forest* demonstrates how eloquently movement
speaks. Man is not born with a knowledge of death. The consciousness of
"death, measured against man's total presence on earth, is a relatively
recent occurrence." In the *Gilgamesh Epic* we encounter "most of the
themes of the meditation on death – the fear of death, the intimation of
the futility of life, and the problem of how to live in view of the bitter
truth that this radical change from life to death is inevitable . . ."[34]
Gilgamesh's sorrow over the death of his companion Enkidu is the first
great lament of western literature. Wilson translated Gilgamesh's discovery of death into a slow and stately march that criss-crossed the stage in
five diagonals. The two friends – Gilgamesh and Enkidu – begin walking
together, slowly. Imperceptibly, Gilgamesh starts walking faster and
leaves his friend behind. Walking on separate diagonals, the actors conveyed, simultaneously, the idea of closeness and distance. On the fifth
diagonal, just before Gilgamesh and Enkidu should pass on parallel lines,
Gilgamesh turns abruptly and walks smack dab into the backdrop.
Turning quickly, he catches sight of his beloved friend, separated forever
by death, living forever in memory. A chorus of hooded pilgrims enters.
Opposite, a woman in Victorian dress approaches. She raises her hand to
stop them. Enkidu stares off-stage into the void. Gilgamesh, realizing he
is alone, turns and faces the wall. Blackout. Gilgamesh – the great king,
the builder of Uruk – confronts nothingness. All the rest is silence.

5   The dream work

Nommer un objet, c'est supprimer les trois-quarts de la jouissance du
poëme . . . le *suggérer*, violà le rêve.
                    Mallarmé, *Réponses à des enquêtes sur l'évolution littéraire*

In Act I of *The Forest*, Wilson's meditation on the Babylonian epic
Gilgamesh, the lights come up on a desolate shore – a strange, primeval
landscape, the earth washed clean by the receding waves of a deluge,
untouched, unpolluted by the hand of man, Yeats's world of "salmon-
falls and mackerel-crowded seas." An old gnome, who brings wisdom
from the days before the flood, sits atop a rock. A jet-black raven perches
beside him. The old man's white face and white hair contrast with his
inky black cloak. Who is he? An ancient bard, a singer of tales, a prophet
who looks inside and sees what is past, is passing, or is to come? From the
opposite side of the stage, a malevolent crocodile bares his teeth and grins
in perpetuity. With a voice from the other side of the tomb, the old man
intones an epic story from the beginning of time about the primordial
energy of nature. Against the distant horizon, Urmother – the great
goddess herself – enters, walks, turns, walks backwards, reaches center,
pours the sands of time through her fingers, retraces her steps, exits. A
hooded soldier, sword brandished, crosses the stage diagonally with a
hesitation goose step. Reaching the old man, he raises the sword over his
neck, ready to strike. A child toddles in and builds a crystal city of Oz in
the sand. Pulsating, exhilarating music by David Byrne pounds the ear
drum. A chorus of women enter – some in Victorian gowns, others
barechested. Ravens, whispering secrets to the women, perch on their
outstretched fingers. In a trance, the women cross the stage. Periodically,
men dart across the horizon. The stage darkens. The old sage continues to
intone his epic. A witch cackles. Or is it a raven? The sky turns violet, the
earth black. The stage empties except for the old man and young boy. A
branch with budding leaves floats up from the ground and slowly
ascends into the heavens. The sky brightens, the stage lightens. Blackout
except for one tight spot on the wizened face of the old prophet, half-
human, half-fossil. He alone can read the runes, but he keeps the enigma
to himself.

The cycles of nature; birth, death, and rebirth; the transition from unreflecting animal life to the disease of consciousness[1] – all this the tableau suggests, but it pricks the memory like a thorn because it refuses to surrender all its secrets. The weird juxtaposition of objects, the dislocations in time, the narrative that hides more than it reveals, the paucity of clues about how to interpret what we see – all this adds up to a universe that beguiles with its riddles, a universe that, like dreams, lets us glimpse meaning through a glass darkly. But whatever it may or may not mean, it exalts, it quickens.

Discussing an image from Eisenstein's *Ivan the Terrible*, Barthes distinguishes three levels of visual meaning: information, symbols, and what he calls "the third meaning." Erratic, obstinate, obtuse, the third meaning "compels an interrogative reading," based, not on intellection, but on "a poetical grasp." This third meaning subverts the practice of meaning. Essentially dramatic in its dialectic, the third meaning is "a multi-layering of meanings which always lets the previous meaning continue, as in a geological formation, saying the opposite without giving up the contrary."[2] Much of Wilson's theatre works on the level of this third meaning.

"Nothing," Wilson affirms again and again, "is as beautiful as a mystery," and mystery runs through his work, flowing up from the unconscious like a secret river, irrigating the images on stage. "I don't like most of Ibsen's plays," the director claimed when starting to tackle *When We Dead Awaken*. "Ibsen usually explains too much. But *When We Dead Awaken* is different. It's so mysterious. The minute you think you understand a work of art, it's dead. It no longer lives in you. This play lives on in the mind like an hallucination. It's Ibsen's dream play."[3] One of the highest praises the director can bestow on an actor is "that was strange." Complimenting Christoph Waltz, who played Edgar in *King Lear*, Wilson said, "I liked your entrance that time. You just sort of appeared. It was very quiet, very strange." During the *When We Dead Awaken* rehearsals Wilson told Alvin Epstein (Rubek) to hold his feet parallel in order to "keep the architectural line of the chair." More than obliging, Epstein, who has studied both dance and mime, turned his leg out in a classic ballet position. "How do you like this?" the actor asked. "Great," Wilson replied. "I like it because it's so weird."

Frequently during the early stages of rehearsals, Wilson will sigh, "This is too realistic. We have to make it more dreamy." Hallucination, mystery, dream. These are Wilson's stock in trade, the hallmark of the world he creates on stage. Understandably, when Louis Aragon, the French poet, stumbled into this wonderland, he levitated in rapture. Penning a letter to the dearly departed André Breton, high priest of Surrealism, he exulted:

The miracle we were waiting for has happened, long after I had stopped believing in it: *Deafman Glance*. I have never seen anything so beautiful. No other spectacle can hold a candle to it because it is, at the same time, waking life and life seen with the eyes closed, the world of every day and the world of every night, reality mixed with dream. Bob Wilson is not a surrealist. He is what we, from whom Surrealism was born, dreamed would come after us and go beyond us.[4]

Many of the characteristics of Wilson's works are outlined in Freud's *The Interpretation of Dreams*.[5] Strange, alien, obscure, dreams stage memories inaccessible to waking life, dredging up material – forgotten or repressed – from childhood. Whereas concepts and language dominate waking life, visual thinking dominates dreams (67). Through condensation and displacement, the dream work translates dream-thoughts, the latent content, into another mode of expression, the pictographic script of the manifest dream-content (311). Dreams think in images (82), and these images reveal "the center of our being," veiled from the conscious mind (69, 103, 642). In dreams, the mind "becomes more conscious of the body" (67), and dreams and insanity "share many features in common" (123). Working through association (122), contradiction (87), and mystery (124), dreams eclipse logic (89) and generate more than one meaning (181, 388). Dreams have their own sense of time, different from waking time (86). In dreams language becomes "a verbal hotchpotch" (331). Dreams suppress causal relations (351), emphasize simultaneity of time zones (349), and invent new languages (338). Dreams have no definite endings (564), and are "most profound when seem most crazy" (480). Freud's gloss on dreams could also serve as a gloss on Wilson: Wilson's theatre stages the unconscious. It is a theatre of primary process.

According to Michel Foucault, Freud, by trying to nag the meaning out of dreams, misses the point. Freud exploits dreams as indexes, pointing to messages hidden from consciousness. In reducing dreams to a utilitarian function, he fails to savor the dream-image in and of itself. "The peculiarly imaginative dimension of . . . [dream] expression is completely omitted [in Freud] . . ." Foucault asserts. "In the density of the image, meaning finds the wherewithal to express itself allusively. The image is a language which expresses without formulating, an utterance less transparent for meaning than the word itself."[6] Entering Wilsonland, one should bear in mind Foucault's insistence on the phenomenology of the dream-image, the experience of dreaming rather than its justification through hermeneutics. Dreams are autotelic, an end in themselves. One need not scrutinize them for hints and clues to external meanings. By psychologizing dream to death, Freud "deprived it of any privilege as a specific form of experience" (43). Freud lost sight of the sensory excitement of dreams, the immanence of value and meaning in the image itself. Foucault sums up his critique of Freud by noting: "If consciousness sleeps during sleep, existence awakens in the dream" (54). It is this secret existence one savors in Wilson. "The dream restores the imagination to its truth and gives it back the absolute meaning of its freedom" (73). All theatre, to be authentic, must learn to dream.

Art, claims the Russian Formalist critic Victor Shklovsky, is a technique of defamiliarization. "The purpose of art is . . . to make objects 'unfamiliar'. . . to increase the difficulty and length of perception because the process of perception is an aesthetic end in itself and must be prolonged. Art is a way of experiencing the artfulness of an object . . . [Art] removes the automatism of perception; the author's purpose is to create the vision which results from that deautomatized perception."[7] Art takes the dross of reality and through a sea-change, turns it into something rich and strange: "Those are pearls that were his eyes." Wilson's productions bewitch because they are mysterious. To create this mystery, Wilson displaces from the norm the visual, verbal, and sonic elements he uses to forge his dream plays. Celebrating their status as art and revelling in their artifice, his plays are at three or four removes from what we see and hear in daily life.

Wilson's distaste for Realism becomes evident in the following remarks:

The fact that I chose a woman to play Lear moves the production away from Realism. We must do this play formally. I don't know what people mean when they talk about Realism in the theatre. Realism on stage looks false and sounds false. It's not real. It's a lie. Theatre is not life. We must acknowledge that theatre is art. Only then can we be truthful. Method actors try to be natural on stage. They try to sound as if they were speaking in a restaurant. So they keep chopping up their lines into little phrases that they mumble. But they're not in a restaurant, they're on a stage and should act as if they're on a stage. The best "realistic" actors aren't "realistic" at all. They're formal. Look at Brando. His performances are very studied. His movements have a formal structure to them. His pout is completely artificial. (*Lear*)

One should distinguish between the oneiric and the surrealistic in Wilson. The surrealistic creates bizarre images by juxtaposing objects that normally do not travel together. The oneiric, through the body's kinesthetic responses, actually puts one into a dream-like trance: even though awake, one's mind begins to function as if dreaming. By influencing the sensorimotor centers of the brain, an altered state of consciousness is induced.[8]

Wilson makes the following observations about dreaming and the mind's eye:

In the womb, the child's eyes are closed, but they move. The fetus sees with the inner eye. We come into this world blind, with eyes closed. We are born dreaming. As adults we blink all the time. During that blink the light of day goes out. What do we see? It happens so quickly, we're not conscious of it, but something is seen when the eyelid closes. In that blink, for a fraction of a second, the world dissolves and we dream. That's what my theatre is about. You must learn to see with your eyes shut. Only the blind really see. Only the deaf really hear. (*Lear*)

Both the surrealistic and the oneiric make their presence felt in Wilson, although the oneiric occurred more often earlier on. Through his manipulation of time and visual and musical rhythms, Wilson's early work frequently put spectators into a twilight zone between waking and dreaming in which they would see and experience events that never happened on stage. Wilson calls it "seeing with an interior screen." The exterior screen takes in the outside world. According to Sutton, the primary goal of the early work was to instill a liminal state that allowed the audience to experience inner visions. Watching *Deafman Glance* was like smoking a hookah: one slipped easily, peacefully over the edge into the beatitude of dreams. In the blink, the exterior world fades into mist. One floats on the dark sea of the mind among shadows and reflections of reflections.

To create the dream work, Wilson marshals a wide array of sophisticated strategies. By tinkering with language, Wilson has already gone far into dreamland.[9] Language gives us the illusion that we understand; it creates the fiction of a predictable, objective "reality"; it fools us into thinking we have tamed a savagely absurd universe. When God let Adam name the beasts of the field and the fowl of the air, He gave him dominion over the earth. To name is assume control. As seen in chapter 2, Wilson's surgery on language led to the collapse of dialog, the destabilization of character, the fragmentation of narrative, and the aura of mystery – all of which contribute to the dreamscape. Connected with this assault on language is the absent exposition. "When individuals attend any current situation, they face the question: what's going on here?" observes sociologist Erving Goffman. In order to make sense out of events, one needs frameworks – rules and references – to interpret and understand.[10]

In classical drama the exposition, usually act I, scene i, provides the information and frame we need to understand what is going on. "My problem with most theatre," Wilson says, "is it gets locked into a frame so its boundaries are boxed in. I'm more interested in theatre without boundaries" (*Lear*). One way to get rid of boundaries is to get rid of exposition. Entering the proscenium theatre for a performance of *The*

39 The hanging man in *The Golden Windows*. Who he is and why he hangs we will never know. The appeal of mystery is endless.

Golden Windows, one saw a man, oddly reminiscent of the somnambulist from *Dr. Caligari*, dangling from a rope high over the stage (see figure 39). Someone started to whistle "A Bicycle Built for Two," jauntily. Who is this man? Why was he hanged? What is the story behind this violence? What is the connection between this macabre scene and the gay, little ditty? We do not know when we come in. We do not know when we leave. No exposition, no frame. The play – a nightmare of danger and despair – hints at an act of violence that may or may not have been an accident. An elegant matron in evening dress enters and says, "I love you and would do anything to hurt you." Later she asks the dangling corpse, "Exactly what do you mean? Exactly what happened?" That neither she nor we will never know. Creating mystery depends on withholding information, and Wilson is a past member of the art, on stage and off.

Wilson is a man of secrets and surprises. Surprises form an important part of his dramaturgy of dreams. To jump start a play, he throws a curveball. Wilson hated Ibsen's little *When We Dead Awaken*. He found it lugubrious and fretted lest the play become "heavy, like this production I saw in Hamburg." He decided to get the play rolling with a vaudeville sketch, written and performed by Honni Coles, the celebrated tap dancer. "The audience will come anticipating this gloomy play," the director ruminated. To baffle the audience's expectation, he came up with several devices:

I'll hit them with a surprise, a prologue that's light and bright, fun and quick, the opposite of the play. To offset that title I'll paint a drop with *When We Dead Awaken* written in cheerful colors. We'll hit a bright yellow chair with a bright yellow spot. When Honni comes out in his elegant white suit and starts singing "I Was Alone When I Met You, Now I Wish I Was Alone," the audience won't know what's up. Let's put a swing dance at the end of Act I. It's such a shock to see all the characters come out in period costume and do a modern dance. It should start immediately after the end of the act to keep the edge of strangeness, that dark, serious first act followed by a funny knee play.

Wilson added three knee plays to *When We Dead Awaken*. Although a surprise, nothing was arbitrary about their selection or placement. Through the blues, tap dance, and swing, the knee plays translated Ibsen's themes into a popular American musical idiom. By taking Ibsen's tragic subject and refracting it through a comic prism, Wilson added a layer of complexity to the situation, inviting the audience to look at it from different and opposed angles (see figure 40).

Similarly, Wilson began *King Lear* with a prolog based on a poem by William Carlos Williams, "The Last Words of My English Grandmother," a contemporary lyric that parallels Lear's story from a tough, comic perspective. "The audience will come to the theatre expecting to see Shakespeare's *King Lear* in German," the director said at rehearsal. "Instead, the first thing they'll hear is this poem in English with those strange words 'rank, disheveled bed.' They'll really wonder what's going on. When you say 'What are all those / fuzzy looking things out there? / Trees? Well, I'm tired / of them . . .' you must give the audience permission to laugh with this old woman, just as they can laugh with Lear" (*Lear*). "Never let it become predictable," Wilson advises actors. "To make theatre you have to know how and when to pull the rug out from beneath the audience's feet. Shock the audience. It makes them listen. It makes them think. Let them figure it all out" (*Quartet*).

Another way Wilson surprises audiences is to set up a pattern – he calls it a code – and then break it and create a new code. "Rules are made to be broken. You set up expectations, then break them. That's what Art is about, breaking the code" (*WWDA*). Catch them off guard, keep them off guard – this sums up Wilson's dramaturgy of surprise.

40 *When We Dead Awaken*, American Repertory Theatre. "Beautiful like
the accidental meeting of an umbrella and a sewing machine on a
dissection table" (Lautréamont). Wilson uses startling juxtapositions to
create an unpredictable and fierce beauty. Ibsen's existential angst
yoked with American vaudeville. In the second knee play the entire
cast in period costume performed a swing dance to one of Coles's
songs. Honni Coles on far right.

Dreams as Freud showed (87, 347, 351) suppress logical connections. Likewise, Wilson separates cause and effect. The text he is working on suggests many of the visual images he uses, but by placing the visual image before or after the words that suggested it, Wilson avoids the obvious, heightens the mystery, and still builds an overall architectural structure that refracts the text but not in a simple, straightforward way (see figure 41). For Wilson the verbal key to *Lear* was the monarch's humble request at the end: "Pray you undo this button. Thank you, sir" (act V, scene iii, line 310) – a line most productions throw away since its simplicity masks its depth. With deep literary sensitivity, Wilson zeroed-in on this line. When the lights came up on Wilson's *King Lear*, the audience saw the entire cast in long blue coats, submerged in an unearthly blue light, unbuttoning for four minutes the top button round their choker collars. The bizarre wedded to the beautiful. If this gesture had accompanied Lear's line – which dramatizes the humanity the king has found through suffering – it would have been banal and redundant, a mere illustration of the text. Placed at the beginning and performed by all members of the cast, it became a mysterious icon from which the entire production would sprout and blossom. Foreshadowing the end, it created an architectural pattern that would be consummated, cyclically, at the close. Wilson also separates cause and effect with stage business. In act I, scene iv, Kent trips Oswald. The conventional director would have Kent stick his leg out and trip the churl. Hardly conventional, Wilson separated cause from effect in both time and space. The director had Kent pound the floor with his foot a few minutes before Oswald fell flat on his face and several paces yonder. No physical contact. Oswald fell, as if by magical thinking. Like a child, to wish is to effect.

To distill the dream mood, Wilson also expands time. Dream time is not waking time, and during rehearsals Wilson reminds actors that the experience of time in the theatre is not the time of ordinary life, not the tick tock of clocks and calendars, but the duration lived and felt by consciousness[11] – the time of Proust, Woolf, and Faulkner: the time of internal meditation, not external action.

Wheeler-dealers hustler-bustlers – those drugged on the frantic pace of modern life that represses the inner world – get the jitters sitting through a Wilson work. "There's no action," they complain. "Nothing happens!" Nothing and everything. These critics – pseudo-realists – are entertained by the action of Hollywood movies. But there are lethal weapons of the spirit, too. Traditionally, western theatre has been oriented towards time measured by external events. Aristotle considered plot with its structuring of incidents the most important element of drama,[12] and time in our

41 The hanging scene in *Quartet* – one of Wilson's most seductive stage pictures – was suggested by Müller's text. But since the visual image took place before the audience heard the verbal motif, Wilson avoided a facile illustration of the text. Charging the stage with eroticism, a refined sadomasochism flickered through the production like the flame of a torch shining against cold steel. Young Woman (Jennifer Rohn), Valmont (Bill Moor), the Marquise de Merteuil (Lucinda Childs). American Repertory Theatre.

theatre has usually been reduced to the dimension in which action takes place. In contrast, Wilson – carrying to an extreme a tendency that started with Maeterlinck and other Symbolist playwrights – moves the theatre towards interior time: the infinity of meditation. Wilson illuminates his concept of time as a process of distension:

Time in theatre is special. Time is plastic. We can stretch it out on stage until it becomes the time of the mind, the time of a pine tree moving gently in the wind or a cloud floating across the sky and slowly becoming a camel, then a bird. I'm the slowest director in the world. You must always give the audience space to see and time to think. The time of my theatre is the time of interior reflection. (*Lear*)

"Slow!" is the word the director screams most often. "Slow, slow, slow, slow. Slower. Slow, slow, slow, slow, slower. I said slow. Much too fast. Stop!" Through time and eternity, these words will echo and re-echo like Poe's raven in every theatre he has ever rehearsed in.

The unhurried use of time also serves the purposes of visual composition, helps to effect a graceful transition from one composition to another, and enables the audience to see and think about what they are experiencing. Dilating time, moreover, is a common mechanism of trauma victims. "Slowing down time enables one to deal with psychic terror."[13]

In addition to time, lights and color enable Wilson to conjure up a dream world. Wilson uses lights to dematerialize matter. One technique is to light objects successively. When one turns on the lights in a room, all objects swim into view simultaneously. Not so in Wilson. Total blackout preceded the "Temple of Apollo" scene from *Alceste*. First a tight spot picked out a person in white robes upstage center. Then the floor came up, a rich cerulean blue. Then, hanging over the white-garbed priest, a cube materialized. The play of lights formed a magical pyramid in the middle of the temple, and, finally, the sacred image itself – Apollo the sun god – took shape in a burst of golden beams. By bringing each object up separately, Wilson created an otherworldly atmosphere.

Wilson used the same technique for act ii of *When We Dead Awaken*: blue river below, white face above, gray rock, red rock, yellow sky. One by one the elements came up and only gradually fell into place as a total composition, making one more aware of the architecture. "This additive process," Wilson said, "is more surrealistic" (*WWDA*). During the *Doktor Faustus* workshop, the director felt the death of Echo looked too realistic. "But with lights, I'll make the whole scene strange. Death must be mysterious," he contended (see figure 42). "My fear," he brooded during the *When We Dead Awaken* workshop, "is that this set is too conventional, too naturalistic. But so much depends on light. I'll make it strange with

42 *Doktor Faustus*. Death, like life, is strange. Death passes like a dream, and the little life of Echo is "rounded with a sleep." Visually, the child in the swing draws the eye upwards. Symbolically, he represents Echo's shadow self.

the lights. *Orlando* ran for two hours, and with the light I changed the sense of space very slowly. It made it all mysterious."

In addition to carving out, then melting space, lights in Wilson also dissolve the real world through unnatural color, as the strange reds, pinks, and oranges disintegrated the well-known contours of Marilyn Monroe's face in Warhol, making the real surreal.[14] The fool in *King Lear*, bathed in an unearthly green spot, seemed more a figment of Lear's feverish brain than flesh and bone. A red spot trained on a red rock in *When We Dead Awaken* turned it into a magical gem, glowing like a rich ruby in Buddha's golden forehead. After the entrance of the two Irenes in the same act, *terra firma* evaporated as teal blue lights turned the earth into an infernal ocean. In *Quartet* Wilson used lights to project spooky shadows across a gauze (see figure 43). The high contrast lighting in *The Golden Windows*, reminiscent of Expressionist movies, created an unreal, nightmare world inhabited not by people but by memories and ghosts. In *When We Dead Awaken*, during the train sequence, Wilson lit the actors' faces from below to make them look "eerie." In Wilson the light of common day goes out, revealing the glory and freshness of dream.

Bizarre behavior – dreams and insanity are next of kin – also helps install the dream state. Dreams, Freud insists, are most profound when they seem most crazy (480). In the train scene from *Death Destruction & Detroit II* (act I, scene ii) (see figure 44), a man, toting a respectable umbrella and suitcase, strolls into a compartment, opens an invisible window, sits down, takes off his beard, stuffs it into his hat. Puts hat back on, attaches large, Dumbo ears over his own. Looks at a man sitting across from him and jumps into his lap. The stranger embraces him, and the two men open their suitcases and dump their clothes on the floor. On a Wilson stage, people break the norm. During the final chorus of *Flute*, which celebrates the union of Pamina and Tamino, Sarastro, the solemn priest of Isis and Osiris, tugs a long red ribbon out of his mouth and wanders distractedly among the joyous celebrants like an inebriated lizard. Suddenly, his ability to govern the Temple of Wisdom comes into doubt, and we wonder who the villain of the opera really is – the Queen of the Night or Sarastro? The libretto is a ragout of contradictions, which most productions varnish over. By problematizing the end, Wilson's staging turned the received interpretation of Mozart's opera on its head.

The director has always had a penchant for the bizarre. "I like *When We Dead Awaken*," Wilson noted, "because everybody in the play is crazy." Consequently, they do strange things. Ulfheim balances a champagne glass on Maya's head. Maya falls into and out of trances. In act III, after a

43 In *Quartet* Wilson used shadows to create a climate of menace and
for psychological doubling. When Merteuil saw her shadow, she
screamed, exposing self-loathing. Young Man (Scott Rabinowitz),
Valmont (Bill Moor), the Marquise de Merteuil (Lucinda Childs).
American Repertory Theatre.

violent, hysterical outburst, she switches abruptly, comically, to a matter-
of-fact, grocery-list voice. Maya's labile mood swings show that Irene is
not the only character in the play with a split personality. The two Irenes
paw the air with strange, cat-like gestures. When one speaks, the other
mouths her words. Quirky, autistic gestures – unmotivated,
decontextualized; slow, formalized movements (at times we do not see
actors move, they float invisibly from one place to another as if in a
trance); walking, crawling, hopping backwards; tics repeated obsessively
– all these strange behavioral patterns lift Wilson's work away from
humdrum reality.

   Much of the behavior seen on a Wilson stage exhibits symptoms psychologists associate with schizophrenia: dissociation and dissonance. The
former leads to a separation of mental processes, a splitting off of mental

44 *Death Destruction & Detroit II.* When strangers on a train meet in a Wilson production, aberrant behavior heightens the enigma. The director suspends rational motivation and the rules that govern normal social intercourse. Note how Wilson turns the back into a powerful emblem of mystery.

components, and often results in hysteria. The latter – a disharmony between speech and affect – characterizes Wilson's approach to dialog. In rehearsal the actress playing the white Irene read the following line like Lady Macbeth, in an obvious dragon-lady voice: "I killed my children. I murdered them ruthlessly." "Smile when you say that line, and let me hear the echo of laughter in your voice," the director said. "It will be more terrifying." Wilson's use of deviant behavior, which many would characterize as insane, enables the director to enlarge our perceptions and challenge fundamental assumptions. Madness can lead to insight. Lear's insanity, for instance, is the avenue to his "self-discovery and his new awareness of suffering and injustice in society."[15] Dramatizing insanity also undermines a fixed concept of reality.

Another strategy Wilson uses to create mystery is to have actors turn their backs to the audience. We automatically look to the face and the eyes as windows of the soul. When these are veiled or averted, an aura of mystery shrouds the figure. The audience rarely saw the face of the

woman in black in *The Golden Windows*. At the entrance to his retrospective exhibit at the Museum of Fine Arts in Boston, Wilson placed a
Victorian statue of Medea with her face to the wall. "I love the back,"
Wilson confesses. "It's as expressive as the face and so mysterious. Make
your back very straight. Feel all the energy in your back. Make your back
very alive" (*Quartet*).

One of the most important ploys Wilson uses to transport us to dreamland is abstraction, which again distances his productions from naturalism, making them both more formal and more bizarre. *The Magic Flute*
typifies Wilson's mature style: abstract, geometric, minimal. Realistic
theatre tries to create the illusion of a slice of life. The fourth wall of a
room dissolves, and the audience – turned into voyeurs – eavesdrops on
a domestic melodrama. The typical set for *Long Day's Journey into Night*
tries to look like a turn-of-the-century summer home in Connecticut. "All
theatre," Wilson asserts, "is artificial. It's never natural. We must accept
the fact." Consequently, a Wilson production never pretends it is a
middle-class American living room. It never pretends it is anything
except a stage, an artificial space. Mozart's *Magic Flute* takes place in
Egypt. Most directors would lug a pyramid or two on stage to represent
the land of the pharaohs. Not Wilson. In his Paris production of this
Masonic opera, a giant vertical line, a square, and a triangle – burning
with pure white incandescence against an azure backdrop – overpowered the spectator with mysterious beauty (see figure 45). Wilson's
stage explores line and color; it does not try to be a documentary photograph. Hence, in the opening scene, the mountain cliff was abstracted to a
blue rectangle set diagonally against yellow sky and chartreuse earth; the
dragon, a swath of red silk, slinking out round the rock. In most *Magic
Flute* productions, the dragon looks like a stuffed animal pilfered from a
nursery. In contrast, Wilson uses visual synecdoche: the red cloth stands
for the dragon's tongue, which stands for the entire dragon.

Thus the river in *When We Dead Awaken* became a ribbon of bright blue
fluorescent light, cutting the stage diagonally; the hotel, three strips of
green fluorescent bars, running on parallel horizontals; the avalanche, a
white gauze drop falling slowly. The citadel in *Lohengrin* was signified by
an apotheosis of T-squares; the guillotine in *Danton's Death*, by a large
wooden square into which the victims slowly sank, forlorn jacks-in-the-
box. "The real guillotine," Wilson noted, "is the white carpet that unrolls
on the floor with the speed of lightning." The cliffs of Dover in *King Lear*
were represented by the outline of a white triangle projected on the floor.
During the discomfiture of the Queen of the Night in *The Magic Flute* rows
of vertical fluorescent lights fell down from on high, driving the Queen,

45 In Wilson's *The Magic Flute*, primary geometric forms signify Egypt.

her attendants, and Monostatos into the ground. It was as if the sky had caved in on them. The forest in *The Forest* became a series of tall black verticals; the nineteenth-century factory, a minimalist grid of horizontals and verticals – a steel cage to trap workers (see figure 46).

This movement towards abstraction disturbed the composer of *Doktor Faustus*, who complained to the director that the first scene of his opera had become so abstract in the staging that no one would know it was a bordello. "You can be in a bordello with your text and your music," Wilson retorted. "But I don't have to be in a bordello visually."

Abstractionism is the great triumph of twentieth-century art. Although stage design usually follows the trail blazed by great painters,[16] abstractionism has not flourished on stage because it is difficult to translate into theatrical terms, and audiences cling nostalgically to Wedgewood tea cups and over-upholstered sofas. It takes the visual acuity of a Wilson linked with his theatrical flair to make abstractionism work, and one of his strongest influences on current theatre is the trend toward greater symbolic abstraction in stage design.

Improbable settings also bewitch us in Wilson. Act I of *When We Dead*

46 *The Forest*. In Wilson's abstract vision of a nineteenth-century
sweatshop – seen as a prison – the director's love affair with verticals
and horizontals reached a paroxysm.

Awaken – in Ibsen a realistic spa with aspidistra in the lobby – became a
surrealistic moonscape. A towering mountain of black lava tumbled diagonally into the sea against a poison green sky. Small lunar craters dotted
the arid earth like small pox. Against this malevolent background, not
Ibsen's comforting bourgeois opulence, Rubeck and Maya spewed forth
their marital venom. Act III of *The Life and Times of Joseph Stalin* took place
in a mystico-Platonic-Freudian-subconscious cave, that, like all good
surrealist images, transcended dichotomies.[17] The wonders of *Deafman
Glance* transpired in a magical, Douanier Rousseauesque forest. The
sexual wars of *Quartet* exploded on triangles of shifting, shimmering
light – orange and blue, violet and red; Müller's stage directions indicate
a "drawing room before the French Revolution. Air raid shelter after
World War III." The last scene of *The Golden Windows* played itself out in
the jaws of an earthquake. Episodes from *the CIVILwarS* unfolded on the

47 *Death Destruction & Detroit II*. Kafka broke one pencil after another –
a neurotic tic of aggression perpetrated against the instrument of
creation.

bottom of the ocean. King Lear confronted madness and stumbled across
his humanity in a labyrinth of industrial walls. Many and marvellous are
the Emerald Cities Wilson has built.

Another tactic Wilson uses to cast his spell is repetition. Since visual
repetition happens rarely in reality, it transports us to another realm.
Death Destruction & Detroit II opened with a woman in a man's suit
(Kafka), seated with her back to the audience. Obsessively, she held out
her hand, broke a pencil, put her fist into the air (see figure 47). This ritual
was repeated until a huge pile of pencils formed a pyramid on the floor.
Any writer will identify with this aggression perpetrated against the
instrument of writing, the instrument of torture. In *The Life and Times of
Joseph Stalin* twenty ostriches cavorted across the stage; eighty black
women waltzed to the "Blue Danube." In *Deafman Glance* eight gorillas
held eight red apples that flew up into the sky. In *Einstein on the Beach*
everyone wore the same deadpan pants and sneakers. In *the CIVILwarS*
eight black scribes strolled round Frederick the Great's deathbed, record-

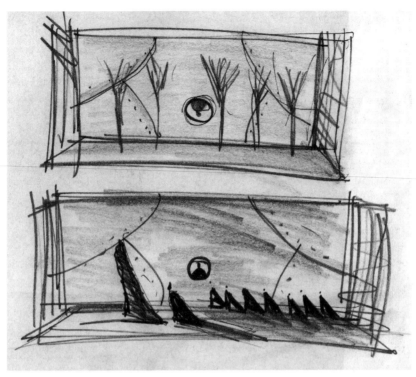

48 Wilson's early drawing for the gospel chorus in the Rome Section of
the CIVILwarS, showing how the director structured the scene visually
by repeating triangles. In the background, Robert E. Lee tumbles
around the port hole of a submarine. In a note to the gospel singers,
Wilson said that the chorus should be "noble" and "uplifting."

ing history in the air. In *The Forest* fifteen hooded pilgrims formed a
funeral cortege, heads bowed. In *When We Dead Awaken* seven women
sported the same Victorian gown, faces veiled in the same mysterious
clouds of gray tulle. "Let's put all the women in the same dress," Wilson
said. "It's stranger and more interesting" (*WWDA*): more interesting
because it deviates from what we see around us in the banal, sublunar
world we inhabit. Repetition, one of the primary devices of minimalism,
also became magical in the hands of Andy Warhol. With his endless series
of coke bottles and soup cans and Brillo boxes, he showed that by simple
repetition, an object, no matter how trite, acquires miraculous power (see
figure 48).

By playing with scale, Wilson also beguiles. The World's Tallest
Woman with dwarf in hand (*the CIVILwarS*). Big turtle, little turtles

(*Deafman Glance*). The doctor's clinic with a backdoor for a giant, a front door for a midget (*Doktor Faustus*). Colossal cat paws – floor to ceiling – stalking across the stage (*The King of Spain*). A monstrous white rat glaring at the audience with beady red eyes (*Death Destruction & Detroit II*). The giant light bulb in *Death Destruction & Detroit*, burning forever with a soft, blue glow. Gargantuan silver spoons – big enough to placate any gourmand – in *Death Destruction & Detroit II*. A sapphire-blue dress trailing half way across the stage (*The Forest*). Abe Lincoln built like a sky-scraper (*the CIVILwarS*). The tiny, burnished-copper door, scaled for Tinkerbell (*Orlando*). By baffling our expectations about size, Wilson creates a never-never land.

Magic objects play an important part in fairy tales, legends, and myths.[18] Wilson also uses mysterious or invisible objects to enchant. "When Maya comes back in," the director said, "she must be holding a strange object in her hand" (*WWDA*). The strange object became a *Star Trek*, intergalactic control box – black with a burning blue button. When Maya pushed the button at odd moments, the box emitted a menacing growl. Irene held a glass of milk illuminated with a green light that disappeared mysteriously into the ground. "Take the glass and look into it as if it were a deep well down to the center of the earth," Wilson directed. "In it you see ghosts from your entire life" (*WWDA*). The fool in *King Lear* carried a tiny chair in his hand, so small the audience had no idea what it was, but thanks to the way the fool fondled it, it became a magic talisman. Wilson gave Goneril a white handkerchief, and after her fight with Albany, he had her spread it on the ground (act IV, scene ii). "The hand-kerchief becomes a little stage. On it you see the action of the entire play unfolding. The tiny stage then becomes an enormous space. You see your husband as a tiny ant you squash with your thumb." Standing on his head, Danton peered into a golden globe embedded in a green couch. In its burnished luster he read his dark fate (*Danton's Death*).

In addition to magical objects, Wilson also uses invisible ones. The director told Edgar, when he entered the blasted heath, to go to the middle of the room, look up, circle round an invisible tree, and inspect it closely. The audience had no clue as to what motivated the perusal of intangible shapes, but it created the atmosphere of a strange, new space Edgar had wandered into. Gloucester stumbled over an invisible rock; the fool stared at invisible geese flying overhead (*King Lear*). When the waitress serves Rubek in *When We Dead Awaken*, the director told him to see on the tray, not caviar and champagne, but a rattlesnake. In the last act Rubek and the two Irenes catch invisible snowflakes and gaze at them while Ulfheim scratches his head in disbelief. "Imagine a snowflake that's falling," Wilson said, "and follow it gently with your hand. You catch it with the tip of the finger and examine it. In it you see a world. Ulfheim knows an avalanche is coming and can't figure out what you're dreaming about." Actors in Wilson see things hidden from the audience. Since the motivation for much of their behavior is veiled, the shadow of mystery falls over it.

Objects in Wilson have an obstinate will of their own. The chairs in *When We Dead Awaken* move to and fro, mysteriously, with their own power and volition. "I want to see the chairs move by themselves on a horizontal plane," the director said during the design workshop. "It makes it more surreal and dreamy." A demonic energy seems to propel many Wilson objects: the descending chair in *The King of Spain*, twirling slowly; the glass coffins darting through space in *Einstein on the Beach*; the door to the little hut creaking open in *The Golden Windows*; the Corinthian columns transforming into smoke stacks in *Alcestis*; the shoe floating miraculously on the river in *When We Dead Awaken*; the strange, white circle gliding through the air in *The Forest*; the crystal pyramid looming up from the ground in *the CIVILwarS*; the Golem suit in *Death Destruction & Detroit II*, breathing life as if touched by the hand of God – or the devil (see figure 49).

Inanimate objects in Wilson lead a hidden life. Objects have secrets; they ward off all attempts to explain them away. We look at them, we use them, but we do not understand them. They contemplate a riddle we cannot penetrate. They escape our control, they refuse to let us anthropomorphize them. In Sartre, Roquentin's waves of nausea erupt from his confrontation with the inscrutability of objects: "Objects are not made for us to touch. It's better to slip through them, avoiding them as much as possible. I exist, the world exists."[19] Paradoxically, objects in Wilsonland serve two diametrically opposed functions. On the one hand, they help create the inner dreamscape. On the other, as Roquentin discovered, they convince us that the exterior world – the world of palpable, tangible objects – also exists, awesome in its indifference and alienation (one of the lessons of Minimalism). In Wilson one must see with an exterior as well as interior screen.

Dreams, Freud points out, have a great fondness for animal figures (65). So does Wilson. Animals, after all, do not talk. Animals – often fantastical – seduce us into sharing his vision. A frog tippling martinis in *Deafman Glance*. An elephant lolling on the roof in *Stations*. Snow owls (*the CIVILwarS*) and snow monkeys (*Le Martyre de Saint Sébastien*). Dinosaurs (*Death Destruction & Detroit*). A crocodile king and a goat god (*Alcestis*). Twenty giraffes (*the CIVILwarS*). A sacred ox, gorillas, ostriches, turtles

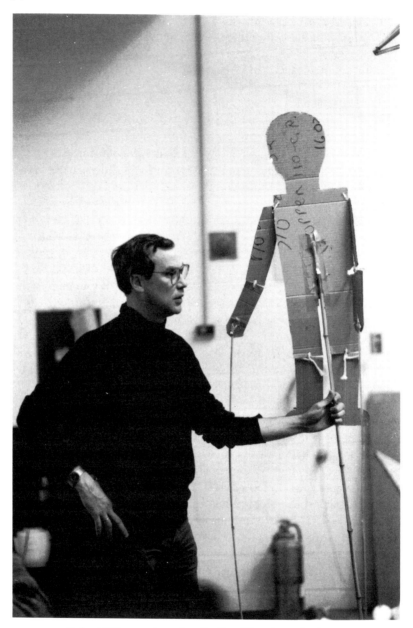

49 Robert Wilson, rehearsing *the Knee Plays* from *the CIVILwarS: a tree is best measured when it is down*. The main performer, a humanoid puppet, acquired superhuman vitality. Wilson with a mock up at the Guthrie Theater.

(*The Life and Times of Joseph Stalin*). Golden fish swimming in a copper tank (*Quartet*). Bears tripping the light fantastic, an eagle soaring into the sky, a carousel horse for the king (*the CIVILwarS*). Penguins toddling through the snow (*I was sitting on my patio*). The ubiquitous raven on the ubiquitous Byrdwoman. The god of death looking like a sinister white moth (*Alcestis*). The list goes on and on and on; outside Barnum and Bailey, Wilson keeps the largest menagerie in show business.

In contrast to figures of fantasy, Wilson also juxtaposes two real objects that do not normally go together to create unexpected, surrealist images: Lautréamont's "accidental meeting of an umbrella and a sewing machine on a dissection table." These visual intersections ignite sparks of poetry that illuminate both objects with a strange, new glow. We see both with new eyes. Wilson calls it his computer-on-a-baroque-table theory. By placing a piece of technological hardware on an antique, one sees each more clearly. In *Alceste* a sleek modern ladder, shining with pristine aluminum purity, rises up from the floor diagonally, pointing to the archaic Greek statue of Apollo. In *Alcestis* Japanese coolies, stooped over in backbreaking labor, gather rice in a field adorned with three Corinthian columns. Later, a fey Edwardian butler, in tails and ascot, dallies with Hercules, draped in lion skins. In *Quartet*, the Marquise de Merteuil, a French aristocrat, speaks with a Texas drawl and packs a Colt 45 round her waist. In *the CIVILwarS* Timon of Athens, aloft, spouts his misanthropy in iambic pentameters while below a rollypolly fatso, samurai sword in hand, boogiewoogies to David Byrne's *The Catherine Wheel*. In *Death Destruction & Detroit II* an elegant blonde woman in red evening gown stumbles into a magical forest and lies down next to a black panther, eyes burning bright like amber coals in the dark. She takes out a wooden puppet and plays with it. A man enters. His hand falls off. He picks it up and screws it back into his arm. A medieval knight appears. In Wilson's forest of the night one hears the silence and sees the invisible (see figure 50).

One of the major devices Wilson uses to create a strange, haunted atmosphere is sound. Auditory images figure prominently in dreams,[20] and the director uses them to conjure the dream state. Wilson, who integrates sound into his pieces as a major component, works frequently with Hans-Peter Kuhn, the leading sound artist in Europe. Of all his collaborators, Kuhn has exercised the most significant influence on Wilson,[21] and the two have radically altered the relationship between sound and image in theatre. Many spectators find the soundscapes Wilson and Kuhn build disorienting. Bizarre noises startle and disturb. Actors may be speaking on stage and standing stock-still, but the sound of their voices jumps

50 *Death Destruction & Detroit II*. Strange bedfellows in Wilson's magic forest of the night: a Medieval knight, a blond woman in red evening gown playing with a puppet, a black panther at large, an old man locked up in a steel cage – these unwonted juxtapositions prick the imagination.

around erratically from location to location in the house. Language dissolves into noise. The sense of acoustical space keeps shifting. One soon feels lost, drifting on a sea of sound. Organizing the auditory information flooding our senses suddenly becomes problematic. As always, Wilson's theatre asks, how do we see? How do we hear? How do we make sense of what we perceive?

Kuhn discloses that he wants to make audiences more sensitive to sounds in themselves:

My goal is not to disorient the audience. I want to wake people up who spend their lives sleepwalking in a perceptual fog. Sound is a miracle. Sound is a beautiful experience, one of the fundamental human experiences. The sound of language carries more meaning than its content. The voice is our most sensitive organ of expression. It communicates much more than words. I'm interested in language as *musique concrète*. I want to make people aware of what the ear tells us.[22]

And what the ear tells us in a Wilson work is complex. "The ear is closely affiliated with man's emotional life . . . Auditory space has the capacity to elicit the gamut of emotions from us, from the marching song to opera. It can be filled with sound that has no "object," such as the eye demands."[23] Since sound, bypassing logic, works directly and potently on the emotions and since sound can be absolutely concrete – dis-associated from representation and meaning – it becomes a formidable tool in the hands of Wilson to create an alternative theatrical space, a space that forges a new relation between sound and image.

To explore the experience of sound, Kuhn builds his acoustical archi-tecture like a symphony. Working with found sounds – he travels with a library of nearly 2,000 sound effects – he likes to take sound out of its original context and yoke together two sounds that, in nature, never sing a duet. "Discordant sounds" Kuhn calls them. Thus, for the entrance of the two Irenes in *When We Dead Awaken*, he juxtaposed the sound of a spoon squeaking against a coffee cup and the heaving of a pneumatic pump recorded in the bowls of a coal mine in the *Ruhrgebiet*. This mix created a strange sonic atmosphere – beautiful, but unsettling because one did not know what the noises were; they seemed to emanate from a tomb, a ghost-like *ostinato* for the appearance of a woman who claims she is dead. "I love industrial sounds," Kuhn says, "and that big pneumatic pump was weird. When it exhaled, it sounded like a wounded animal. It gave me the sound I needed – powerful, mysterious, dangerous."

The ambient sound environment in Wilson is complicated. For *When We Dead Awaken*, Wilson and Kuhn used three reel-to-reel tape decks, a computer sampler, a computer sequencer, six body mikes (that change the quality and source of the actor's voice), two special-effects decks, one on-stage mike (for weird off-stage voices), a live guitarist to accompany Honni Coles's vaudeville songs, and twenty-one speakers scattered throughout the house to bombard the audience with sound from many different locations. There were 168 different sound cues; 75 percent of the time three or four different things happened on each cue.

The sound log page for Maya's dream sequence shows how compli-cated the soundscape can become. The text was spoken by eight women on stage simultaneously with eight different recorded tracks – each reading the same line differently. Wilson told the women in the chorus "each voice must be distinct and clear, but when they blend together the language must shine like rubies and emeralds, sapphires and diamonds in a king's treasure chest." Some of the different qualities he wanted included: a high nasal, like a cat; an exorcist with heavy inhalations; a staccato, mid-range monotone, breaking the words into discrete syllables; a high ghost-like whisper; a speech impediment; a cold, dispassionate voice; someone speaking only the consonants; someone speaking only the vowels. Wilson read the passages in the various voices he wanted, and the actresses imitated him. The recorded voices hit the audience from all over the theatre, surrounding the ear with a constantly shifting sense of acoustical space.

Special effects during this scene included the sound of breaking glass, three different sounds of crystal being struck, the squeaking spoon, and the low droning sound of a string bass. Dealing with many different layers of acoustical perception, the ear was both stimulated and perplexed. "I'm not interested in the obvious," Kuhn confesses. Neither is Wilson, and their collaboration has led to the most innovative, complex, and beautiful use of sound in contemporary theatre, creating a magical soundscape that bewitches and bewilders.

Maribeth Bank, former sound designer of the American Repertory Theatre, points out that:

The Wilson-Kuhn collaboration is amazing. They're pioneers. Most theatre people haven't figured out how to use sound creatively. For the past seven years new technological capabilities – for example digital-audio samplers and sequencers – have permitted more sophisticated control over sound information. But most directors are stuck in traditional ruts. They think of sound as dropping a needle on a record. They use sound as movies use sound. When the scene is sad, you play sad music or, for ironic contrast, cheerful music. Wilson and Kuhn do not use sound in such a banal, programmatic way. Wilson and Kuhn have liberated sound, finding new ways to use it theatrically.[24]

One of the new ways that Wilson and Kuhn use sound is to create an acoustical space that can displace and subvert not only the image, but also the speaking subject. Barthes's theory of the grain of the voice helps explain what Wilson is up to. For Barthes, the grain of the voice is, "a site where language works *for nothing*."[25] It is related to his theory of *writing aloud*:

Writing aloud is not expressive; it leaves expression to the . . . regular code of communication . . . it is carried not by dramatic inflections, subtle stresses, sympathetic accents, but by the *grain* of the voice, which is an erotic mixture of timbre and language . . . its aim is not the clarity of messages, the theatre of emotions; what it searches for [is] . . . language lined with flesh, a text where we can hear the grain of the throat, the patina of consonants, the voluptuousness of vowels, a whole carnal stereophony: the articulation of the body, of the tongue, not that of meaning . . . This vocal writing . . . make[s] us hear in their materiality, their sensuality, the breath, the gutturals, the fleshiness of the lips, a whole presence of the human muzzle (that the voice, that writing, be as fresh, supple, lubricated, delicately granular and vibrant as an animal's muzzle), to succeed in shifting the signified a great distance and in throwing, so to speak, the anonymous body of the actor into my ear; it granulates, it crackles, it caresses, it grates, it cuts, it comes: that is bliss.[26]

In Wilson and Kuhn's soundscapes (*the CIVILwarS, Alcestis, The Golden Windows, When We Dead Awaken* are prime examples), the mix of live and recorded voices, bombarding the ear from all quarters, gives the voice a strange autonomy. The voice no longer represents a character, no longer utters a speaking subject. The speaking voice is simply and beautifully a voice speaking. The conventional relationship between person and voice, actor and voice, and voice and audience breaks down. The voices are not speaking to us. They are not speaking to each other. They are simply speaking, unaware that anyone is listening. We seem to be eavesdropping on someone else's half-forgotten dream. Who is speaking? We do not know who these voices are. They have sound, but no identity. Coming from afar, the voices echo and re-echo like memory drifting up from the subconscious. What we hear disrupts what we see, widening the gap between sound and image. Realistic dialog anchors us to a prosaic, commonsense world. These anonymous, autonomous voices turn our sense of reality on its head. We lose our moorings, and the tide carries us out on an open sea of sound. Leaving meaning behind on the shore, sound becomes pure pleasure, pure enchantment, what Barthes calls "bliss."

Artaud exhorted directors to become "managers of magic."[27] Wilson has answered the call, but the dream-vision in Wilson does not turn its back on "reality." Rather, it exists in a dialectic with it. In his notes for *Death Destruction & Detroit II*, Wilson jotted down: "Contrast between fantastical images and things very real. Some elements bizarre and unreal. Others like photographs" (11 September 1985). This contrast between the high "fantastical" and the "very real" informs Wilson's vision. Thus, in *Doktor Faustus* when the child Echo dies in one corner of the stage – a dream sequence with a beautiful angel of death – in another corner Frau Schweigestill stands at a counter in the kitchen, chopping carrots and celery with crisp efficiency. During Maya's dream in *When We Dead Awaken*, a waitress enters with a tray of food. The staccato beat of her utilitarian steps sets off the bizarre gestures and floating movements of the seven identical women who peregrinate across the stage, murmuring Maya's thoughts.

Wilson layers different zones of reality against each other. The dialectic he sets in motion between realism and fantasy is not innocent: it violates our assumptions about how the universe works. A flight into pure fantasy does not threaten as much as a juxtaposition of the familiar and the unfamiliar. By juxtaposing the real and the bizarre, the normal and the abnormal, Wilson creates tension. By confronting the audience with discordant realities taking place simultaneously, he dramatizes how we mobilize subjective interpretations to fabricate our sense of reality. The reassuring, mechanical universe invented by Newton and governed by rational laws gives way to a revelation of mystery.

Realism as an artistic category depends on vraisemblance, the precise and "objective" duplication of the everyday world. Realism, dominant for nearly one hundred and fifty years, mirrors perfectly the world view of the petty bourgeois. It reinforces the positivistic values of the dominating class by its celebration of the material world, its belief in cause and effect, its depiction of a world "capable of scientific explanation".[28]

Building on van Gennep's notion of liminality in *rites de passage*, Victor Turner has elaborated a theory of the liminoid. According to van Gennep, the liminal is a transitional realm of the betwixt and between.[29] During this threshold period the cultural order is inverted; the bizarre becomes normal. By making the familiar strange and the strange familiar, this liminal phase contains the seeds of social change and cultural creativity. For Turner, the liminoid represents spaces on the margins of post-industrial societies where individual creative activity can question cherished values and play with the possibilities of form and meaning to liberate human potential. Like ritual, the liminoid transforms. It spreads the seeds of change. It also provides a metacommentary that enables society to understand itself: "We have to go into the subjunctive world of monsters, demons, and clowns, of cruelty and poetry, in order to make sense of our . . . lives."[30] Wilson's theatre is both liminal and liminoid.

Wilson's theatre derives from the wisdom of the irrational. By juxtaposing different and dissonant realities, Wilson estranges the familiar world, dislocates our sense of reality, and dramatizes the inability of reason to encompass or explain human experience. By trespassing the border between the real and the surreal, between male and female, between normal and abnormal, between meaning and absurdity, Wilson's productions provoke anxiety. The binary oppositions that structure our sense of reality crumble. Old certainties dissolve. The world "ceases to be reliable."[31] We lose our sense of control. The earth cracks, and underneath the predictable order of daily life, the abyss grins. As Poe warned us, at the heart of the universe dwells an imp of the perverse.

Wilson's theatre makes many spectators twist, squirm, and itch in their seats. During performances of *Quartet*, which probes with sang-froid the destructive energy released by love and the social construction of gender identity, half the audience would sometimes leave. Wilson's world unsettles. His theatre interrogates, destabilizes, subverts. It calls reason and reality into question. It challenges how our culture establishes meaning[32] and value. It explodes the structural frame of officially promulgated pieties. Wilson denies political intent.[33] But by radically questioning social norms and by disrupting cultural assumptions, his theatre resonates with social and political implications. Wilson's world is magic, but social revolt and metaphysical anguish tinge that magic.

6 The valley of the shadow: trauma and transcendence

> The loud lament of the disconsolate chimera.
>
> T. S. Eliot, *Burnt Norton*

In Wilson, life is trauma. Existence poses itself as a problem. The major existential preoccupations – the absurd, alienation, anxiety, loneliness, and a confrontation with death – roll through his theatre like a drum beat. The train insert in *When We Dead Awaken* shows how Wilson dramatizes these concerns. Ibsen's plays are among the first to reveal the influence of Kierkegaard, and Wilson steeped this scene in existential angst:

Although absolutely nothing happened, I knew that we had crossed the border, that we were really home again because it stopped at every little station. No one got off and no one got on, but the train stood there, silently, for what seemed like hours. At every station I heard two railmen walking along the platform – one of them carrying a lantern – and they mumbled quietly to each other in the night, without expression or meaning. There are always two men talking about nothing at all.[1]

In *When We Dead Awaken*, this reminiscence of returning to one's native soil occurs casually in realistic dialog between an aging husband and his spry wife. Ibsen's existential irony is twofold; his sense of alienation, physical and metaphysical. Coming home, the couple discover they have no home. Strangers abroad, strangers at home. Exiled on earth, they continue to search for what the universe will not give them: meaning, clarity, unity. According to Camus, our yearning for meaning and the absence of it leads to a discovery of the absurd. Uprooted, the couple feel ill at ease in their home and in their skin. A train held in the dark, language without meaning, a deep-seated sense of loneliness – this passage, one of the most haunting Ibsen wrote, reads like a scene from Ingmar Bergman's movie *The Silence*.

By turning Ibsen's dialog into monolog, Wilson deepens the malaise. In Wilson, the world becomes, to use Camus's words, "dense and strange." Wilson relocates the train text between Maya's question, "Are you saying I'm the one who's changed?" and Rubek's answer, "Yes, I am. The others back here too. And not for the better."[2] Between question and answer falls the shadow of Wilson's bizarre insert in which he dramatizes Ibsen's retrospective narration. The stage darkens. Man and wife walk stage front and face each other, but, sitting in different planes, are oblivious to the other's presence. Only in love does one feel truly alone. All we can make out are the heads of Maya and Rubek, lit with tight spots and eerie lights from below. Detached from the body, the faces float in space. A mechanical noise pierces the silence. Slowly, sadly, a faraway voice whistles a song. A disembodied voice-over – a tape of Rubek's voice – reflects rather than projects the train text, like an interior monolog. An elegant man, sporting morning coat and walking cane, ambles on, looks at the couple, ambles off. No contact made. The voice of the live actor repeats the last phrase of the tape: "at all," emphasizing the sense of futility, the collapse of communication, the mood of alienation. "There are always two men talking about nothing *at all.*" Rubek gets up, disappears into the darkness upstage. Maya pulls her hair, raises her palm over her nose as if to claw it. The spidery shadows of her fingers form a black tarantula across her face. She rejoins Rubek. Lights up. After this glimpse into the abyss, the naturalistic, cup-and-saucer dialog resumes as husband and wife fall again into the battle of holy matrimony.

Dialog turned into monolog – a characteristic feature of Wilson – drenches the stage with loneliness. In *King Lear* act I, scene iii – the scene between Goneril and Oswald – Wilson removed the steward from the scene and had Goneril, literally, talking to herself, This made her seem not only lonely, but also deranged. "In the end," Nietzsche sighed, "one experiences only oneself." In Wilson, as in all existential artists, loneliness is a given of human existence. During the rehearsals of *When We Dead Awaken*, Wilson asked Kuhn for some music in act II, when Maya confronts the debris of her marriage. The next day Kuhn brought in his rendition of a melancholic Swedish folksong, played so slowly that the shape of the melody almost disintegrated. "That music is beautiful," Wilson responded, "it's so lonely. It's perfect." And commenting on the last knee play, "Love's the Doggonest Feeling," Wilson asked Sheryl Sutton, who had her back to the singer Honni Coles, to leave the stage. "At the end of the song, it's better if you're all alone, sitting on the edge of the bed, singing to yourself. I'll stream blue moonlight through the window so it will all be sad and lonely and beautiful."

To dramatize loneliness, Wilson unfurls many devices. The breakdown of language, dialog, and, consequently, communication (analyzed in chapter 2) leads, inevitably, to an acute sense of loneliness. "Loneliness is caused not by being alone but by being without some definite needed relationship or set of relationships."[3] Wilson intensifies this mood of

loneliness by seldom letting actors interrelate: each inhabits a solipsistic –
some would say autistic – cocoon. Wilson creates this cutting stab of loneliness by not letting the actors look at each other, touch each other, speak
to each other. And often by putting enormous space between actors
supposedly engaged in dialog. This distancing violates our sense of
social space. "Spatial changes give a tone to a communication, accent it,
and at times even override the spoken word. The flow and shift of distance between people as they interact with each other is part and parcel of
the communication process. The normal conversational distance between
strangers illustrates how important are the dynamics of space interaction."[4] Thus Lear in act I, scene iv stood on one side of a large stage while
Goneril, whom he berated, stood on the other. In act II, scene iv, Wilson
directed Lear to turn his back to Gloucester and look far off into the
auditorium when speaking to him. "Let the audience figure out you're
talking to him," the director explained. In act II, scene ii, when Gloucester
finds the self-wounded Edmund, he instructed the father not to look at
the son: "Don't look at Edmund when you're talking to him. Look at the
palm of your hand. Examine it intently. In it you can read the entire
history of the world. Don't relate to Edmund, especially when you're
talking to him. Keep reading the palm of your hand." Since it goes against
the grain – most people instinctively relate to whomever they're speaking
to – actors must rehearse this alienated style diligently.

In act II of *When We Dead Awaken*, Wilson asked the two Irenes to enter
from opposite corners, running on a diagonal towards each other to stage
center. When they were approximately five feet apart, Wilson ordered
them to stop abruptly. "The audience will expect you to meet. It creates
more tension if you don't make contact." Not letting actors touch rendered the tragedy of Lohengrin and Elsa much more poignant. They
came close, but not once – not even on their wedding night – did they
have the consolation of touch (see figure 51). Wilson also etches the stage
with loneliness by leaving the main character alone and quiet after
moments of great intensity – Lear after the division of the kingdom, like a
tiny, frail bird dwarfed by that vast expanse of empty space, recently
teeming with the pomp and circumstance of court; Rubeck at the end of
acts I and II after tense confrontations with Irene. Left suddenly alone,
loneliness embraces him.

Wilson's interior acting style also charges the atmosphere with loneliness. The actors seem not to be projecting their words to the audience, not
to be speaking to each other, but meditating to themselves. "My acting
style," Wilson counseled the actors in *King Lear*, "depends on the time of
interior reflection. On the subway in New York, a blast of noise constantly

51 Even on their wedding night, Elsa (on left, Lucia Popp) and Lohengrin are denied the consolation of touch. The marriage bed was abstracted into a shimmering square of light against which Lohengrin's silhouette (Gösta Winbergh) stands out as an emblem of solitude.

assaults you. You just turn it off. You become deaf. You withdraw into your own dreams. That's how I want you to act in this play. Turn off the exterior world." A world where people talk not to each other, look not at each other, relate not to each other, touch not each other is a world of severed connections. It is a world of psychic terror. "The individual," Kierkegaard writes, "absolutely cannot make himself intelligible to anybody."[5]

Wilson works hard with actors so that they do not pick up each other's speaking rhythms in dialog. By making it non-responsive and non-reactive, the director shreds dialog into monolog, emphasizing the fault lines in communication. The autistic gestures, out of context and seemingly unrelated to the dialog, also sharpen the feeling of alienation. The actors at the Schauspiel, Frankfurt, were so addled by this new acting style that one fine day at rehearsal they put on for the director a comic dance entitled "The No Touch Ballet." Contact between bodies would almost, but not quite, take place, resulting in one pratfall after another. But these devices that isolate the individual render more powerful those rare moments when emotional and/or physical contact is made: Lear and Cordelia in death (see figure 52); Rubek and the two Irenes just before the shroud of snow falls.

52 When Lear (on left, Marianne Hoppe) finally touches his/her daughter Cordelia (on right, Alexandra von Schwerin), the emotion overwhelms.

As auteur director, Wilson will deconstruct the text he is working with to cut the mood of loneliness deeper. Reunited with her husband at the end of Gluck's opera, Alceste drowns the memory of her tribulations with joyful chorus. Most productions stage this happy scene with a banquet in the palace. Hand in hand, Alceste and her husband Admetus, joined by loving children and loyal subjects, raise their voices in harmonious song. What a sea change in Wilson's production! Heracles and Admetus enter the palace, but at the threshold Alceste turns unexpectedly away. The walls close in, blocking her out. The chorus of celebration continues inside, but Alceste has become an outsider. The experience of death has changed her, forever. Her shadow self – a death imprint – enters, and Alceste, cut off from the happy crowd inside, remains alone. In Wilson's production, Alceste has discovered that marriage is a *solitude à deux*. At times Wilson plays against the obvious meaning of a text to see the material from more than one angle. "The music at the end of the opera was a problem for me. It's so joyous. But the myth of Alcestis existed long before Gluck. I wanted to put back into the story the mystery of

Euripides, the mystery of Eleusis. Gluck's end is too closed. I don't like plays that conclude something. Leave the situation open ended so the audience continues to think about it" (*Alcestis*).

Similarly, the mood of Woolf's *Orlando*, shifted. Woolf's novel sprawls with boisterous rogues, elbowing their way through Orlando's life and English history. In Wilson's monodrama, this teeming gallery fades into memory; Orlando is always alone on stage. The novel ends by celebrating two types of community, one public, one private. The first binds a nation together in collective consciousness, the sense of a shared past. The second binds man and woman together in the emotional intimacy of marriage. On the last page, Orlando's husband comes home, like the wild goose, to still the dark imaginings of his wife. At the end of Wilson's play, no one comes to comfort Orlando, who lies motionless on the ground: "The cold breeze of the present brushes my face with its little breath of fear. But I am alone." Wilson's play ends as it began, with the word "alone." Wilson refracted Orlando's happy end through the prism of Woolf's own tragedy.

The sense of loneliness in *Alice* is overwhelming. Wilson's saturnine musical weaves together characters from *Alice in Wonderland* with the biography of Charles Dodgson, who wrote as Lewis Carroll. "What attracted me to *Alice*," says Wilson, "was the personality of Dodgson as mathematician, writer, photographer, cleric, and gentleman of the nineteenth century, an age of propriety and hypocrisy." Wilson's *Alice* is a tragedy of sexual obsession. Dodgson, a pedophile, would feel right at home in this polymorphous-perverse production that features sexual desire as self-laceration, love as mirage, and human beings – lonely and adrift – rushing headlong toward death. *Alice* sounds a disconsolate note. Images of violence, sexual despair, and passing time stud the lyrics of Tom Waits, whose surrealistic songs express the plangent mood of the piece: "Hang me in a bottle like a cat / Let the crows pick me clean but for my hat / Where the wailing of a baby / Meets the footsteps of the dead / We're all mad here."[6] "*Alice*," says Waits in his sandpaper voice, "is a love story, so I wrote romantic songs about snakes in a jar." Dodgson's love for Alice becomes a prison of solitary confinement.

Closely related to this sense of loneliness are Wilson's perambulations in the inner world. Wilson's work – a theatre of introspection – privileges interior mental processes over external events. It is a theatre of mood, not action. The director describes *Orlando* as a "journey in Orlando's mind"; *Quartet* as "a memory in Merteuil's mind"; *When We Dead Awaken* as "Rubek's inner landscape"; *Deafman Glance* as a "fantasy in Raymond's mind"; *Doktor Faustus* as "Esmeralda's dream"; *The Golden Windows* as "a collective nightmare." "I try to dramatize how the mind works," the director says, "and it doesn't work sequentially; it works symphonically" (*Alcestis*). Wilson's theatre, then, tries to render visible and audible this invisible and inaudible symphony of the mind.

Ever since Hegel, western art has drawn further and further inward. We now inhabit a world "in which the relations between within and without, between the truth and the sign, the meaning and the word, have suffered a formidable disturbance."[7] As a result, the thrust of twentieth-century art has been to depict the "play of consciousness."[8] External action evaporates into the flickering shadows of the mind; the subject, not the object, becomes the focus of study. "Examine for a moment an ordinary mind on an ordinary day. The mind receives myriad impressions – trivial, fantastic, evanescent, or engraved with the sharpness of steel. From all sides they come, an incessant shower of innumerable atoms . . . they fall . . . they shape themselves . . . into a luminous halo, a semi-transparent envelope surrounding us from the beginning of consciousness to the end."[9] It is this "luminous halo" that Wilson puts on stage, and in so doing, he enables the theatre to catch up with the novel, which has a much easier time portraying the ebb and flow of consciousness. Wilson explores the margins of theatre, searching the outermost reaches of what drama, as a genre, can do.

Traditionally, theatre has dramatized man imbricated in a social world, what Szondi calls the realm of the "between." The drama creates an artistic reality in which man mirrors "himself on the basis of interpersonal relationships . . . Man entered the drama only as a fellow human being."[10] Theatre enacts, and whereas it is easy to enact the exterior world of dialog, action, and social relations, it is difficult to enact the interior world in which nothing physical transpires. Theatre is a physical medium. How does one physicalize the intangible? Unconscious feelings, unspoken thoughts, inchoate sensations – how does one stage the vortex of the soul? Poetry, novels, music, and abstract art have conquered this territory, and ever since Mallarmé the theatre has grappled with the problem of putting on stage the swirling eddies of the mind, eddies that resist communication through dialog and action – the pillars of theatre. The stream-of-consciousness novel explores "mental and spiritual experience – both the whatness and the howness of it."[11] But how can drama probe and plumb the dark crannies of the inner world? This conundrum has teased playwrights for more than a century. The form of theatre yields reluctantly to this content. How does one make silence speak? In response to this dilemma, Wilson has concocted an arsenal of strategies. Wilson cites Faulkner as an influence, and many of the devices the direc-

tor uses resemble those of stream-of-consciousness novels: free association, images, symbols, discontinuity, formal patterns, and time as duration. Wilson exploits all these techniques to suggest the mysterious
freight of consciousness.

What Maeterlinck dreamed of – an interior theatre of silence that
reveals the secret places of life – Wilson achieves through non-verbal
means.[12] As in the cinema,

> not to speak does not mean that one has nothing to say. Those who do not speak
> may be brimming over with emotions which can be expressed only in forms and
> pictures, in gesture and play of feature. The man of visual culture uses these not as
> substitutes for words . . . The gestures of visual man are not intended to convey
> concepts which can be expressed in words, but such inner experiences, such non-
> rational emotions which would still remain unexpressed when everything that
> can be told has been told. Such emotions lie in the deepest levels of the soul and
> cannot be approached by words that are mere reflections of concepts, just as our
> musical experiences cannot be expressed in rationalized concepts. What appears
> on the face and in facial expression is a spiritual experience which is rendered
> immediately visible without the intermediary of words.[13]

Wilson uses visual devices unavailable to language. Some of these
devices originated in the cinema: montage, time dilation, close-ups, and
microphysiognomy. During rehearsals, Wilson often uses cinematic
terms to describe the effects he wants. When the stage falls dark except
for one tight, bright light on an object (the champagne glass Maya
smashes in *When We Dead Awaken*, for instance), Wilson calls the effect a
close-up, and like a cinematic close-up, this stage device imbues the
object with poetic symbolism – in this case Maya's bubbling rage, her
vulnerability, her simultaneous desire to preserve and destroy her marriage. Similarly, at the end of the train insert, when the bright spot focuses
on Maya's hand clawing her nose, we read in the microdrama of her face,
her anxiety and self-loathing. Since these are unconscious emotions, they
cannot be expressed in language; Wilson uses visual means to speak the
unspoken. By an uncanny fusion of sounds and visual symbols, Wilson
turns the stage into a landscape of the soul.

"Each man," Pascal reminds us, "dies alone." Linked to his acute sense
of loneliness and exploration of consciousness is Wilson's meditation on
death. "All consciousness," Unamuno contends "is consciousness of
death." Greek tragedy began as a cry of outrage against the mystery of
death, and the presence of death hovers over Wilson's work.
Consequently, Wilson is drawn to the Greek legend of Alcestis in which a
wife dies to give her husband the gift of life. Wilson, who has directed both
Euripides' play and Gluck's opera, explains why this story appeals to him:

I like the myth of Alcestis because it's about the poetry of death. I'm not morbidly obsessed by the idea of death in my own life, but death is a thread that runs through all my work. When I started *Life and Times of Sigmund Freud*, I was thinking about the death of Freud's grandson. The death of a child is especially tragic. Freud said "When Heinerle died, something in me passed away for ever." Freud fell into a depression he had never known before. Certain moments of being have great weight. Death is one of those moments. (*Alcestis*)

This meditation on death infuses Wilson's work with a sense of loss.

In *the CIVILwarS* Wilson wrote the following exchange between Mme. Curie and Robert E. Lee: Curie, "In modern society the meaning of death is completely forgotten." Lee, "No, it's not forgotten. Rather, the subject is avoided." In our secular, materialistic world, death provokes an anxiety without consolation; therefore, it is denied. Denied in polite society, but not in Wilson's theatre. The biggest crisis the living have to face is dying; without facing it, life has no meaning. Kübler-Ross observes that contemporary society refuses to face death and that "in our unconscious, death is never possible in regard to ourselves. It is inconceivable for our unconscious to imagine an actual ending of our own life here on earth, and if this life of ours has to end, the ending is always attributed to a malicious intervention from the outside by someone else. In simple terms, in our unconscious mind we can only be killed."[14] The conscious fear of death shrinks from suffering and separation – being wrenched away from those one loves. The unconscious fear of death dreads the unknown evil that blots one out.

The death of Frederick the Great in *the CIVILwarS* bodies forth these concerns (see figure 53). The stage a palpable black. The Black Scribes – those writers whose lamentation we call history – distribute themselves throughout the auditorium, whispering a litany of destruction: Guernica, Auschwitz, El Alamein, Verdun, Dachau. Recumbent against his golden throne, the King sleeps. Eyes closed, lips pinched, face a living death mask. A white hussar enters, marches stiffly to king, snaps heels, stands at attention, bayonet erect. An organ reverberates: low, insistent, funereal. A black-garbed servant raises a candelabra over the dying king. The sputtering flames cast eerie, serpent-like blades of light across his face. The head of the king drops to one side. With difficulty he heaves himself up. His eyes stare into the void. Like Richard III at Bosworth Field, the past haunts him with one message: "Despair and die." He collapses. Raises himself up again. Mouth falls open in a silent scream. Face a whorl of pain. Meeting death, Frederick is terrified by his life. Aghast at the blood he has shed, he freezes into a statue of bronze. In death he wakes from the nightmare of life. A black-robed doctor closes the monarch's eyes. In that

53 *the CIVILwarS*. The death of Frederick the Great in rehearsal at the American Repertory Theatre. Courtier (on left, Jeremy Geidt) attends King (on right, Priscilla Smith). "Men die like animals," wrote Hemingway. In life, perhaps, but not on a Wilson stage, where death is mysteriously beautiful.

mysterious moment of transition, when the spirit flees the body, when one feels death pass by, the king becomes an object, a corpse with no more life in it than the throne he sits on. From being to nothingness, from nature to eternity. The court files out in stately ceremony. In this dense scene, no words are spoken. The silent drama of the human face carries the meaning.

As always, death in Wilson is beautiful. *When We Dead Awaken* ends with the death of Rubek and Irene. Wilson cautioned the actors not to become lugubrious. "Even if theatre deals with depressing ideas, it should never depress. I saw this production in Hamburg. I hated it. It was so heavy and gloomy. You must keep it light. Death must be luminous." For Merteuil's death in *Quartet*, the director had Childs walk slowly into a wall of blazing white light, accompanied by a stately baroque pavane. The metaphor he gave her to color the moment was: "It is the clearest, brightest, most sparkling day in the history of the world. You're in the Arctic and can see infinity." She had just finished speaking her last line, "Now we are alone, cancer my lover."

In Wilson, death is the ultimate confrontation with self, the ultimate confrontation with life. "I see Frederick," Wilson says, "as a prototype of all the military dictators who've come since – Napoleon, Mussolini, Stalin, Hitler" (*Alcestis*). With a blinding realization, Frederick, in death, sees the horror of life, of his life. But the realization comes too late. Like Tolstoy's dying Ivan Ilych, Wilson's Frederick passes his life in review and comes to the same conclusion: "It can't be that life is so senseless and horrible. But if it really has been so horrible and senseless, why must I die and die in agony? There is something wrong . . . Why, and for what purpose, is there all this horror . . . What if my whole life has really been wrong?"[15] The modern world, trying to hide from death, hides from life. Only by acknowledging death as the end of life, only by considering how one lives can one give life value. "He who teaches men to die," Montaigne reminds us, "teaches them to live."

Cordelia's death wields special power over Wilson. The director has staged *King Lear* twice, put the scene in *the CIVILwarS*, made a video of it in which he plays Lear, and often acts out the scene at parties and lectures. In *the CIVILwarS* the body of Cordelia became a roll of old newspapers. During rehearsals he went to extraordinary lengths – even for Wilson – to get the size and weight of the newspapers just so. He tried out sixteen different configurations before the sheaf satisfied him. Striking to the core of our being, the death of a loved one shatters all our defenses. Robert Jay Lifton says the experience leaves a "death imprint," an indelible memory leaving in its wake anxiety, guilt, depression, distrust of life, and a struggle to find meaning in the face of death.[16] Confronting and transcending this sense of loss lie at the heart of Wilson's theatre.

Also at the heart is the contrast between the cool, elegant surface and an angry subtext. In a Wilson work, the performance style is chiseled from ice: cold, aloof, unemotive. Over and over during the *When We Dead Awaken* rehearsals, the director warned the actors about displaying too much emotion: "Cut the crying, Rubek. It's sentimental." "That gesture is too expressive. The more expressive it becomes, the less it expresses." "I don't want any emotion in that voice. Keep the emotion private." "Make that voice cooler. When you put so much emotion into your voice you sound like an actor." To Valmont in *Quartet*, he counseled, "Müller's text is hot and sexual and cruel. So speak it with a cold voice. Outside you're controlled and contained. Inside you're boiling. The contrast will make the speech more intense, more erotic." Rehearsing *Great Day in the Morning*, he told Jessye Norman to "use your face more like a mask in Noh." Presenting a false face to the world, a mask hides what one thinks and feels.

Wilson tells the following anecdote about performing with Meredith Monk:

Meredith called me one afternoon and said she needed me to perform with her that night. There was no time to rehearse, but to help her out, I agreed. There was a series of blackouts in the piece. When the lights came up after the first blackout, I was in the wrong place. I was standing in front of her, so during the next blackout, she bit me. During the next blackout I slapped her, and so it continued the rest of the evening. Lights out we kicked and pinched and hit, but whenever the lights came up we were cool, like two cucumbers. (*WWDA*)

This story explains much about Wilson's performances: they are the ultimate in emotional control. Not letting on what you're feeling is one way to throw the audience off, and making theatre, Wilson claims, means "pulling the rug out from underneath. Keep it unpredictable" (*Quartet*). The anti-histrionic style of Wilson's theatre – his actors act like Balanchine's dancers dance – misleads inadvertent spectators into believing that Wilson's works have no emotion. "What I liked in Balanchine was the distance," Wilson says (*Quartet*). He's referring to emotional distance. There is deep emotion in Wilson, but distanced through formal patterns and metaphors. Almost never is it communicated directly. But underneath the shimmering surface of formal beauty boils a cauldron of anger, rage, hate, aggression, destruction, and self-destruction. This contrast gives Wilson's work texture and tension and richness.

It is disconcerting to see Wilson work out a beautiful moment and then give the actor a malevolent subtext to accompany it. In *Quartet* Merteuil had an elegant hand gesture, which he explained thus: "Lucinda, you just dropped an atom bomb. Watch it go down. Enjoy the explosion." Repeatedly, he'll tell an actress to smile sweetly at someone while thinking inside, "I want to kill you"; "Drop dead"; "You stupid thing"; "I hate your fucking guts"; and, most frequently, "Fuck you." "It's stranger and more interesting" Wilson claims, "if something different is going on under the surface" (*WWDA*).

What is going on under the surface is not sweetness and light. It is a volcano of anger and hostility. Wilson told Maya to imagine a dot on the floor. "That dot is your husband. Imagine he's a tiny insect. Squash him with your shoe and smile." Earlier, when he wanted an elegant, sexy walk he said, "Put more fun into the walk. Sway your hips. Think that you're trampling on your husband. You're stepping all over him and enjoying it. Then pick up his body with your toe and toss it away."

Other subtexts the director gives actors define relationships in terms of the games people play to control and dominate. "The two Irenes are boxing you in now, Rubeck, with their mind games, just like you boxed Maya in." But the violence is physical as well as psychological. When Maya goes into her trance, Wilson told the actress, "You want to stab Honni Coles [who was playing the spa manager]. Direct the knife in your thought at him. Then turn and face the audience. You have the whole audience to stab too." Again and again, Wilson instructs actors to think about murdering the audience. Rehearsing *Quartet*, he told Lucinda Childs to pick out particular people she wanted to kill: "I've got a gun. I'm going to shoot the lady in the red sweater in the second row. But make sure you smile sweetly at her." On the surface impeccable manners. Underneath destructive rage.

The world Wilson puts on stage is a world of terror, a world of severed connections, a world where human relationships are painful, and loneliness is the only faithful companion. The disruption of language mirrors the unravelling of the social fabric. Wounded and bruised, consciousness withdraws into itself. Much of the behavior one sees in a Wilson production would be diagnosed as schizoid. Wilson's theatre stares into a psychic abyss; the theme of madness runs through his work.[17] Some critics dismiss Wilson's theatre as a series of "pretty pictures," signifying nothing. But Wilson's stage images resonate with a beauty born in sorrow. Wilson's theatre exults not because it denies tragedy but because it transcends tragedy. It heals the trauma.

Evidence – already ample and steadily growing – demonstrates the therapeutic value of art – therapeutic in a literal sense. Wilson began his career as a teacher and therapist, working with brain-damaged children, terminally ill patients in iron lungs, paraplegics, and others who needed physical therapy. Both Raymond Andrews, a deaf-mute, and Christopher Knowles, an autistic child, matured, flourished, and healed under his tutelage.

Erik Erikson maintains that children dramatize their traumas to overcome them.[18] The goals of psychodrama as defined by J. L. Moreno are to act out inner conflicts and traumas in a group; to replay painful experiences from the past and rewrite them; and to vent unconscious feelings and destructive urges so that they can be integrated into the personality in a healthy way.[19] Psychodrama can solve emotional problems too deep for the conscious mind to face. Psychodrama achieves what all great theatre achieves – insight and catharsis.

Ingmar Bergman sees his cinema as psychodrama, therapy, and catharsis, and when discussing his movies, he posits art as the healing alternative to madness:

Making films is a drive for me. It is a need like eating, drinking, making love, sleeping. It is integrated into every cell of my body. I believe that if one tried to remove it from me, there would be almost nothing left. Perhaps there would remain some little asparagus-like madman, wandering about without being able to take care of himself.[20]

Threatening and overwhelming, the most painful issues an individual or society faces are seldom expressed directly. Yet express them we must. Collectively and individually, we turn to metaphors.[21] Metaphors are used "to distance and protect the individual" from the psychic pain that seeks expression.[22] And for the most traumatic experiences, those metaphors are often visual, not verbal. Under the strain of the strongest emotion, language breaks down. Visual metaphors enable a patient "safely to represent in pictorial form that which he finds frightening";[23] consequently, psychologists use art therapy regularly. "It is through the more metaphorical and non-discursive of our symbolic modes that our thoughts and feelings find their fullest expression."[24]

"Great artists do us the service," Proust writes, "of showing us what richness, what variety lies hidden, unknown to us, in that vast, unfathomed and forbidding night of our soul which we take to be an impenetrable void."[25] Wilson's theatre explores that void, and in doing so it exorcises our demons.

Wilson's theatre heals through the miracle of communication. Without saying anything, it says everything. "An artist," François Mauriac notes, "is a man who refuses to surrender to solitude. Each of us lives in a desert. A work of art is a cry in that desert."[26] Art is an escape from solitude. When speaking of Raymond, a deaf-mute, Wilson explains that communication and friendship were impossible between them until Wilson learned Raymond's language: "By meeting him halfway and speaking his language, something happened in the exchange. I think that's basic to theatre. It's a forum where people come together, people from different backgrounds, people with different ideas politically, socially, artistically. And together we share something" (Quartet). For Wilson, then, art is not just communication. It is also community and communion.

David Hume argued that the pleasure we get from tragedy derives from the consolation of beauty. If Wilson's theatre gives us release through communication, it also gives us the balm of beauty, a desperate beauty. Art celebrates the joy of creation, the ability to create order and meaning from the debris of life. Wilson's images console because they dramatize the triumph of order, balance, and harmony over the psychic disorder seething underneath. Pain pitted against pleasure, chaos against meaning. In act I of *When We Dead Awaken*, Irene describes to Rubek the emotional trauma she suffered as a result of their separation. During this retrospective narration of incarceration in an asylum, Sutton leaned over and with a stylized gesture started kicking a chair. A hauntingly beautiful moment thanks to the gracefully controlled movement. Yet the voice-over told the tale of mental collapse: "I was dead for many years. They came and bound me. They strapped my arms together behind my back. Then they lowered me into a tomb, with iron bars and padded walls. No one was allowed to hear my shrieks from the grave."

Beauty is its own consolation. Add humor to the equation, and one comes closer to understanding why Wilson's theatre, which deals with tragic themes, does not depress. Wilson himself is a funny man and an accomplished raconteur who can amuse his interlocutor to the wee hours of dawn. "Never do a play without humor" (*Quartet*), Wilson tells his actors, and he never does. The frantic butler hurling dishes on the banquet table for Hercules in *Alcestis*; the boogie-woogie to David Byrne's "The Catherine Wheel" during Timon of Athens's tirade in *the CIVILwarS*; the erotical–comical, hide-and-seek minuet between the garden walls when Goneril dallies with Edmund in *King Lear* (act IV, scene ii). Rehearsing *Quartet*, *King Lear*, and *When We Dead Awaken* – grave texts all – the director worked assiduously to prevent the productions from becoming macabre. He introduced the song-and-dance knee plays into *When We Dead Awaken* to cheer the play up. "To be a great tragedy, *King Lear* must be light," Wilson told his Lear. "You must let the audience know that they can laugh with him." And to Gloucester: "Try a Mr. Magoo walk. It's more comic. Play him as a jolly old man, slap happy. Begin the play as comedy. Let the tragedy overtake you by surprise. *King Lear* is not a tragedy unless first it's a comedy." Humor, like beauty and communication, works its own therapy. Laughter reconciles us to tragedy.

On a deeper level still, Wilson's theatre transcends the human condition. His staging of act I, scenes iii–vii of *Alceste* shows how. The scene takes place in the temple of Apollo, where the queen, grieved that her husband must die, comes to implore the god. Total blackness on stage. Then, as if by magic, light comes up on individual objects: a priest in white robes, a large white cube suspended high above. We have entered the temple of light, the temple of life. By penetrating the darkness, light creates the world. Mysteriously – Wilson alone has the secret – concentric pyramids of light form around the priest, creating a holy of holies. The large cube – like a rune stone falling from paradise – descends to the floor and becomes an altar. Deep blue light washes the floor. With stylized gestures, the hierophant invokes Apollo – the god of light – to spare the king. Alceste's shadow self – an inscrutable doppelganger – enters stage right. The Delphic priest walks backwards stage left. Entering upstage right, Alceste walks on a diagonal to the altar, stage center. The three form a perfect pyramid, repeating the pyramids of light streaming down from the heavens. In a golden burst, more radiance than reality, the god appears – a colossal nude kouros, his yellow glow set off by the deep blue backdrop. A cortege of black-robed mourners – carrying large panes of glass – enters. Mysteriously, the panes float into the air and turn slowly. A flame soars up from the altar. Reflecting it, the rotating panes flash rainbows of fire. Like a voice from the whirlwind, the god speaks: the king must die unless someone sacrifices himself in his place. Offering her life to save her husband's, Alceste kneels, then lies on the ground, arms stretched up to heaven in prayer. Except for a tight spot on her face the stage disappears in darkness as she sings to the divinities of the Styx. Lights up. The altar ascends to the heavens and an upside-down pyramid of light – reversing the pattern that opened the scene – forms over the queen. Overhead, a small cube, turning slowly, appears like an oracle in the sky.

Mystery and majesty, awe and terror – these characterize the holy,[27] a feeling that cannot be conveyed by language. "Like the erotic, the holy has no words."[28] It talks in signs and symbols. Wilson's theatre stirs the soul. While singing the still, sad music of humanity, it longs for something eye has not seen nor ear heard. It yearns for something beyond. It insists on the divine in human life. In *Grace for Grace*, a benefit for the homeless Wilson offered in New York's Episcopal Cathedral, the director flooded the soaring Gothic arches with an unearthly blue light. From the highest reaches of the clerestory, Chris Knowles, like a wounded angel, read Shakespeare's "Sonnet 73," a poem about time and the transcendence of time. Wilson's dilation of time – his theatre slows time down until a moment is no longer a moment but a glimpse of eternity – approaches the still point of the turning world, a point beyond time. Tragedy, Nietzsche contends, is reconciliation with another world.[29]

Wilson's production of *Lohengrin* shows how the spirit keeps the flesh alive. The director turned Elsa and Ortrud into warring sides of the same, all-too-human self (see figure 54). Although the costumes were diametrically opposed, the gestures and movements of the one mirrored the other. They crossed, simultaneously, on a diagonal; they circled the stage together; and as Elsa entered the Minster for her wedding, she turned back, staring at Ortrud, staring at her. Ortrud as Elsa's alter ego – a daring and incisive stroke – gave the end new resonance. After Lohengrin's

54 *Lohengrin*. Elsa (on right, Lucia Popp) and Ortrud (on left, Anja
Silja) – antagonistic sides of a divided self – locked in battle.

farewell, the two women faced the audience – Elsa holding her husband's ring; Ortrud, her husband's shroud. As the stage darkened, the two women fell in death at the same time, in the same position. By turning Ortrud into the doubting self – the eloquent Mephistopheles who negates life – Wilson dramatized the necessity of belief. At the beginning, Elsa has faith that grace can work its miracles in a dark world. Ironically, when the miracle happens, when the divine touches the human, she doubts. In Wilson, Elsa dies because she loses faith in life, a faith that can be sustained only by faith in something beyond life. Light and life give way to darkness and doubt, and Elsa's physical existence – from which the spiritual has ebbed – collapses. By accepting the sacred, Wilson's theatre transcends trauma. Transfigured at the edge of doom, it blesses life.

7 An eye with a mind of its own: the revolution continues

> You should dream more. Reality in our century is not something to be faced.
>
> Graham Greene, *Our Man in Havana*

Via del bambino Gesù is the most exclusive address in Milan. Outside, the houses lining the street look like forbidding stone fortresses. Inside, after one has safely passed through the portcullis, passed the growling German shepherds with chiseled teeth, passed the armed guards, after one has ascended the grand staircase to the piano nobile, one is transported to a *palazzo* of baroque splendor: marble on the floor, gold-framed mirrors on the wall, crystal chandeliers suspended in the air. It all looks like an ornate fantasy concocted by Franco Zefferelli, but, in fact, this *palazzo* is the grandiose residence of Gianni Versace.

A long Renaissance table, elaborately carved with garlands and cornucopia, stands against one wall in Versace's conference room. At its head a sheaf of papers and a silver goblet with freshly sharpened pencils sit. Expectantly, nervously, people fidget, waiting for Robert Wilson to arrive. They have gathered for the first production meeting of a new opera at La Scala based on Thomas Mann's *Doktor Faustus*. Versace is designing the costumes. Those who have never worked with Wilson pump the others for clues about the enigmatic director who has dominated European theatre for the past fifteen years. Words like "odd," "weird," "bizarre" buzz through the room.

Wilson – a towering six foot four with luminous blue eyes and sandy hair – strides through the door an hour late. He stalks over to the table, sits down, takes a long pencil, examines the point, starts drawing. The others slowly gather round and sit down. The director's brooding presence imposes an unearthly silence. No one dares speak. The minutes drag by in a tension that soon becomes excruciating. Sitting quietly, people squirm, twist, itch. Wilson continues to draw, lost in absolute concentration, seemingly oblivious to everything around him. After an eternity, he shows us a drawing: a milk bottle with nails stuck all over it. "I thought I would have a screen over the stage with a film of someone driving nails into a milk bottle, but the milk doesn't run out."

Giacomo Manzoni, the befuddled composer asks what the milk bottle means. "I draw pictures," the director returns, "I don't draw meanings." "That milk bottle doesn't have anything to do with my opera," the composer grumbles. "This milk bottle is interesting to look at," the director shoots back, terminating the discussion. Versace stares blankly at the two men. Nine months later, *Doktor Faustus* opens to roaring cheers.

Wilson, who started out as a teacher, has now reached a point in his career where he wants to pass on to the next generation the tricks of the theatrical trade he has learned. Wilson has always enjoyed working with students, and in March, 1993, he returned to the University of Texas, Austin, where, to please his father, he had once studied business administration. He had agreed to direct drama students in a workshop of Genet's *The Balcony*. This masterpiece of the absurd takes place in a bordello as a bloody revolution explodes; the house of illusion inside mirrors the political tumble outside. Like all forms of make-believe, Genet suggests, politics and sex are a willing suspension of disbelief in which hope triumphs over experience. With iron fist, fantasy rules Parliament and the bedroom. "I like this play," Wilson says, grinning like the Cheshire cat, "because it's so crazy."

He establishes an easy rapport with students, who take to his playful humor. Each morning the students, seated around Wilson, beg the accomplished raconteur for another story. Their favorite deals with Lady Bird Johnson and German Chancellor Konrad Adenauer, who visited Austin when Wilson was an undergraduate. Telling the anecdote, Wilson slips back into a broad Texas drawl that sends the students into gales of giggles. The long-winded chancellor delivered a two-hour speech in German, which no one understood. In a fuchsia straw hat, Lady Bird, sitting next to Adenauer on the dais in the Texas State Capitol, could not hide her boredom. During his interminable oration, she kept waving wildly to people she recognized in the audience, screaming out over the chancellor, "Howdy." That night Lady Bird threw a barbecue for 2,500 people. The Chancellor was fiddling with knife and fork. Picking up a chicken breast slathered with barbecue sauce, Lady Bird shoved it into his hands. "Use your fingers," she ordered with down-home, no-nonsense authority.

While Wilson can be playful, his formal workshop methods take some getting used to. Since the students want to talk about what *The Balcony* means in literary terms, Wilson lets them. Meanwhile, not looking at anyone, he sits at a long table and draws. After the students have their say, he gets up, walks over to an easel covered by an enormous six foot-by three foot sheet of paper. He diagrams the stage of Houston's Alley Theatre, which wants to mount the production.

"The first thing you must know as an actor or director is the space you will inhabit. See the architecture, imagine where things can happen in space." He then shows them the drawings he made while they were babbling away about the lack of sexual fulfillment in Genet's cathouse. "There will be open elevators and closed boxes to create different kinds of spaces. I want screens of lace, chicken wire, curtains of red velvet and gold lamé, glass beads and mosquito nets that can fly down and up and constantly change the sense of space. I also want oversized props rolled on stage, like a big pistol that can shoot, and a jungle gym."

Wilson asks a student to direct the first scene. The student has the three characters clustered together downstage – Madame Irma, dominatrix of the brothel; the prostitute; and the client, who dresses up as a bishop to hear the whore's confession, which acts as an aphrodisiac.

All three have their scripts in hand and read the scene. Wilson jumps up. "Put your scripts down – no text," he commands. "Just look at the spatial relationships." Gently, Wilson points out the weaknesses in the student's visual composition and his uninteresting use of stage space. The director seats the bishop on a high platform at center stage to draw the eye up and give the composition a strong focal point. He turns the bishop around. "It's more mysterious to see his back," he says. He places the two women far off, huddled downstage left. The separation of the women from the man creates tension and dramatizes the intimacy between the females and the underlying antagonism between them and the male. "That's an opening look," Wilson says. "What do you want to happen next?"

"Wilson is inspiring because he taught me not to be afraid of my imagination and that there are other ways of doing theatre beyond realism," says Carey Russell, an acting student. "I'll never be an avant-garde director," chimes in Nina LeNoir, a directing student, "but Bob opened my eyes and taught me how to see space, and that's important no matter what style you work in."

Like any good teacher, Wilson empowers students to explore their own creativity. He does not dictate. He unlocks the secret chambers of the mind. Like any southern gentleman, he knows charm is the most potent weapon of coercion.

Wilson has purchased an abandoned Western Union laboratory in Water Mill, Long Island, which he plans to turn into an interdisciplinary center for theatre research. He hopes to bring together students and professionals from many countries to develop projects – his own as well as other's. Water Mill will house workshops, archives, libraries, art exhibits, and installations. Visual artists, choreographers, directors, actors, dancers, composers, singers, filmmakers, and video artists will cross-fertilize each other, and students will learn by working with seasoned professionals.

"Water Mill," says Wilson, "will further my interest in working with young people. Young people are more open, not so set in their thinking. And they laugh more readily." In July, 1993, Wilson workshopped several projects at Water Mill: his one-man version of *Hamlet*, in which he acts and directs; *Monsters of Grace*, a new musical work with Glass; Marguerite Duras's *The Malady of Death* with Lucinda Childs; *The Meek Girl*, a dramatization of a Dostoevsky short story, in which he acts and directs; and a new piece with Hans-Peter Kuhn. Wilson is a monomaniac who eats, breathes, drinks, dreams work.

On Long Island, Wilson will have a studio, and he hopes to devote more time to sculpting, drawing, and painting. European museums and private collectors have been asking for more work. "My career is turning full circle," Wilson ruminates. "I started out as a painter, then I went into theatre. Now painting and sculpting are taking up more of my time. I had to do theatre to learn about myself and discover my aesthetic. On stage I found my signature – my way of seeing space and time."

Wilson's signature – he has altered the course of drama – is impossible to miss. But sitting on the patio of a cafeteria at the University of Texas, Wilson falls pensive. After long silence, he speaks. "I've been thinking a lot about Andy Warhol lately. Five hundred years from now people – whether they're from America or China or Mars – will stare in fascination at his portrait of Marilyn [Monroe] because it's so mysterious. The depth is on the surface. My work doesn't have a future. A production is created in and for a moment, not for eternity." In art, in life, Wilson cuts short any drift toward sentimentality. "Theatre," says the director, "is the art of the emphemeral."

There is no conclusion to this book. Wilson will continue to evolve, continue to astound. How will he change? Not even he knows. But no matter what surprises the future holds, he will remain faithful to his unique vision. Ours is a tragic age. But we fail to see its tragedy. In a cruelly materialistic world – blind to its own ugliness – we need Wilson's eye. His theatre is manna from heaven. It feeds the soul by ravishing the senses.

What astonishes Wilson the most about his career? Forthwith comes the forthright answer. "That my work ever found an audience."

Notes

1 Contextualizing Wilson: from semiotics to semantics

1. Jean-Marie Blanchard, letter to the author, 24 May 1993, trans. Holmberg.
2. Julie Archer, personal interview, 17 February 1991.
3. For a detailed description of the early work, see Stefan Brecht, *The Theatre of Visions: Robert Wilson* (Frankfurt, 1978).
4. Robert Wilson "Production Notes on *The King of Spain*," *New American Plays*, III, ed. William Hoffman (New York, 1970).
5. To place Wilson's career in the evolution of American theatre, see Arthur Holmberg, "Artistic Profile," in *The World Encyclopedia of Contemporary Theatre*, II (London, 1996) 424–35.
6. Richard Schechner, *The End of Humanism* (New York, 1982) 18–27.
7. See John Cage, *Silence* (Middletown CT, 1973) 94–95.
8. Wilson, Learning from Performers, Harvard, 9 February 1982.
9. *New York Times*, 16 March 1975.
10. Sheryl Sutton, personal interviews, February 1991. Sutton first worked with Wilson on *Deafman Glance*. During the early period, many considered her the quintessential Wilson performer.
11. Fred Kolo, personal interviews, May 1994.
12. Louis Aragon, "Lettre ouverte à André Breton," *Les Lettres Françaises*, June 2–8, 1971, trans. Arthur Holmberg.
13. Susan Sontag, personal interview, March 1993.
14. René Girard, *Violence and the Sacred* (Baltimore, 1984) 19.
15. In the first half of the century, a similar shift occurred in the novel. Ralph Freedman, *The Lyrical Novel* (Princeton, 1963) 16–41.
16. Brecht, *Theatre of Visions*, 143.
17. Robert Brustein, "Theatre in the Age of Einstein: The Crack in the Chimney," *Critical Moments* (New York, 1980) 121–22.
18. Carol Donley and Alan Friedman, *Einstein as Myth and Muse* (Cambridge, 1985).
19. Henri Bergson, *The Creative Mind* (New York, 1992) 11–29.
20. Keir Elam, *The Semiotics of Theatre and Drama* (New York, 1983) 119.
21. David Bordwell, *Narration in the Fiction Film* (Madison, 1985) 49.
22. These texts can be found in Philip Glass, *Music by Philip Glass* (New York, 1987) and in the libretto that accompanies the recording of *Einstein on the Beach*, CBS Masterworks, M4 38875.
23. Lucinda Childs, personal interviews, March 1988.
24. Holmberg, "Emotion in Pure Form: An Interview with Philip Glass," *ART News*, May 1988.

25. Alan Kriegsman, *The Washington Post*, 21 November 1992.
26. Alan Rich, *Newsweek*, 31 December 1984.
27. John Rockwell, *The New York Times*, 17 December 1984.
28. Glass, personal interview, April 1993.
29. Wilson, personal interview, February 1980.
30. Holmberg, "A Warning from Heiner Müller," *The New York Times*, Sunday, 8 July 1990.
31. For an account of *the CIVILwarS*, see Janny Donker, *The President of Paradise* (Amsterdam, 1985).
32. Wilson, Learning from Performers, Harvard, 9 February 1982.
33. Holmberg, "Another Opening, Another Show?" *The Antioch Review*, 44 (1986): 228.
34. Linda Nochlin, "Why Have There Been No Great Women Artists?" in *Art and Sexual Politics*, ed. Elizabeth Baker (New York, 1973) 36.
35. Michael Foucault "What Is an Author?" in *Twentieth-Century Literary Theory*, ed. Vassilis Lambropoulos (Albany, 1987) 132.
36. Stephen Greenblatt, "Culture" in *Critical Terms for Literary Study*, ed. Frank Lentricchia (Chicago, 1990) 226.
37. Lawrence Shyer, *Robert Wilson and His Collaborators* (New York, 1989) 280.
38. Howard Brookner, *A Minute with Bob Wilson*, BBC, 1985.
39. Wilson, personal interview, March 1993.
40. For an account of Wilson's attempts to work in America, see Holmberg, "Merlin of the Avant-Garde," *Los Angeles Times Sunday Magazine*, 8 August, 1993.
41. Dan Sullivan, *The Los Angeles Times*, 10 March 1985.
42. Robert Brustein, introduction, *When We Dead Awaken* by Henrik Ibsen (Cambridge MA, 1991) 9.
43. David Mamet, personal interview, 28 April 1992.
44. Arthur Holmberg, "Proust Is Filmed at Last," *Sunday New York Times*, 24 July 1983.
45. Jonathan Miller, *Subsequent Performances* (New York, 1986) 247.
46. Robert Wilson and Darryl Pinckney, *Orlando*, unpublished script.
47. Virginia Woolf, *Orlando* (New York, 1956) 156–57.
48. Suzanne Lambert, née Wilson, personal interview, 24 July 1991.
49. On the style of boys' weeklies and their importance in British culture, see George Orwell, "Boys' Weeklies" in *Collected Essays* (London, 1975) 88.

2 The cracked kettle

1. "Language is a cracked kettle on which we beat out a tune for a dancing bear when we want with our music to move the stars." Gustave Flaubert, *Madame Bovary*, trans. Arthur Holmberg (Paris, 1979) 196.
2. Vladimir Nabokov, *Lolita* (New York, 1989) 32, 97.
3. Virginia Woolf, *Jacob's Room* (New York, 1959) 68–73.
4. Ludwig Wittgenstein, *Tractatus Logico-Philosophicus* (London, 1988) 62. Anglo-

American philosophy has been particularly hypnotized by the language problem.

5. Chris Baker, Dramaturg, Alley Theatre, personal interview, 14 November 1992.

6. Wilson's privileging architecture over color reveals much about his aesthetic, analyzed in chapter 2.

7. Holmberg, "Another Opening, Another Show?" *The Antioch Review*, 44 (1986): 228. See also, Holmberg, "*Lear* Girds for a Remarkable Episode," *The New York Times*, 20 May 1990.

8. Stephane Mallarmé, "Le Tombeau d'Edgar Poe," in *Œuvres complètes*, trans. Holmberg (Paris, 1965) 189.

9. Tom Waits, personal interview, 7 June 1993.

10. In pre-sleep monologs, toddlers play with the sounds of words, creating surrealistic rondos with little referential function. Ellen Winner, *Invented Worlds: The Psychology of the Arts* (Cambridge MA, 1982) 308.

11. On the tangible nature of language – word as object – see Ferdinand de Saussure, *Course in General Linguistics* (New York, 1959), 15, 102–3.

12. Rudolf Arnheim, "Language, Image, and Concrete Poetry," in *New Essays on the Psychology of Art* (Berkeley, 1986), 91.

13. On the concept of speech community see Dell Hymes "Modes of the Interaction of Language and Social Life," in *Directions in Socioliguistics: The Ethnography of Communication* (New York, 1972) 35–71.

14. Ludwig Wittgenstein, *Philosophical Investigations* (New York, 1968) 11–12; 20; 33–35; 126.

15. Noam Chomsky, *Language and Mind*, (New York, 1968) 1–24.

16. J. L. Austin, *How to Do Things with Words* (Cambridge MA, 1975) 109.

17. Wittgenstein, *Philosophical Investigations*, 47.

18. Jacques Derrida, "Signature Event Context," *Glyph* 1 (1977): 172–97.

19. Mikhail Bakhtin, *Rabelais and His World* (Bloomington, 1984) 49.

20. Sheryl Sutton, personal interview, 26 February 1991.

21. Suson Sontag, "The Aesthetics of Silence," in *Styles of Radical Wills* (New York, 1969).

22. W. J. T. Mitchell, *Iconology: Image, Text, Ideology* (Chicago, 1986) 110–13.

23. Holmberg, "Machiavellis of the Bedroom – An Erotic Endgame," *ART News* February 1988. In this issue, see Holmberg's "Robert Wilson Rehearses" for an account of the creation of this production.

24. T. S. Eliot, *On Poetry and Poets* (New York, 1961) 93.

25. Ernst Cassirer, *Language and Myth* (New York, 1953) 74.

26. Eugene Ionesco, Interview in *Književne novine*, Beograd, Year XXIII, Number 399, 16 September 1971.

27. Susan Sontag, *Against Interpretation* (New York, 1966) 19, 23.

28. Barthes, *Image–Music–Text* (New York, 1977) 32–51.

29. Heiner Müller, personal interview, May 1990.

30. The number of theatrical codes depends on one's system of classification; one

can subdivide codes and invent new ones *ad infinitum*. The important fact to bear in mind is the vast number of theatrical codes and their heterogeneity. Keir Elam, *The Semiotics of Theatre* (New York, 1983).

31. Michel Foucault, *This Is Not a Pipe* (Berkeley, 1983).
32. Childs generated this monolog during rehearsals. "Bob asked me to improvise a speech about the beach. The play, after all, is called *Einstein on the Beach*, and the word 'beach' had not been mentioned. 'I have nothing to say about the beach,' I answered. 'Say whatever you think,' he replied. 'I never think about the beach,' I said. 'I don't like the beach. I don't go to the beach.' 'It doesn't matter' he returned. 'Talk about the beach anyway. Say whatever pops into your head.' So I started babbling away, free associating, and came up with that paragraph about not going to the beach." Lucinda Childs, personal interview, March 1988.
33. Cued visually and musically, the actual number of repetitions varied from performance to performance.
34. It is not without psychological significance that Wilson sends up the courtroom, the world of his father.
35. Bertrand Russell, *The Problems of Philosophy* (Oxford, 1967) ch. 5. John Searle, *Speech Acts* (Cambridge, 1985). Saul A. Kripke, *Naming and Necessity* (Cambridge MA, 1980).
36. Jacques Lacan, *Ecrits* (New York, 1977) 94, and Martin Heidegger, *Being and Time* (New York, 1962) 211–13.
37. Benjamin Lee Whorf, *Language, Thought, Reality* (Cambridge MA, 1989) 263.
38. Derrida, *Of Grammatology* (Baltimore, 1976) 15.
39. Barthes, *Mythologies* (New York, 1972) 110.
40. Michel Foucault, *The Order of Things* (New York, 1973) 9.
41. Robert Venturi, *Complexity and Contradiction in Architecture* (New York, 1988) 25, 41.
42. Robert Wilson and Heiner Müller, *the CIVILwarS* (Cambridge MA, 1985) 35. This passage was written by Wilson.
43. Albert Camus, *The Myth of Sisyphus* (New York, 1955) 10–13.
44. Roman Jakobson, *Fundamentals of Language* (Hague, 1975) 69–96. Barthes, *Writing Degree Zero*, (Boston, 1967) 47–49.
45. Wilson, Learning from Performers, Harvard, 9 February 1982.
46. Barthes, *Image*, 146.
47. Bakhtin, *The Dialogic Imagination* (Austin, 1981) 263 and *Problems of Dostoevsky's Poetics* (Ardis, 1973) 13, 23.
48. Alain Robbe-Grillet, *For a New Novel* (Evanston, 1989) 33.
49. Jean-François Lyotard, *The Postmodern Condition* (Minneapolis, 1984) 26–41.
50. Harold Rosenberg, *Art on the Edge* (Chicago, 1983) 176, 178.
51. Peter Burger, *Theory of the Avant-Garde* (Minneapolis, 1984) 81.
52. Barbara Johnson, *The Critical Difference* (Baltimore, 1980) 75.
53. Lyotard, *Postmodern Condition*, xix, 3, 60–67.
54. Wolfgang Iser, *The Act of Reading: A Theory of Aesthetic Response* (Baltimore,

1984) 5, 37. Stanley Fish, *Is There a Text in This Class?* (Cambridge MA, 1980) 303–37. Umberto Eco, *The Role of the Reader* (Bloomington, 1984) 3–5.

55. Barthes, *S/Z* (New York, 1974) 5–6.

56. Lacan, *Ecrits*, 155.

57. Hans Robert Jauss, *Toward an Aesthetic of Reception* (Minneapolis, 1982) 30.

58. Barthes, *S/Z*, 14.

59. Wilson, *I was sitting on my patio*, *The Drama Review*, 21.4 (1977) 75.

60. Umberto Eco, *The Open Work* (Cambridge MA, 1989).

61. Barthes, *Image*, 42.

62. Jauss, *Toward an Aesthetic*, 19.

63. E. H. Gombrich, *Art and Illusion: A Study in the Psychology of Pictorial Representation* (Princeton, 1972) 202.

64. Woolf, *The Captain's Deathbed and Other Essays* (New York, 1950) 96.

65. "As the archaeology of our thought easily shows, man is an invention of recent date. And one perhaps nearing its end." Michel Foucault, *The Order of Things* (New York, 1973) 387. Robbe-Grillet, 27–29.

66. Jean-Paul Sartre, *The Transcendence of the Ego* (New York, 1977) 36, 40, and Erving Goffman, *The Presentation of Self in Everyday Life* (New York, 1959) 252–53.

67. Lacan, *Ecrits*, 165, 284–85. Emile Benveniste, *Problems in General Linguistics* (Miami, 1971) 67.

68. Jerome Bruner, "Narration and Life," Susan Wise Memorial Lecture, Harvard, 26 April 1986. Daniel Stern, *Interpersonal World of the Infant* (New York, 1985) 177, 226–30.

69. Language was heard sporadically in earlier work, but it is with *A Letter for Queen Victoria* that Wilson's intense scrutiny of language begins.

70. Wilson, Learning from Performers.

71. Müller, *Hamletmachine* (New York, 1984) 54.

72. See also, Jiri Veltrusky, "Contribution to the Semiotics of Acting," in *Sound, Sign, and Meaning*, ed. Ladislav Matejka (Ann Arbor, 1976) 556–57.

73. Eco, "Semiotics of Theatrical Performance," *The Drama Review*, 21.2 (1977): 115–16. J. Urmson, "Dramatic Representation," *The Philosophical Quarterly*, 22 (1972): 336. Benveniste, *Problems*, 218, 224–27.

74. Isabelle Huppert, personal interview, 27 June 1993.

75. Saussure, *Course in General Linguistics*, 6, 14.

76. Colin Cherry, *On Human Communication* (Cambridge MA, 1982) 78, and Peter and Jill de Villiers, *Early Language* (Cambridge MA, 1979) 4, 39, 97, 114.

77. Peter Szondi, *Theory of the Modern Drama* (Minneapolis, 1987) 7–10.

78. Heidegger, *Being and Time*, 205.

79. Søren Kierkegaard, *Fear and Trembling* (Princeton, 1974), 81, 122–29.

80. Samuel Beckett, *Proust* (New York, 1931) 46–47.

81. See Paul Grice's theory of conversational implicature, "Logic and Conversation," *The Logic of Grammar*, ed. Donald Davidson (Encino, 1976). Cherry, *On Human Communications*, 75. Pierre Bourdieu, *Outline of a Theory of Practice* (Cambridge, 1977) 72–87.

82. Simone de Beauvoir, *Pour une morale de l'ambiguité* (Paris, 1961) 22 and Kierkegaard, *Either/Or* (Princeton, 1987) 134.

83. Vicente Molina Foix, *Don Juan último, Primer Acto*, 246, November–December 1992, 71–101. In the margin of his script next to this speech, Wilson penciled in, "Farewell to Language."

84. Cherry, *On Human Communication*, 157. Saussure, *Course in General Linguistics*, 103–5.

85. Hans-Peter Kuhn, personal interview, 31 January 1990.

86. Wilson, interview, *Semiotexte* 3 (1978): 20–27.

87. Freud, *A General Introduction to Psychoanalysis* (New York, 1935) 19 and Lucien Lévy-Bruhl, *How Natives Think* (Princeton, 1985) 174–80.

88. Bronislaw Malinowski and James Fox, "Our Ancestors Spoke in Pairs," in *Explorations in the Ethnography of Speaking*, ed. Richard Bauman (Cambridge, 1974) 83 and Malinowski, *Coral Gardens and Their Magic* (Bloomington, 1965) 137–57.

89. Michelle Rosaldo, "It's All Uphill: The Creative Metaphors of Ilongot Magical Spells," in *Sociocultural Dimensions of Language Use*, ed. Ben Blount (New York, 1975) 177–203.

90. Annette Weiner, "From Words to Objects to Magic," in *Dangerous Words*, ed. Donald Brenneis (New York, 1984) 1–29.

91. S. J. Tambiah, "The Magical Power of Words," *Man* 3 (1968): 178–79.

92. "Newspapers," recalls Jeremy Geidt, who played Lear, "were much easier to carry than a fat Cordelia, and, mysteriously, they made the scene more abstract and purer." Personal interview, 4 January 1988.

93. According to Claude Lévi-Strauss, the principal aim of magical narrative is to relieve pain through symbolic expression. Lévi-Strauss, *Structural Anthropology* (New York, 1963) 186–205. See also, Bruno Bettelheim, *The Uses of Enchantment: The Meaning and Importance of Fairy Tales* (New York, 1976) and Max Luethi, *Once Upon a Time: On the Nature of Fairy Tales* (Bloomington, 1976).

94. Heidegger, *Poetry, Language, Thought* (New York, 1975) 211–29.

95. Camus, *Myth of Sisyphus*, 90–91.

3 Alchemy of the eye

1. Barthes, *Mythologies* (New York, 1972) 90.

2. Rudolf Arnheim, *Visual Thinking* (Berkeley, 1969) vi, 18; *Art and Visual Perception* (Berkeley, 1974) 166. T. Bower, *The Perceptual World of the Child* (Cambridge MA, 1977) 56, 66. At least "75 percent of the information entering the brain is from the eyes." Jarice Hanson, *Understanding Video* (Newbury Park, 1987) 39. Some medical researchers put the figure at 90 percent.

3. Wassily Kandinsky, *Concerning the Spiritual in Art* (New York, 1977) 41.

4. Ingmar Bergman, *Film: A Montage of Theories*, ed. Richard Dyer MacCann (New York, 1966) 144.

5. Artaud, a voice crying in the wilderness, pointed the way: *The Theatre and Its*

Double (New York, 1958) 37–41. See also Derrida's two essays on Artaud in *Writing and Difference* (Chicago, 1978) 169, 232.

6. On the importance of images to consciousness, see Sartre, *The Psychology of Imagination* (Seacaucus, n.d.) 134–38.

7. Arnheim, *Art and Visual Perception*, 37–41.

8. Erle Loran, *Cézanne's Composition* (Berkeley, 1985). Clement Greenberg, *Art and Culture* (Boston, 1969) 50–58.

9. Arnheim, *The Dynamics of Architectural Form* (Berkeley, 1977) 37, 45, 65.

10. Kenneth Baker, *Minimalism* (New York, 1988) 9. The geometric aesthetic has played a crucial role in twentieth-century American art. *The Geometric Tradition in American Art, 1930–1990*, Whitney Museum of American Art, New York, February 1993. See also, Los Angeles County Museum of Art, organized by Maurice Tuchman, *The Spiritual in Art: Abstract Painting* (New York, 1986) 313. The prototype for this aspect of minimalism is Kazimir Malevich. *Malevich* (Los Angeles, 1990).

11. In Cologne the branch was a straight horizontal. In the ART remounting, it became more diagonal.

12. According to Jeff Muscovin, ex-technical director of the ART for three Wilson productions, the most difficult miracle he had to produce for the director was the Lincoln colossus: "It was a gigantic puppet with two people literally built into it, a woman standing on a platform on top for the face and a man below for the legs and for stability. As the puppet strode along, it swang its arms. Stage hands actually did the movements, using traveller lines that ran across a complex set of riggings. People on one side of the stage pulled the puppet; on the other side, they let it go, keeping it straight up at the same time. The size and movements made the process enormously tricky. And Wilson was not happy with the way it had been done in Germany and Rome. He found the heavy cables they used too distracting." Personal interview, June 1988.

13. Arnheim, *Art and Visual Perception*, 461, 97, 458. Arnheim, *The Power of the Center* (Berkeley, 1988) ix, 54. Maurice Merleau-Ponty, *The Primacy of Perception* (Evanston, 1964) 172: "For Descartes . . . the real power of painting lies in design, whose power in turn rests upon the ordered relationship existing between it and space-in-itself as taught to us by perspective–projection."

14. Although Glass granted permission to Achim Freyer to restage *Einstein* in Germany, the composer has second thoughts about the sagacity of that decision. "I persuaded Bob that we should let other people do this work. Eventually they will be done by others, I thought, so why not get on with it. Now I'm beginning to wonder if that's true, having seen one example. I'm not convinced anymore that these collaborative works that Bob and I have done can really be staged by other people. I've changed my mind. When Bob and I come together, we create a joint work. I'm not sure it's a good idea to take that apart. I won't let any other director stage *Einstein* again." Personal interview, 19 April 1993.

15. *Hiroshima mon amour*, dir. Alain Resnais. Screenplay by Marguerite Duras, Argo Films, 1959.

16. Henrik Ibsen, *When We Dead Awaken*, English version by Robert Brustein, adapted by Robert Wilson (Cambridge MA, 1991) 23.

17. Ibsen, *WWDA*, trans. Rolf Fjelde (New York, 1978) 1038.

18. "Playing the world's biggest woman," reminisces Sutton, "was the most fun I ever had in a theatre. The hydraulic fork lift inside the giant puppet was an amusement park ride, and the midget who played William made me laugh; he was obnoxious – a typical actor: verbose, egotistical, and forever complaining that he didn't have enough lines. He wanted more and longer speeches, but Bob wouldn't budge, so each night the dwarf would sit in the palm of my out-stretched hand, cursing Wilson in Flemish."

19. A. Saxon, *P. T. Barnum: The Legend and the Man* (New York, 1989) 101. Robert Bogdan, *Freak Show: Presenting Human Oddities for Amusement and Profit* (Chicago, 1988) 206–7.

20. See also, Roger Shattuck, *The Banquet Years: The Origins of the Avant-garde in France*, (New York, 1968) 325–52, and Frederick Karl, *Modern and Modernism* (New York, 1985) 270.

21. T. S. Eliot, introduction and translation of *Anabasis* by St.-John Perse (New York, 1949) 10–11.

22. Wilson has long expressed the desire to stage *The Waste Land*, and *T.S.E.* was a meditation on Eliot's life.

23. John Barth, "The Literature of Replenishment: Postmodernist Fiction," *The Atlantic Monthly*, January 1980, 69.

24. Marvin Carlson, *Theatre Semiotics* (Bloomington, 1990) 98.

25. My discussion of montage as a collision of successive images is based on Sergei Eisenstein's *Film Form* (New York, 1949) 5, 27, 36–8, 239; and *Film Sense* (New York, 1947) 7, 10, 63. Eisenstein often uses the word "conflict" to mean the visual contrast of colors, scales, shapes, volumes, masses.

26. My discussion of the function of the image in Wilson's theatre is indebted to the methodology Stephen Ullmann employs in *The Image in the Modern French Novel* (Oxford, 1963). See also, Eugene Falk, *Types of Thematic Structure: The Nature and Function of Motifs in Gide, Camus, and Sartre* (Chicago, 1967) 11–12.

27. Anton Chekhov, *The Brute and Other Farces* (New York, 1958) 11.

28. Francois Lesure, "Naissance et destin du *Martyre de Saint Sébastien*" Paris National Opera program *Le Martyre de Saint Sébastien* (Paris, 1988) 6–8.

29. Gabriele D'Annunzio, *Le Martyre de Saint Sébastien* (Paris, 1911), 267–68.

30. HMI is an acronym for hydrargyrum, medium-arc length, iodide discharge lamps, which are mercury-vapor lamps.

31. See, for example, Giovanni di Paolo's *Paradise* in the Metropolitan, New York.

32. Ibsen, *When We Dead Awaken*, adap. Wilson, 53.

33. *Ibid.*, 47.

34. Carl Jung, "On the Relation of Analytical Psychology to Poetry," *Dramatic*

Theory and Criticism, ed. Bernard Dukore (New York, 1974), 845. Maud Bodkin, *Archetypal Patterns in Poetry* (London, 1963) 1–4.

35. Müller *Quartet* in *Hamletmachine and Other Texts for the Stage*, trans. Carl Weber (New York, 1984) 117–18.

36. Wilson has an extensive art collection, which often suggests the images he uses. This image derives from a pot he owns.

37. Jean Miller, "Psychological Consequences of Sexual Inequality," *American Journal of Orthopsychiatry* 41 (1971): 767–70.

38. Wilson, Guild of Stage Designers and Choreographers, New York, 18 December 1987.

39. Wilson, personal interview, 9 March 1993.

40. Charles Baudelaire, "Les Phares," *Œuvres complètes* (Paris, 1961) 12–14.

41. Ray Birdwhistell, *Kinesics and Context* (Philadelphia, 1970) 56–57.

42. Yoshio Yabara, who designed the costumes, says Wilson gave him instructions to create "a timeless, archetypal American family," personal interview, 3 February 1990.

43. The English translation, "slowly burned," does not convey the humor of either the original French, "à petit feu" or the German.

44. Erik Erikson, *Identity: Youth and Crisis* (New York, 1968) 49, 130.

45. Alice Miller, *The Drama of the Gifted Child* (New York, 1981) 14–15.

46. Miller, *The Untouched Key: Tracing Childhood Trauma in Creativity and Destructiveness* (New York, 1990) 52–53.

47. Robert Wilson, *Alice*, Thalia Theatre Program (Hamburg, 1992) 48. Text by Paul Schmidt. Music and lyrics by Tom Waits.

48. This rage against parents has been repressed in most adults, who no longer have any conscious recollection of it. Miller, *Untouched Key*, 73–74. Through the psychological defense mechanism of splitting, an overidealized image of the parent usually prevails. Bodkin *Archetypal Patterns*, 13–16.

49. Margaret Mahler, *The Psychological Birth of the Human Infant: Symbiosis and Individuation* (New York, 1975).

50. Donald Burnham, *Schizophrenia and the Need–Fear Dilemma* (New York, 1969) 44–48.

51. Wilson, *the CIVILwarS* (Cambridge MA, 1985) 52.

52. Norman Paul, "Parental Empathy," in *Parenthood: Its Psychology and Psychopathology*, ed. Therese Benedek (Boston, 1970) 337.

53. On 22 May 1973 Wilson wrote the following letter to Dallas Pratt: "My mother died last Thursday. I was with her holding her hand." And on 4 July 1973: "I think about my mother all the time and almost every night I dream about her." Columbia University Rare Book and Manuscript Library.

54. H. F. Harlow, "The Nature of Love," *The American Psychologist* 13 (1958) 675–76; "The Maternal Affectional System of Rhesus Monkeys," in *Maternal Behavior in Mammals*, ed. Harriet Rheingold (New York, 1963); "Primary Affectional Patterns in Primates," *American Journal of Orthopsychiatry* 30 (1960): 676.

55. John Bowlby, "Grief and Mourning in Infancy and Early Childhood" *The Psychoanalytic Study of the Child*, 15 (1960) 9–10. René Spitz, *The First Year of Life: A Psychoanalytic Study of Normal and Deviant Development of Object Relations* (New York, 1965) 267–84.

56. Kandinsky *Concerning the Spiritual*, 8–9. Holmberg, "Waning of Spirituality Perplexes Artists Today," *American Theatre* June 1991: 44.

57. Baudelaire, "Le Voyage," *Œuvres complètes*, 127.

58. Freud, *Civilization and Its Discontents* (New York, 1961) 65.

59. Holmberg, "Greek Tragedy in a New Mask Speaks to Today's Audiences," *New York Times*, 1 March 1987.

60. David Perkins *The Quest for Permanence: The Symbolism of Wordsworth, Shelley and Keats* (Cambridge MA, 1959) 114; 1–62.

4 The deep surface

1. Wilson, personal conversation, July 1988. Wilson has a large collection of native American pottery. "I love pottery," he says. "It's so silent."

2. My analysis of Wilson's lighting is based not only on my conversations with him and observing him work, but also on interviews with three lighting designers who have frequently collaborated with him: Howell Binkley (May, 1989); Jennifer Tipton (March, 1990); and Steven Strawbridge (June, 1991).

3. Tom Kamm, personal interview, May 1990.

4. Steen Rasmussen, *Experiencing Architecture* (Cambridge MA, 1986) 208–9.

5. Priscilla Smith, personal interview, February 1992. Bumping into Wilson at the ART two years after *the CIVILwarS*, Ms. Smith mumbled, "Oh, it's you." "Is that all you can say?" asked Wilson. "What do you want me to say to the worst director I ever worked with?" Smith queried. "The same thing I say to the second worst actress I ever worked with. Hello, how are you, nice to see you again."

6. The Boston Museum of Fine Arts held a major retrospective in 1991; the show traveled to Houston and San Francisco. The catalog *Robert Wilson's Vision*, ed. Trevor Fairbrother (Boston, 1991), has excellent photographs of many of the director's sculptures and drawings. The Pompidou Center, Paris, also held a major exhibit in 1991.

7. Wilson's aesthetic shares affinities with many of the sculptors exhibited, especially Richard Serra. Richard Armstrong, ed., *The New Sculpture 1965–75: Between Geometry and Gesture* (New York, 1990).

8. David Denby, *Dance Writings* (New York, 1986).

9. "You must see the music and hear the dance," claimed Balanchine. Don McDonagh, *George Balanchine* (New York, 1983) 2.

10. Merce Cunningham, Learning from Performers, Harvard, April 1988.

11. Joseph Mazo *Prime Movers: The Makers of Modern Dance in America* (New York, 1977) 200.

12. I mentioned to Cunningham that Wilson cited him as a major influence. I asked

the choreographer if he had seen Wilson's work and if he discerned any influence. "I saw the early pieces like *The Life and Times of Joseph Stalin* and *Einstein on the Beach*, and I was struck by the use of stillness in *Deafman Glance*. Stillness is an important part of my work. But I think less about influence than sharing. Great artists share ideas that are in the air. People perceive the ideas differently and use them differently. So it's not really a question of influence." April 1988.

13. Benveniste, *Problems in General Linguistics* (Miami, 1971) 49–54.
14. Lillian Lawler, *The Dance of the Ancient Greek Theatre* (Iowa City, 1964) 22.
15. Allardyce Nicoll, *Film and Theatre*, (New York, 1936) 57.
16. Thomas Derrah, personal interview, January 1988.
17. Seth Goldstein, personal interview, March 1992.
18. Marianne Hoppe, personal interview, January 1990.
19. Stephanie Roth, personal interview, October 1990.
20. Honni Coles, personal interview, 16 February 1991.
21. Elzbieta Czyzewska, personal interview, March 1991.
22. Isabella Huppert, personal interview, June 1993.
23. Ann-Christin Rommen, personal interview, January 1990. Ms. Rommen works regularly with Wilson as his assistant director. Their collaboration began with the Cologne Section of *the CIVILwarS*.
24. Stephane Mallarmé, *Œuvres Complètes*, trans. Holmberg (Paris, 1965) 304.
25. Sally Banes, *Terpsichore in Sneakers* (Middletown, 1987) xxi, xxxi.
26. Judith Hanna, *To Dance Is Human* (Chicago, 1987) 4, 60.
27. On exemplification, see Selma Jeanne Cohen, *Next Week, Swan Lake* (Middletown CT, 1982) 87, 88; and Nelson Goodman, *Languages of Art* (Indianapolis, 1976) 52 and "How Buildings Mean," *Critical Inquiry* 11 (1985): 642–53.
28. Susan Foster, *Reading Dance* (Berkeley, 1986), xiv.
29. Birdwhistell, *Kinesics and Context* (Philadelphia, 1970) p. 158.
30. Arnheim, *Art and Visual Perception* (Berkeley, 1974) 372, 409.
31. Foster *Reading Dance*, 59.
32. Jurgen Ruesch and Weldon Kees, *Non-verbal Communication* (Berkeley, 1974) 52.
33. Suzushi Hanayagi, personal interview, January 1990.
34. Jacques Choron, *Death and Western Thought* (New York, 1963) 19.

5 The dream work

1. "Man, by the very fact of being man, of possessing consciousness, is, in comparison with the ass or the crab, a diseased animal. Consciousness is a disease." Miguel de Unamuno, *The Tragic Sense of Life* (New York, 1954) 18.
2. Roland Barthes, *Image–Music–Text* (New York, 1977) 52–68. See also Barthes's discussion of *studium* and *punctum* in *Camera Lucida* (New York, 1981) 26–28.
3. Holmberg, "The Disease of Art," *ART News*, February 1991.
4. Louis Aragon, "Lettre ouverte à André Breton," trans. Holmberg, *Les Lettres Françaises*, 2–8 June 1971.

5. Sigmund Freud, *The Interpretation of Dreams*, trans. James Strachey (New York, 1965). All further references to this work appear in the text.

6. Michel Foucault and Ludwig Binswanger, *Dream and Existence* (Seattle, 1986) 34–36. All further references to this work appear in the text.

7. Victor Shklovsky, "Art as Technique," in *Russian Formalist Criticism*, ed. Lee Lemon (Lincoln, 1965) 3–24.

8. Vlada Petric, "Bergman and Dream," Harvard, 9 May 1991. J. Allan Hobson, *The Dreaming Brain* (New York, 1988).

9. See also, Freud, *Interpretation of Dreams*, 330–31, 338, 347, 454.

10. Erving Goffman, *Frame Analysis: An Essay on the Organization of Experience* (Boston, 1986) 5–8, 27.

11. Henri Bergson *Time and Free Will* (New York, 1959) 90–106.

12. Aristotle, *Poetics*, Gerard F. Else, translator (Ann Arbor, 1978) 26–27.

13. Gail M. Price, Clinical Psychologist, personal interview, February 1993. The following chapter on trauma expands the idea of psychic terror in Wilson.

14. *Quartet*, the production in which Wilson, the architect obsessed with line, went furthest in this direction, was dedicated to the memory of Andy Warhol, colorist supreme.

15. Lillian Feder, *Madness in Literature* (Princeton, 1980) 120.

16. George Kernodle *From Art to Theatre* (Chicago, 1970) 217.

17. "It is urgent to reveal the artificial character of the old antinomies . . ." André Breton, *Manifestes du Surréalisme*, trans. Holmberg (Paris, 1972) 76.

18. Vladimir Propp, *Morphologie du conte* (Paris, 1965) 55.

19. Jean-Paul Sartre, *La Nausée*, trans. Holmberg (Paris, 1966) 173. Robbe-Grillet, *For a New Novel* (Evanston, 1989) 19, 68–73.

20. Freud *Interpretation of Dreams* 82, 67, 134.

21. For interviews with other collaborators, see Laurence Shyer, *Robert Wilson and His Collaborators* (New York, 1989).

22. Hans-Peter Kuhn, personal interviews, January 1990, February 1991.

23. Marshall McLuhan, "Acoustic Space," in *Explorations in Communication* (Boston, 1960) 69.

24. Maribeth Back, personal interview, January 1993.

25. Barthes, *Image–Music–Text* (New York, 1977) 187.

26. Barthes, *The Pleasure of the Text* (New York, 1975) 66–67.

27. Artaud *The Theater and its Double* (New York, 1958) 60.

28. Wolfgang Kayser, *The Grotesque* (Gloucester MA, 1968) 126.

29. Arnold van Gennep, *The Rites of Passage* (Chicago, 1975).

30. Victor Turner, *From Ritual to Theatre: The Human Seriousness of Play* (New York, 1982) 122.

31. Kayser *The Grotesque* (Gloucester MA, 1968) 185, 31–33.

32. Rosemary Jackson, *Fantasy: The Literature of Subversion* (New York, 1984) 69.

33. Holmberg, "A Conversation with Robert Wilson and Heiner Müller," *Modern Drama*, 31 (1988): 455.

6 The valley of the shadow: trauma and transcendence

1. Ibsen, *When We Dead Awaken*, English version by Robert Brustein, adapted and directed by Robert Wilson, Cambridge MA, 1991, 19–21.
2. The train sequence had been deleted from the English version Wilson was working with. During the Stage B rehearsals, Wilson put it back, relocating it to make a typical Wilsonian intertext and once again demonstrating the director's acute literary sensitivity.
3. Robert Weiss, *Loneliness: The Experience of Emotional and Social Isolation* (Cambridge MA, 1973) 17.
4. Edward T. Hall, *The Silent Language* (Greenwich, 1959) 160.
5. Kierkegaard, *Fear and Trembling* (Princeton, 1974) 81.
6. Robert Wilson, Tom Waits, Paul Schmidt, *Alice*, Thalia Theatre Program, Hamburg, 53. "Hang me in a bottle like a cat" comes from *Much Ado about Nothing* (act I, scene i, line 259). Benedict swears never to fall prey to love. The elegant surface of Shakespeare's play, like that of Wilson's production, is pierced by images of violence.
7. Erich Heller, *The Artist's Journey into the Interior* (London, 1966) 143.
8. Erich Auerbach, *Mimesis* (Princeton, 1953) 534–35.
9. Woolf, *The Common Reader* (New York, 1953) 154.
10. Szondi, *Theory of the Modern Drama* (Minneapolis, 1987) 7.
11. Robert Humphrey, *Stream of Consciousness in the Modern Novel* (Berkeley, 1972) 7.
12. Maurice Maeterlinck, *Le Trésor des humbles* (Paris, 1904) 9, 21, 200.
13. Béla Balázs, *Theory of the Film* (New York, 1970) 40.
14. Elisabeth Kübler-Ross, *On Death and Dying* (New York, 1976) 2.
15 Leo Tolstoy, *The Death of Ivan Ilych* (New York, 1960) 148–52.
16. Robert Jay Lifton, *The Future of Immortality* (New York, 1987) 236–42.
17. Wilson had a nervous breakdown in 1966 and attempted suicide.
18. Erik Erikson, *Childhood and Society* (New York, 1963) 216–18; Bruno Bettelheim "The Importance of Play," *The Atlantic Monthly*, March, 1987; Ellen Winner *Invented Worlds: The Psychology of the Arts* (Cambridge MA, 1982) 373–76. D. W. Winnicott, *Playing and Reality* (New York, 1982) 46, 50, 54.
19. J. L. Moreno, *Psychodrama* (Ambler, 1985).
20. Petric, ed., *Film and Dreams: An Approach to Bergman* (New York, 1981) 55.
21. Clifford Geertz, "Deep Play," *The Interpretation of Cultures* (New York, 1973) 412–53.
22. David Johnson, "Drama Therapy and the Schizophrenic Condition" in *Drama in Therapy*, ed. Richard Courtney (New York, 1981) 52.
23. John Birtchnell, "Art Therapy as a Form of Psychotherapy," in *Art as Therapy*, ed. Tessa Dalley (New York, 1984) 38. Janek Dubowski "Art Versus Language," in *Working with Children in Art Therapy*, ed. Caroline Case (New York, 1990).
24. John Henzell, "Art, Psychotherapy, and Symbol Systems" in Dalley, *ibid*.

25. Marcel Proust, *Swann's Way* (New York, 1989) 380.
26. François Mauriac, *Dieu et Mammon*, trans. Holmberg (Paris, 1958) 51–52.
27. Wilson's theatre fits perfectly the definition of holy theatre Christopher Innes elaborates in *Holy Theatre: Ritual and the Avant-Garde* (Cambridge, 1984).
28. Rudolf Otto, *The Idea of the Holy* (Oxford, 1973) 47.
29. Friedrich Nietzsche, *The Birth of Tragedy* (Garden City, 1956) 107.

Select bibliography

Wilson has maintained monumental archives – letters, notebooks, correspondence, drawings, videos, research files, books, programs, slides,
photographs, and articles. The Rare Book and Manuscript Library at
Columbia University holds a large portion of this material; the Theatre
Collection at Harvard, a small portion. Much of the visual material
remains at Wilson's New York office, the Byrd Hoffman Foundation.
None of these collections is open to the public.

Works by or about Wilson

Aragon, Louis. "Lettre ouverte à André Breton." *Les Lettres Françaises*. 2–8 June
    1971.
Brecht, Stefan. *The Theatre of Visions*. Frankfurt, 1978.
Brookner, Howard. *A Minute with Bob Wilson*, BBC, 1985.
Brustein, Robert. "Theatre in the Age of Einstein *The Crack in the Chimney*." *Critical
    Moments*. New York, 1980.
Childs, Lucinda. Personal interviews. 6 January and 16 March 1988.
Coles, Honni. Personal interview. 16 February 1991.
Derrah, Thomas. Personal interviews. 3 January 1988 and 14 November 1992.
Donker, Janny. *The President of Paradise: A Traveller's Account of the CIVILwarS*.
    Amsterdam, 1985.
Fairbrother, Trevor, ed. *Robert Wilson's Vision*. Boston, 1991.
Geidt, Jeremy. Personal interview. 4 January, 1988.
Glass, Philip. *Einstein on the Beach*. CBS Masterworks, M4 38875.
  Music by Philip Glass. New York, 1987.
  Personal interviews. 2 April 1988 and 19 April 1993.
Goldstein, Seth. Personal interview. 29 March, 1992.
Hanayagi, Suzushi. Personal interview. January 1990.
Holmberg, Arthur. "Another Opening, Another Show?" *The Antioch Review* 44
    (1986).
  "A Conversation with Robert Wilson and Heiner Müller." *Modern Drama* 31
    (1988).
  "The Disease of Art." *ART News*, February 1991.
  "Emotion in Pure Form: An Interview with Philip Glass." *ART News*. May 1988.
  "Greek Tragedy in a New Mask Speaks to Today's Audiences." *New York Times*.
    1 March 1987.
  "Lear Girds for A Remarkable Episode." *New York Times*. 20 May 1990.

"Machiavellis of the Bedroom – An Erotic Endgame." *ART News* February 1988.

"The Merlin of the Avant-Garde." *Los Angeles Times Magazine* 8 August 1993.

"Objects Speak Volumes." *American Theatre* April 1991.

"Wilson Rehearses." *ART News* February 1988.

Hoppe, Marianne. Personal interview. 1 February 1990.

Huppert, Isabelle. Personal interview. 27 June 1993.

Ibsen, Henrik. *When We Dead Awaken*. English version by Robert Brustein. Adapt. by Wilson. Cambridge, MA, 1991.

Johnston, Jill. "Family Spectacles." *Art in America*. December 1986.

Kolo, Fred. Personal interviews. May 1994.

Kuhn, Hans-Peter. Personal interviews. 31 January 1990 and 12 February 1991.

Lambert, Suzanne. Personal interview. 24 July 1991.

Lesure, François. "Naissance et destin du *Martyre de Saint Sébastien*." Paris National Opera Program. Paris, 1988.

Müller, Heiner. Personal interview. 1 June, 1990.

Müller, Heiner, and Wilson, Robert. *the CIVILwarS*. Cambridge, MA, 1985.

Rockwell, John. Intro. *Robert Wilson: The Theater of Images*. New York, 1984.

Rommen, Ann-Christin. Personal interview. 20 January 1990.

Shyer, Laurence. *Robert Wilson and His Collaborators*. New York, 1989.

Simmer, Bill. "Robert Wilson and Therapy." *The Drama Review* March 1976.

Sutton, Sheryl. Personal interviews. 22 and 26 February 1991 and 27 November 1992.

Waits, Tom. Personal interview. 7 June, 1993.

Wilson, Robert. *A Letter for Queen Victoria. The Theatre of Images*. Ed. Bonnie Marranca. New York, 1977.

Alice. Music and lyrics by Tom Waits. Text by Paul Schmidt. Thalia Theater Program. Hamburg, 1992.

the CIVILwarS. Cambridge MA, 1985.

Einstein on the Beach, CBS Masterworks, M4 388 75.

I was sitting on my patio. The Drama Review 21.4 (1977).

Interview. *Semiotexte* 3 (1978).

King of Spain. New American Plays. Ed. William Hoffman, New York, 1970.

Learning from Performers, Harvard. 9 February 1982.

Spencer Memorial Lecture. Harvard. 14 February 1985.

Wilson, Robert, and Müller, Heiner. *the CIVILwarS*. Cambridge MA, 1985.

Wilson, Robert, and Pinkney, Darryl. *Orlando*, unpublished script.

Yabara, Yoshio. Personal interview. 3 February 1990.

Secondary sources

These secondary sources, drawn from anthropology, linguistics, semiotics, communication studies, psychology, sociology, kinesics, theories of visual communication, philosophy, literary theory, music, art history, architecture, film theory, dance, and drama criticism demonstrate the wide range of contemporary concerns Wilson's theatre reflects and the necessity of using an interdisciplinary approach when studying his work.

Aristotle. *Poetics*, Gerald F. Else, trans. Ann Arbor, 1978.

Armand Hammer Museum of Art, *Kazimir Malevich*. Los Angeles, 1990.

Armstrong, Richard, ed. *The New Sculpture 1965–75: Between Geometry and Gesture*. New York, 1990.

Arnheim, Rudolf. *Art and Visual Perception*. Berkeley, 1974.
  The Dynamics of Architectural Form. Berkeley, 1977.
  New Essays on the Psychology of Art. Berkeley, 1986.
  Visual Thinking. Berkeley, 1969.

Artaud, Antonin. *The Theatre and Its Double*. New York, 1958.

Auerbach, Erich. *Mimesis*, Princeton, 1953.

Austin, J. L. *How to do Things with Words*. Cambridge MA, 1975.

Baker, Kenneth. *Minimalism*. New York, 1988.

Bakhtin, Mikhail. *The Dialogic Imagination*. Austin, 1981.
  Problems of Dostoevsky's Poetrics. Ardis, 1973.
  Rabelais and His World. Bloomington, 1984.

Balázs, Béla. *Theory of the Film*. New York, 1970.

Banes, Sally. *Terpsichore in Sneakers*. Middletown CT, 1987.

Bann, Stephen. *Concrete Poetry*. London. 1967.

Barth, John. "The Literature of Replenishment: Postmodernist Fiction." *The Atlantic Monthly* January 1980.

Barthes, Roland. *Camera Lucida*. New York, 1981.
  Critical Essays. Evanston, 1972.
  Image–Music–Text. New York, 1977.
  Mythologies. New York, 1972.
  S/Z. New York, 1974.
  Writing Degree Zero. Boston, 1967.
  The Pleasure of the Text. New York, 1975.

Baudelaire, Charles. *Œuvres complètes*. Paris, 1961.

Beckett, Samuel. *Proust*. New York, 1931.

Benveniste, Emile. *Problems in General Linguistics*. Miami, 1971.

Berger, John. *Ways of Seeing*. London, 1984.

Bergman, Ingmar. "Film Has Nothing To Do with Literature." *Film: A Montage of Theories*. Ed. Dyer MacCann. New York, 1966.

Bergson, Henri. *The Creative Mind*. New York, 1992.
  Time and Free Will. New York, 1959.

Bettelheim, Bruno. "The Importance of Play." *Atlantic Monthly* March 1987.
  The Uses of Enchantment: The Meaning and Importance of Fairy Tales. New York, 1976.

Birdwhistell, Ray. *Kinesics and Context*. Philadelphia, 1970.

Birtchnell, John. "Art Therapy as a Form of Psychotherapy." *Art as Therapy*. Ed. Tessa Dalley. New York, 1984.

Bluestone, George. *Novels into Film*. Berkeley, 1968.

Bodkin, Maud. *Archetypal Patterns in Poetry*. London, 1963.

Bogdan, Robert. *Freak Show: Presenting Human Oddities for Amusement and Profit*. Chicago, 1988.

Bordwell, David. *Narration in the Fiction Film*. Madison, 1985.

Bourdieu, Pierre. *Outline of a Theory of Practice*. Cambridge, 1977.

Bower, T. *The Perceptual World of the Child*. Cambridge MA, 1977.

Bowlby, John. "Grief and Mourning in Infancy 2nd Early Childhood." *The Psychoanalytic Study of the Child* 15 (1960).

Breton, André. *Manifestes du Surréalisme*. Paris, 1972.

Bruner, Jerome, "Narration and Life." Susan Wise Memorial Lecture. Harvard, 26 April 1986.

Burger, Peter. *Theory of the Avant-Garde*. Minneapolis, 1984.

Burnham, Donald. *Schizophrenia and the Need–Fear Dilemma*. New York, 1969.

Cage, John. *Silence*. Middletown, 1973.

Camus, Albert. *The Myth of Sisyphus*. New York, 1955.

Carlson, Marvin. *Theatre Semiotics*. Bloomington, 1990.

Cassirer, Ernst. *Language and Myth*. New York, 1953.

Chekhov, Anton. *The Brute and Other Farces*. New York, 1958.

Cherry, Colin. *On Human Communication*. Cambridge MA, 1982.

Chomsky, Noam. *Language and Mind*. New York, 1968.

Choron, Jacques. *Death and Western Thought*. New York, 1963.

Cohen, Selma Jeanne. *Next Week, Swan Lake*. Middletown CT, 1982.

Copeland, Roger, ed. *What Is Dance?* New York, 1983.

Cunningham, Merce. Learning from Performers. Harvard, 25 April, 1988.

D'Annunzio, Gabriele. *Le Martyre de Saint Sébastien*. Paris, 1911.

Danto, Arthur. "Description and the Phenomenology of Perception." *Visual Theory*. Ed. Norman Bryson. New York, 1991.

Denby, David. *Dance Writings*. New York, 1986.

Derrida, Jacques. *Of Grammatology*. Baltimore, 1976.

"Signature Event Context." *Glyph* 1 (1977).

Spurs Nietzche's Styles. Chicago, 1979.

Writing and Difference. Chicago, 1978.

Donley, Carol, and Friedman, Alan. *Einstein as Myth and Muse*. Cambridge, 1985.

Dubowski, Janek. "Art Versus Language." *Working with Children in Art Therapy*. Ed. Caroline Case. New York, 1990.

Eco, Umberto, *The Open Work*. Cambridge, 1989.

The Role of the Reader. Bloomington, 1984.

"Semiotics of Theatrical Performance." *The Drama Review* 21:1 (1977).

Eisenstein, Sergei. *Film Form*. New York, 1949.

Film Sense. New York, 1947.

Elam, Keir. *The Semiotics of Theatre*. New York, 1983.

Eliot, T. S. Intro. *Anabasis*. By Saint-John Perse. New York, 1949.

On Poetry and Poets. New York, 1961.

Ellis-Fermor, Una. *The Frontiers of Drama*. London, 1964.
Erikson, Erik. *Childhood and Society*. New York, 1963.
 Youth: Identity and Crisis. New York, 1968.
Falk, Eugene. *Types of Thematic Structure: The Nature and Function of Motifs in Gide, Camus, and Sartre*. Chicago, 1967.
Feder, Lillian. *Madness in Literature*. Princeton, 1980.
Fish, Stanley, *Is There a Text in This Class?* Cambridge MA, 1980.
Foster, Susan. *Reading Dance*. Berkeley, 1986.
Foucault, Michel. *The Order of Things*. New York, 1973.
 This is Not a Pipe. Berkeley, 1983.
 "What Is an Author?" *Twentieth-Century Literary Theory*. ed. Vassilis Lambropoulos. Albany, 1987.
Foucault, Michel, and Binswanger, Ludwig. *Dream and Existence*. Seattle, 1986.
Freedman, Ralph. *The Lyrical Novel*. Princeton, 1963.
Freud, Sigmund. *A General Introduction to Psycho-Analysis*. New York, 1935.
 Civilization and Its Discontents. New York, 1961.
 The Interpretation of Dreams. New York, 1965.
 On Creativity and the Unconscious. New York, 1958.
Geertz, Clifford. *The Interpretation of Cultures*. New York, 1973.
Girard, René. *Violence and the Sacred*. Baltimore, 1984.
Goffman, Erving. *Frame Analysis: An Essay on the Organization of Expenditure*. Boston, 1986.
 The Presentation of Self in Everyday Life, New York, 1959.
Gombrich, E. H. *Art and Illusion: A Study in the Psychology of Pictorial Representation*. Princeton, 1972.
Goodman, Nelson. "How Buildings Mean." *Critical Inquiry* 11 (1985).
 Languages of Art. Indianopolis, 1976.
Greenberg, Clement. *Art and Culture*. Boston, 1969.
Greenblatt, Stephen. "Culture." *Critical Terms for Literary Study*. Ed. Frank Lentricchia. Chicago, 1990.
Grice, Paul. "Logic and Conversation." *The Logic of Grammar*. Ed. Donald Davidson. Encino, 1976.
Hall, Edward T. *The Silent Language*. Greenwich, 1959.
Hanna, Judith. *To Dance Is Human*. Chicago, 1987.
Hanson, Jarice. *Understanding Video*. Newbury Park, 1987.
Harlow, H. F. "The Maternal Affectional System of Rhesus Monkeys." *Maternal Behavior in Mammals*. Ed. Harriet Rheingold. New York, 1963.
 "The Nature of Love." *The American Psychologist* 13 (1958).
 "Primary Affectional Patterns in Primates." *The American Journal of Orthopsychiatry* 30 (1960).
Harper, Robert. *Nonverbal Communication*. New York, 1978.
Heidegger, Martin. *Being and Time*. New York, 1962.
 Poetry, Language, Thought. New York, 1975.
Heller, Erich. *The Artist's Journey into the Interior*. London, 1966.
Henzell, John. "Art, Psychotherapy, and Symbol Systems." *Art as Therapy*. Ed. Tessa Dalley. New York, 1984.

Hobson, J. Allan. *The Dreaming Brain*. New York, 1988.

Holmberg, Arthur. "Artistic Profile." *The World Encyclopedia of Contemporary Theatre*, II. London, 1996.

"Waning of Spirituality Perplexes Artists Today." *American Theatre* June 1991.

"A Warning from Heiner Müller." *New York Times*. 8 July 1990.

Humphrey, Robert. *Stream of Consciousness in the Modern Novel*. Berkeley, 1972.

Hymes, Dell. *Directions in Sociolinguistics: The Ethnography of Communication*. New York, 1972.

Innes, Christopher. *Holy Theatre* 343. Cambridge, 1984.

Ionesco, Eugene. Interview, *Književne novine*, Beograd, Year XXIII, Number 399, 16 September 1971.

Iser, Wolfgang. *The Act of Reading: A Theory of Aesthetic Response*. Baltimore, 1984.

Jackson, Rosemary. *Fantasy: The Literature of Subversion*. New York, 1984.

Jakobson, Roman. *Fundamentals of Language*. Hague, 1975.

"Linguistics and Poetics." *The Structuralists*. Ed. Richard de George. Garden City, 1972.

Jauss, Hans. *Toward an Aesthetic of Reception*. Minneapolis, 1982.

Johnson, Barbara. *The Critical Difference*. Baltimore, 1980.

Johnson, David. "Drama Therapy and the Schizophrenic Condition." *Drama in Therapy*. Ed. Richard Courtney. New York, 1981.

Jung, Carl, "On the Relation of Analytical Psychology to Poetry." *Dramatic Theory and Criticism*. Ed. Bernard Dukore, New York, 1974.

Kandinsky, Wassily. *Concerning the Spiritual in Art*. New York, 1977.

Karl, Frederick. *Modern and Modernism*. New York, 1985.

Kayser, Wolfgang. *The Grotesque*. Gloucester MA, 1968.

Kernodle, George. *From Art to Theatre*. Chicago, 1970.

Kierkegaard, Søren. *Either/Or*. Princeton, 1987.

Fear and Trembling. Princeton, 1974.

Kripke, Saul. *Naming and Necessity*. Cambridge MA, 1980.

Kübler-Ross, Elisabeth. *On Death and Dying*. New York, 1976.

Lacan, Jacques. *Ecrits*. New York, 1977.

Lawler, Lillian. *The Dance of the Ancient Greek Theatre*. Iowa City, 1964.

Lévi-Strauss, Claude. *Structural Anthropology*. New York, 1963.

Lévy-Bruhl, Lucien. *How Natives Think*. Princeton, 1985.

Lifton, Robert, Jay. *The Future of Immortality*. New York, 1987.

Loran, Erle. *Cézanne's Composition*. Berkeley, 1985.

Los Angeles County Museum of Art. *The Spiritual in Art*. New York, 1986.

Luethi, Max. *Once Upon a Time: On the Nature of Fairy Tales*. Bloomington, 1976.

Lyotard, Jean-François. *The Postmodern Condition*. Minneapolis, 1984.

Maeterlinck, Maurice. *Le Trésor des humbles*. Paris, 1904.

Mahler, Margaret. *The Psychological Birth of the Human Infant: Symbiosis and Individuation*. New York, 1975.

Malinowski, Bronislaw. *Coral Gardens and Their Magic*. Bloomington, 1965.

"Our Ancestors Spoke in Pairs." *Explorations in the Ethnography of Speaking*. Ed. Richard Bauman. Cambridge, 1947.

Mallarmé, Stephane. *Œuvres complétes*. Paris, 1965.

Mamet, David. Personal interview. 28 April 1992.
Mauriac, François. *Dieu et Mammon*. Paris, 1958.
Mazo, Joseph. *Prime Movers: Makers of Modern Dance*. New York, 1977.
McDonagh, Don. *George Balanchine*. New York, 1983.
McLuhan, Marshall. *Explorations in Communication*. Boston, 1960.
Merleau-Ponty, Maurice. *The Primacy of Perception*. Evanston, 1964.
Miller, Alice. *The Drama of the Gifted Child*. New York, 1981.
    The Untouched Key: Tracing Childhood Trauma in Creativity and Destructiveness.
    New York, 1990.
Miller, Jean. "Psychological Consequences of Sexual Inequality." *American Journal
    of Orthopsychiatry* 41 (1971).
Miller, Jonathan. *Subsequent Performances*. New York, 1986.
Mitchell, W. J. T. *Iconology*. Chicago, 1986.
Molina Foix, Vicente. *Don Juan último. Primer Acto* 246 (November–December
    1992).
Moreno, J. *Psychodrama*. Ambler, 1985.
Neale, John. *Contemporary Readings in Psychopathology*. New York, 1978.
Nicoll, Allardyce. *Film and Theatre*. New York, 1936.
Nietzsche, Friedrich. *The Birth of Tragedy*. Garden City, 1956.
Nilsen, Vladimir. *Cinema as a Graphic Art*. New York, 1959.
Nochlin, Linda. "Why Have There Been No Great Women Artists?" *Art and Sexual
    Politics*. Ed. Elizabeth Baker. New York, 1973.
Orwell, George. "Boys' Weeklies." *Collected Essays*. London. 1975.
Otto, Rudolf. *The Idea of the Holy*. Oxford, 1973.
Norman, Paul. "Parental Empathy." *Parenthood: Its Psychology and
    Psychopathology*. Ed. Therese Benedek. Boston, 1970.
Perkins, David. *The Quest for Permanence: The Symbolism of Wordsworth, Shelley and
    Keats*. Cambridge, 1959.
Petric, Vlada, ed. *Film and Dreams: An Approach to Bergman*. New York, 1981.
Propp, Vladimir. *Morphologie du conte*. Paris, 1965.
Rasmussen, Steen. *Experiencing Architecture*. Cambridge MA, 1986.
Resnais, Alain. *Hiroshima mon amour*. Screenplay by Marguerite Duras. Argo
    Films, 1959.
Robbe-Grillet, Alain. *For a New Novel*. Evanston, 1989.
Rosaldo, Michelle. "It's All Uphill: The Creative Metaphors of Ilongot Magical
    Spells." *Sociocultural Dimensions of Language Use*. Ed. Ben Blount. New York,
    1975.
Rosenberg, Harold. *Art on the Edge*. Chicago, 1983.
Ruesch, Jurgen and Kees, Weldon. *Non-Verbal Communication*. Berkeley, 1974.
Russell, Bertrand. *The Problems of Philosophy*. Oxford, 1967.
Sartre, Jean-Paul. *La Nausée*. Paris, 1966.
    The Psychology of Imagination. Seacaucus, n.d.
    The Transcendence of the Ego. New York, 1977.
Saussure, Ferdinand de. *Course in General Linguistics*. New York, 1959.

Saxon, A. *P. T. Barnum: The Legend and the Man*. New York, 1989.

Schechner, Richard. *The End of Humanism*. New York, 1982.

Searle, John. *Speech Acts*. Cambridge, 1985.

Shapiro, Dr. Theodore. "Normal and Pathological Language Development." McLean Hospital, Belmont, 8 December 1989.

Shattuck, Roger. *The Banquet Years: The Origins of the Avant-Garde in France*. New York, 1968.

Shklovsky, Victor. "Art as Technique." *Russian Formalist Criticism*. Ed. Lee Lemon. Lincoln, 1965.

Solt, Mary Ellen. *Concrete Poetry*. Bloomington, 1970.

Sontag, Susan. *Against Interpretation*. New York, 1966.

   Styles of Radical Will. New York, 1969.

Spitz, René. *The First Year of Life: A Psychoanalytic Study of Normal and Deviant Development of Object Relations*. New York, 1965.

Stern, Daniel. *Interpersonal World of the Infant*. New York, 1985.

Szondi, Peter. *Theory of the Modern Drama*. Minneapolis, 1987.

Tambiah, J. J. "The Magical Power of Words." *Man* 3 (1968).

Tolstoy, Leo. *The Death of Ivan Ilych*. New York, 1960.

Turner, Victor. *From Ritual to Theatre*. New York, 1982.

Ullmann, Stephen. *The Image in the Modern French Novel*. Oxford, 1963.

Unamuno, Miguel de. *The Tragic Sense of Life*. New York, 1954.

Urmson, J. "Dramatic Representation." *The Philosophical Quarterly* 22 (1972).

van Gennep, Arnold. *Rites of Passage*. Chicago, 1975.

Veltrusky, Jiri. "Contribution to the Semiotics of Acting." *Sound, Sign, and Meaning*. Ed. Ladislav Matejka. Ann Arbor, 1976.

Venturi, Robert. *Complexity and Contradiction in Architecture*. New York, 1988.

Villiers, Peter and Jill de. *Early Language*. Cambridge MA, 1979.

Webster, T. B. L. *The Greek Chorus*. London, 1970.

Weiner, Annette. "From Words to Objects to Magic." *Dangerous Words*. Ed. Donald Brenneis. New York, 1984.

Weiss, Robert. *Loneliness: The Experience of Emotional and Social Isolation*. Cambridge MA, 1973.

Winner, Ellen. *Invented Worlds: The Psychology of the Arts*. Cambridge MA, 1982.

Winnicott, D. W. *Playing and Reality*. London, 1982.

Wittgenstein, Ludwig. *Philosophical Investigations*. New York, 1968.

   Tractatus Logico-Philosophicus. London, 1988.

Whorf, Benjamin Lee. *Language, Thought, Reality*. Cambridge MA, 1989.

Woolf, Virginia. *The Captain's Deathbed and Other Essays*. New York, 1950.

   The Common Reader. New York, 1953.

   Jacob's Room. New York, 1959.

   Orlando. New York, 1956.

Index